AF505429

The Italian general election of 2006

Manchester University Press

The Italian general election of 2006

Romano Prodi's victory

edited by

James L. Newell

Manchester University Press
Manchester and New York
distributed exclusively in the USA by Palgrave

Published by Manchester University Press
Oxford Road, Manchester M13 9NR, UK
and Room 400, 175 Fifth Avenue, New York, NY 10010, USA
www.manchesteruniversitypress.co.uk

Distributed exclusively in the USA by
Palgrave, 175 Fifth Avenue, New York,
NY 10010, USA

Distributed exclusively in Canada by
UBC Press, University of British Columbia, 2029 West Mall,
Vancouver, BC, Canada V6T 1Z2

British Library Cataloguing-in-Publication Data
A catalogue record for this book is available from the British Library
Library of Congress Cataloging-in-Publication Data applied for

ISBN 978 0 7190 75025 *hardback*

First published 2008

17 16 15 14 13 12 11 10 09 08   10 9 8 7 6 5 4 3 2 1

Typeset
by Action Publishing Technology Ltd, Gloucester
Printed in Great Britain
by Biddles Ltd, King's Lynn

Contents

IV THE OUTCOME

Figures

Tables

Contributors

Roberto Biorcio is Professor of Sociology in the Dipartimento di Sociologia e Ricerca Sociale at the Bicocca University of Milan. He is the author of *La Padania promessa* (Il saggiatore, 1997) and of *Sociologia politica. Partiti, movimenti sociali e partecipazione* (Il Mulino, 2003), as well as of numerous articles and book chapters on social movements, political participation, parties and electoral behaviour.

Donatella Campus is Associate Professor of Politics in the Faculty of Political Science 'Roberto Ruffilli' at the University of Bologna. She is the author of *L'elettore pigro. Informazione politica e scelte di voto* (Il Mulino, 2000) and of *L'antipolitica al governo* (Il Mulino, forthcoming) as well as of numerous articles dealing with political communication and electoral politics.

Michele Capriati is Professor of Economic Policy at the University of Bari. His research interests lie in the areas of regional development and processes of innovation in the organisation of enterprises with particular reference to economically disadvantaged areas. His recent articles include: 'Sviluppo regionale e libertà effettive: prime verifiche empiriche' (XXV Conferenza italiana di Scienze regionali, Naples, 16–19 October 2005); 'Expenditure in R&D and local development: an analysis of Italian provinces' (45th Congress of the European Regional Science Association, Vrije Universiteit, Amsterdam, 23–27 August 2005); 'The Italian Economy 2001–2003' (*Modern Italy*, vol. 10, no. 1, May 2005).

Alessandro Chiaramonte is Associate Professor of Political Science in the University of Florence. He has published numerous articles on elections and electoral systems. He is the author of *Tra maggioritario* *e proporzionale. L'universo dei sistemi elettorali misti* (Il Mulino, 2005).

Mark Donovan is a Senior Lecturer in the School of European Studies, Cardiff University. He edited the reader *Italy* (Ashgate, 1998) and co-edited, with David Broughton, *Changing Party Systems in Western Europe* (Pinter, 1998). From 2000 to 2005 he co-edited *Modern Italy*, the journal of the Association for the Study of Modern Italy.

Giovanna Antonia Fois has a PhD in European and Comparative Politics from the University of Siena. She is attached to the University's Centre for the Study of Political Change and her research interests are mainly focused on the European integration process and government elites.

Rachel Gibson is a political scientist and Professor of New Media Studies in the Department of Media and Communication at the University of Leicester. Her main research interests centre on political parties and voters' use of new media technologies by political organisations and candidates in campaigns and elections.

Wainer Lusoli is Lecturer in Social and Communication Studies at the University of Chester. Over the last five years he has worked on a number of projects regarding citizen participation, elections, political representation and the new media. He is a member of the Internet and Elections Project, reporting on the use of the Internet in electoral campaigns worldwide. He has published numerous articles on the new media and politics, and his volume on electronic democracy in Britain (details of which can be found at www.lusoli.info) is forthcoming from Hampton Press.

James L. Newell is Professor of Politics at the University of Salford. His recent books include *Parties and Democracy in Italy* (Ashgate, 2000), *The Italian General Election of 2001: Berlusconi's Victory* (ed., Manchester University Press, 2002), *Corruption in Contemporary Politics* (ed. with M. Bull, Palgrave, 2003), *Italian Politics: Adjustment Under Duress* (with M. Bull, Polity Press, 2005), and *Scandal in Past and Contemporary Politics* (ed. with J. Garrard, Manchester University Press, 2005). He is co-editor of the European Consortium for Political Research's journal of the political science profession, *European Political Science*, and co-convenor of the UK Political Studies Association's Italian Politics Specialist Group.

Licia Papavero holds a PhD in Comparative and European Politics from the University of Siena and she is currently Teaching Assistant in Political Science at the University of Milan. Her research interests include the comparative analysis of parliamentary elites and women's representation processes in Italy and in other Mediterranean countries.

Gianfranco Pasquino is Professor of Political Science at the University of Bologna. He also teaches at the Bologna Center of the Johns Hopkins University. He is author of many books, among which *Il sistema politico italiano* (Bononia University Press, 2002) and, most recently, *Sistemi elettorali* and, with Riccardo Pelizzo, *Parlamenti democratici* (both Il Mulino, 2006).

Franca Roncarolo is Associate Professor of Political Science at the University of Turin. She has written on the changes that have occurred in the political communication systems of America and Italy and has been monitoring Italian election campaigns in the media since the 1990s.

Sarah Rose is a PhD candidate in the Department of Political Science and International Studies, University of Birmingham.

Luca Verzichelli is Associate Professor of Political Science in the University of Siena. His research interests are the comparative analysis of political elites and parliamentary politics. His recent books include *Il Parlamento. Le assemblee legislative nelle democrazie contemporanee* (Laterza, 2006) (with Alfio Mastropaolo) and *Italian Politics 2006* (Berghahn, 2006) (co-edited with Grant Amyot).

Stephen Ward is a Research Fellow at the Oxford Internet Institute at the University of Oxford. His research interests include politics and new information communication technologies, in particular online campaigning and political participation. He is currently co-editing a book on election campaigning and the Internet (Lexington, 2007).

Acknowledgements

I would like to thank each of the authors for their contributions and for their swift responses to requests for suggestions and comments on edited versions of initial drafts. Financial support for production of the book came in the form of a Study Abroad Fellowship awarded to me by the Leverhulme Trust in 2005–2006. The help of the staff at Manchester University Press in seeing the book through the various stages of the production process is also gratefully acknowledged. Naturally, responsibility for any errors remaining in the text at the end of the process lies with me. Finally, a debt of gratitude is owed to Serena for her usual considerable forbearance. Once again, it is to her that I wish to dedicate this book.

James L. Newell

Abbreviations

AN	National Alliance (Alleanza Nazionale)
CCD-CDU	Christian Democratic Centre–Christian Democratic Union (Centro Cristiano Democratico–Cristiani Democratici Uniti)
CdI	House of Freedoms (Casa delle libertà)
CDU/CSU	Christian Democratic Union/Christian Social Union (Germany)
CEI	Central Energy Italia
CGIE	General Council for Italians Resident Abroad
CGIL	General Confederation of Italian Labour (Confederazione Generale Italiana del Lavoro)
CISL	Italian Confederation of Workers' Trade Unions (Confederazione Italiana dei Sindacati dei Lavoratori)
CONSOB	Securities and Exchange Commission (Commissione Nazionale per le Società e la Borsa)
DC	Christian Democratic Party (Democrazia Cristiana)
DE	European Democracy (Democrazia Europea)
DS	Left Democrats (Democratici di Sinistra)
EMU	Economic and Monetary Union
Enel	National Electricity Corporation (Ente nazionale per l'energia elettrica)
ENI	National Hydrocarbon Corporation (Ente Nazionale Idrocarburi)
EPP	European People's Party
Fed	Federation of the Olive-tree Alliance (Federazione dell'Ulivo)
FI	Go Italy! (Forza Italia)
GAD	Great Democratic Alliance (Grande Alleanza Democratica)
GDP	Gross Domestic Product

GSP	Growth and Stability Pact
IAEA	International Atomic Energy Agency
ICI	local property tax (Imposta comunale sugli immobili)
IdV	Italy of Values (Italia dei Valori)
IRPEF	Personal Income Tax (Imposta sul Reddito delle Persone Fisiche)
IRAP	Regional Business Tax (Imposta Regionale sulle Attività Produttive)
ISTAT	Italian National Institute for Statistics (Istituto Nazionale di Statistica)
LFV	League of the Venetian Front (Liga Fronte Veneto)
LN	Northern League (Lega Nord)
MPA	Movement for Autonomy (Movimento per l'Autonomia)
MRE	European Republican Movement (Movimento Repubblicani Europei)
MS–FT	Social Movement – Tricoloured Flame (Movimento Sociale – Fiamma Tricolore)
Pacs	Civil solidarity agreements (Patti civili di solidarietà)
PCI	Italian Communist Party (Partito Comunista Italiano)
PdCI	Party of Italian Communists (Partito dei Comunisti Italiani)
PPI	Italian People's Party (Partito Popolare Italiano)
PR	proportional representation
PRI	Italian Republican Party (Partito Repubblicano Italiano)
PSI	Italian Socialist Party (Partito Socialista Italiano)
RAI	Italian Radio and Television (Radiotelevisione Italiana)
RC	Communist Refoundation (Rifondazione Comunista)
SDI	Italian Democratic Socialists (Socialisiti Democratici Italiani)
SI	Italian Socialists (Socialisti Italiani)
SMCs	single member constituencies
SVP	South Tyrolese People's Party (Südtirolervolkspartei)
TARSU	Solid Waste Management Tax (Tassa per lo smaltimento dei Rifiuti Solidi Urbani)
UD	Democratic Union (Unione Democratica)

UDC	Union of Christian Democrats and Centre Democrats (Unione dei Democratici Cristiani e dei Democratici di Centro)
UDEUR	Union of Democrats for Europe (Unione Democratici per l'Europa)
UDR	Democratic Union for the Republic (Unione Democratica per la Repubblica)
UIL	Union of Italian Workers (Unione Italiana del Lavoro)

Introduction: an ambiguous outcome?

James L. Newell

The victory of the centre left

The general election of 9 and 10 April was one of the closest fought in Italy's history. In the Chamber of Deputies, the centre-left Unione coalition emerged ahead of the centre-right Casa delle libertà (House of Freedoms; Cdl) by just 24,755 votes in the largest of the two domestic arenas (though owing to the electoral law, the majority in terms of seats was a comfortable 66). In the Senate the Unione won just two seats more than the Cdl (and was marginally behind in terms of votes). Besides its narrowness, what also struck observers about the outcome was its unexpected quality. Throughout the campaign, published poll figures had varied little, consistently putting the centre left ahead by some 4 or 5 percentage points and giving rise to expectations of a comfortable victory that were supported by the results of the exit polls announced on 10 April itself. Only with the initial projections later that day did it become clear that what had seemed like a certain outcome would instead remain uncertain until almost the last of the votes had been counted. It is not surprising, then, that surprise was widespread, nor, therefore, that the outcome has, as Italian psephologists Renato Mannheimer and Paolo Natale (2006: 9) note, given rise to an unusually large number of interpretations and comments.

As Mannheimer and Natale (2006: 10) go on to note, the vote was the product of a reality that was 'multifaceted, complex and rich in fine distinctions'. As they would almost certainly be the first to agree, this is undoubtedly true of all election outcomes. This means that the causes and significance of such events are almost never immediately obvious and can be grasped only through *interpretation* of the reality underlying them. We will offer one such interpretation later in this introduction, and in the conclusion, and the reader will find others in the chapters that form the core of this book. Before that, however, there is another issue we have to deal with. Our intended audience consists mainly of non-Italian speakers who, for one reason or another, need to know about the current political situation in a country that is among the half-dozen or so of the world's largest and most successful democracies. This being the case it behoves us to begin by offering a description of the political background against which the election took place to provide the reader with the basic factual material required to appreciate the more detailed analyses in each of the chapters that follow.

The background

The period since the party-system upheavals of the early 1990s and the resulting change of electoral law in 1993 has seen the gradual consolidation of a bi-polar system built around two electoral coalitions each competing for overall majorities of parliamentary seats. In 2001, the centre right's leader and prime-ministerial candidate, media magnate Silvio Berlusconi, achieved a convincing victory for the Cdl, whose four main components were, and remain: Italy's largest party, Berlusconi's Forza Italia (literally, 'Go Italy!'; FI), established immediately prior to the 1994 elections as a vehicle for the entrepreneur's political ambitions; the autonomist Northern League, whose immediate predecessor, the Lombard League, came to prominence in the late 1980s; heirs to the far-right Italian Social Movement, the National Alliance (AN); Christian Democrat heirs, the Christian Democratic Centre–Christian Democratic Union (CCD-CDU) (now the Union of Christian Democrats and Centre Democrats (UDC) following their merger, together with European Democracy, in 2002).

On the other side, a not insignificant role in the centre left's defeat in 2001 appeared to have been played by the fact that ideological and policy divisions had prevented some of its component parties from reaching the stand-down arrangements necessary to enable them to prevent the Cdl taking seats at their joint expense in the single-member constituencies created by the 1993 electoral law. Thus it was that the years following 2001 saw previously divided forces come together. The process was paradoxical because if, on the one hand, it represented a growing unity of intents, on the other each addition only reduced cohesion by rendering the coalition ever larger and more heterogeneous. The result was that the Unione that went into the 2006 campaign consisted of nine principal parties: Communist Refoundation (RC), the Party of Italian Communists (PdCI), the Left Democrats (DS), the Greens, the Socialists (SDI), the Radicals, the Margherita (the Daisy), Italy of Values, the Union of Democrats for

Europe (UDEUR). For the Chamber contest, the DS and the Margherita fielded a joint slate of candidates – the Ulivo (Olive Tree) – as the precursor to what, outwardly at least, the two parties' leaders hope will before long be a formal merger. Meanwhile, the PdCI and the Greens fielded a joint slate of candidates ('Together with the Unione') for the Senate contest. The SDI and the Radicals fielded a joint slate of candidates, the Rosa nel pugno (literally, 'the Rose in the fist'), for both contests.

Extreme fragmentation has always deprived the centre left of a coalition maker – that is, a party which, by virtue of its relative size, is able to dictate the terms on which negotiations within the coalition will take place and therefore to impose a minimum of discipline on its allies – and by the same token has always prevented any one party from imposing on the others a coalition leader drawn from its own ranks. Despite being its principle architect, the coalition's leader – economics professor and former EU Commission President Romano Prodi – is thus essentially a non-party figure whose position is inherently exposed to the interlocking vetoes of the party leaders who originally chose him. This combination of features has always left the coalition vulnerable to accusations that it is inherently incapable of providing cohesive government – accusations that appeared to be supported after the 1996 elections, which produced a Prodi government incapable of surviving beyond October 1998 and that was followed by three other governments before the 2001 election. The October 2005 primary elections which Prodi managed to insist upon for the choice of centre-left leader were thus extremely important. In winning these elections handsomely, Prodi acquired a source of legitimacy for his position that went beyond the coalition's parties. By demonstrating the sheer weight of the popular support he was able to mobilise, the elections considerably strengthened, at least in the short term, the project for coalition unity that he represents. This had then enabled the centre left to go on to publish a 281–page election manifesto which, while the object of some ridicule for its length, was presented as a coalition-wide agreement the very detail of which offered assurances that a centre-left government could remain united.

Ideological heterogeneity on the centre left is mirrored on the centre right. However, the greatest difficulty for the Cdl is Berlusconi's leadership. On the one hand, the extraordinary degree to which FI depends for its image, its finances and its organisation on its leader makes it difficult to imagine – though not all scholars agree on the point – the party continuing to have a meaningful existence after Berlusconi (who is now 70) leaves the political scene; and this has always reinforced the aspirations of AN and the UDC to capture leadership of the coalition for themselves given that they might expect to capture parts of the entrepreneur's party in the process. On the other hand, while Berlusconi was in an extraordinarily powerful position immediately after the 2001 election (which he could claim had been won largely thanks to him) the sheer weight of campaign emphasis on his supposedly extraordinary personal qualities subsequently became a distinct liability – leaving few alternative means of retaining voter loyalty when economic difficulties began tarnishing the leader's image. For these two reasons, Berlusconi's capacity to impose discipline on his coalition declined as time went by – and especially after the 2004 European elections with their revelation that, if a government in difficulties was going to have to pay an electoral price, then, in the context of a proportional electoral law such as that used for the European Parliament, it would be paid by FI rather than its allies and that they rather than the opposition parties would be the principal beneficiaries.[1]

It was in this context that, towards the end of 2005, the centre-right parties reached agreement on a new electoral law, whose details are explained by Chiaramonte in chapter 10 but whose most important features for present purposes are the fact that the vast majority of seats in both chambers are distributed through large multi-member constituencies via the closed-list system of proportional representation and that there is a majority premium that goes to the party, or the coalition of allied parties, that wins the most votes.

The new law appeared to offer the centre right at least three specific advantages. First, by allowing the allied parties to compete in relative independence, each with its own prime-ministerial candidate, it considerably reduced the likely significance of Berlusconi's personal popularity for the prospects of his allies and those of the coalition as a whole. As the 2005 regional elections appeared to confirm, had the parties been obliged – as they would have been had the 1993 electoral law remained in force – to line up behind single candidates representing the coalition as a whole, then they might have suffered badly; for in such a situation voters dissatisfied with Berlusconi and FI would have had no means of giving expression to their dissatisfaction other than by action (abstention or voting for the centre left) also damaging to the entrepreneur's allies.[2] Second, therefore, the new law held out the prospect of considerably reducing the leadership issue as a source of friction and instability within the centre right. Third, the 1993 electoral law had provided for three-quarters of the seats in the two chambers of Parliament to be distributed according to the single-member, simple plurality formula, and one-quarter proportionally – at both of the two previous general elections, in 1996 and 2001, the sum of the votes received by the centre right's parties individually in the proportional arena had been larger than the number of voters willing to support their joint, single candidates in the plurality arena. This therefore provided an additional argument in favour of the new law.[3]

The CdL went into the campaign with a lacklustre record to defend and it was this above all that underpinned confidence in predictions of a comfortable centre-left victory; for if Berlusconi had won in 2001 on the basis of his personal charisma and therefore of considerably heightened expectations of what he would be able to achieve, then subsequent economic stagnation and the government's difficulties in delivering on its promises (especially in the area of taxes) had created widespread disillusionment and pessimism. Why was it, then, that the centre left's victory was so unexpectedly narrow? At this point we leave the world inhabited predominantly by facts to enter, as we said we would, the more uncertain realms of interpretation.

The interpretation

One apparently rather popular account is that which explains the outcome as a kind of failure of the centre left. Though it has not been asserted in a single text in terms as straightforward, it is an account that has been lurking in various comments published since the election's aftermath. Reduced to its essentials it amounts to the claim that the better campaign was actually the one run by Berlusconi who, in the final weeks before polling, managed to mobilise voters who would otherwise have abstained, in the process wrong-footing the centre left, which was only saved (just) by its alliance decisions and the electoral system.

There is no doubt that the centre right's campaign was striking and, monopolised as it was by Berlusconi, considerably more colourful than that of the centre left. Indeed, the entrepreneur's decision to ensure that the election acquired the significance of a referendum for or against himself may be judged as shrewd in the extreme. While the pressure to defend his government's record meant that it would have been difficult to avoid being at the centre of media attention, it allowed him to turn a necessity into a distinct virtue. Thus it was that faced with evidence of his record that was difficult to explain away, he adopted the tactic of straightforward denial, claiming that perceptions of economic stagnation were false impressions put about by 'the usual' commentators working for the left-wing press. By thus insisting on the image of a leader hampered and unjustly attacked from all sides, Berlusconi was in fact able to avoid fighting the campaign on his government's record for much of the time and to assume, instead, the appearance of an *opposition* leader whose dynamic qualities could still deliver much once freed, through a second term, from the shackles of his left-wing tormentors.

It is true, too, that the fiscal aspects of the centre left's programme allowed the Cdl to push it onto the defensive for the last ten days of the campaign – thus reinforcing the impression of a reversal of governing and opposition roles, with the centre left, not the centre right, being forced to account for its policy choices. On the one hand, the centre left proposed the reintroduction of inheritance tax for 'large estates' – but without saying what 'large estates' were. The inevitable consequence was that interpretations of what these amounted to differed as between the coalition's spokespersons thus fuelling uncertainty about how far down the scale the tax might extend. On the other hand, the Unione proposed to harmonise the tax rates on financial activities by introducing a uniform rate of 20 per cent. Although this apparently left no room for ambiguity, the centre right was able to claim that since the Unione also wanted to reduce by 5 per cent the gap between net salaries and employers' labour costs (the so-called *cuneo fiscale*), the centre left would inevitably be obliged to attack the interests of small savers despite its protestations to the contrary. Finally, at the end of the concluding television debate, when nearness of the vote meant that his allies were in no position publicly to question policy improvisations, Berlusconi made sure that the high tax label thoroughly stuck to his opponents by unexpectedly announcing his intention of abolishing ICI (Imposta comunale sugli immobili), the local property tax, in the event that he was victorious.

Finally, given the sheer slenderness of the gap by which the Unione emerged in front of the Cdl, the argument for the significance of the two coalition's alliance decisions seems irrefutable. For example, the significance of the Cdl's failure to embrace the small Project Northeast seems compelling given its 92,002 votes and the 24,755 votes separating the two coalitions in the Chamber contest. Equally compelling appears to be the significance of several other features of the way in which the coalitions were constructed – such as the centre left's decision to field coalition-wide candidates in the constituency for Italians resident abroad (without which its two-seat majority in the Senate might not have materialised) or its 'luck' in incorporating as tiny a formation as Alleanza Lombarda, whose voters, as Chiaramonte notes in chapter 10, are not of the left.

But despite the apparent persuasiveness of what we shall for conven-
ience call 'the standard account' we have a number of problems with
it. First, with respect to the nature and impact of Berlusconi's
campaign, it is important not to let one's impressions be coloured by
one's knowledge of the election outcome. Given that the Cdl did better
than observers assumed it would, it was natural for them, in the election's aftermath, to evaluate positively such features of the Berlusconi
campaign as his colourful outbursts and use of populist rhetoric thus
finding in them (some of) the explanation required. But *at the time*, to
many who actually witnessed the campaign, including the author,
these same features appeared less the likely passport to a (near) victory
than the signs of a prime minister who was desperate – especially when
they were set alongside other events, such as the enforced resignation
of two cabinet ministers in the middle of the campaign,[4] or when they
were juxtaposed to what with as much reason could be called the calm
confidence and the unusually united quality of the centre left's
campaign. And if it is admissible to attribute the centre left's victory in
large measure to 'chance' factors linked with coalition construction,
then it is at least as admissible to argue, on exactly the same grounds,
that the margin of victory could have been much larger. For example,
had the minor formations Alternativa Sociale and Gianfranco
Rotondi's Democrazia Cristiana remained independent of the rest of
the centre right in Piemonte and Lazio, as they had been at the 2005
regional elections, then the Cdl might not have achieved their slender
victories in these regions – in which case the Unione would have had
the much more comfortable Senate majority of fourteen. How effective then would the Berlusconi campaign have seemed?

Second, if one of the most widely accredited hypotheses concerning
the outcome is that concerning the electoral impact of the tax issue in
the final stages of the campaign, then the evidence that supports it
raises a puzzle. Mannheimer (2006: 24) cites polling evidence showing
that while the centre left was ahead of the centre right by 4 per cent on
22 March, by 5 April the lead had declined to 1.5 per cent. Now, since
the publication of poll findings is illegal during the last two weeks of a
campaign, this supports the hypothesis according to which the poll
results showing a comfortable centre-left lead almost throughout the
campaign were largely accurate, and that there was a significant shift
of support in favour of the centre right in the final stages of the
campaign that was not publicly registered because of the ban on
publishing poll findings after 24 March. But in that case one is left
with having to explain why it was that the exit polls failed to register
this shift and were instead in line with the earlier findings. The most

likely explanation is that the exit polls were inaccurate for reasons all of their own; but still, the issue remains puzzling: exit polls are conducted by asking voters to 're-cast' their ballot fill by filling in 'dummy' voting slips given to them by the pollster. One would not therefore expect them to be subject to the range of errors to which pre-election polling is potentially subject given its reliance on questions about future behaviour.

Finally, if the centre left was 'saved' from defeat by 'lucky' or 'fortuitous' alliance decisions, then it is difficult to see how one can establish the relative weight to be attributed to this factor or, indeed, to know what status to attribute to the suggestion. The very meaning of a claim that we can 'know' by empirical means what a past and unrepeatable outcome 'would have been' had this or that factor been different is obscure. True, we can advance and test hypotheses about the likely (past or future) consequences of alliance decisions in the way that Segatti (2006) does when he hypothesises that the centre left's decision to take on board the Radicals towards the end of 2005 cost the coalition votes among practising Catholics. In support of the suggestion is the evidence of voting intentions showing a decline in support for the centre left among practising Catholics between the autumn of 2005 and January 2006. And I suppose that implicit in this hypothesis is the claim that things 'would have been' different had the alliance with the Radicals not materialised. Still, there remains a fundamental difference between this sort of hypothesis and the one that involves noting that the centre left won by 24,755 votes and that Project Northeast took 92,002 and concluding from this that, allied with the Cdl, Project Northeast would have deprived the Unione of victory. And the difference is that the latter kind of hypothesis rests on the implicit but highly implausible assumptions that when parties move they take all their supporters with them and that the decisions of other parties' supporters remain unaffected. The fact is that we have no very convincing way of knowing what the distribution of the vote 'would have been' had the placement of Project Northeast – or, for that matter, any of a large number of other similar placements – been different.

In light of these difficulties, the preference of the author is for an alternative interpretation, one that is almost certainly as problematic in its way (and in some of the same ways!) as the one just described, but which in the author's view at least has the advantage of parsimony. It is the interpretation which says that the most appropriate benchmark against which to judge the centre left's performance is not the pre-polling-day expectations of how it would perform but its past performance. On this basis it was unreasonable to expect more than a narrow victory, the latter being obtained thanks to the simple fact that, faced with the choice between two potential governing coalitions, voters were on balance more persuaded by the offering of the Unione than by the Cdl.

At all of the three previous elections, the centre left trailed the centre right in terms of votes, while in 2006, for the first time, its Chamber vote moved from a position 3.8 per cent behind the centre right to a position 0.3 per cent ahead (Newell, 2006: Table 1).[5] We also know that, at any election, by far the largest single pool of voters is the one consisting of loyal supporters of one or the other of the two coalitions with very few voters ever switching directly between them. That 2006 was no exception in this respect is shown by the figures in Table I.1. A modest victory is therefore all that one was entitled to expect.

Table I.1 Vote flows 1996–2001 (Chamber plurality arena) and 2001–2006

Column per cent	Vote in 1996				
Vote in 2001	Centre right	Centre left	Other	Abstention/ blank ballot	Too young
Centre right	84.7	9.0	40.4	29.3	34.2
Centre left	4.9	80.7	17.3	15.3	27.6
Other	1.5	1.4	28.8	1.3	4.8
Abstention/blank ballot	9.0	8.8	13.5	54.1	33.4

Column per cent	Vote in 2001				
Vote in 2006	Centre right	Centre left	Other	Abstention	Too young
Centre right	77.2	7.2	32.0	26.9	34.6
Centre left	8.1	80.7	40.5	25.6	42.1
Abstention	14.4	11.8	25.4	47.3	23.3

Source: Figures for vote flows 1996–2001 based on author's own elaboration of Italian National Election Study (Itanes) data available at: http://csa.berkeley.edu:-7502 /cattest.html; figures for vote flows 2001–2006 taken from the results of an Swg survey published in *La Repubblica*, 13 April 2006, p. 13.

The figures can also be drawn upon to make the case for a swing of the electoral pendulum, with disappointment in the outgoing government, combined with the centre left's offering, driving a net shift in the distribution of support from centre right to centre left: in essence, while at the 2001 election the centre right had been more successful than the centre left in capturing the votes of those who, at the previous election had voted for 'third' forces, had abstained or been too young to vote – and while it had been favoured by the net flow of votes between the two coalitions – in 2006 the corresponding shifts were of a very similar entity, but this time took place in the opposite direction: that is, they favoured the centre left.

Finally, this interpretation of the result is fully consistent with the most well-established theories concerning the nature of the electoral 'market' in Italy – that is, the theories for which the latter is populated by voters for whom ideological and other socio-cultural divisions are of decreasing relevance for their choices; and the theories according to which elections are increasingly 'open' contests decided by a 'third Italy' (Mannheimer, 2006) consisting of those who are most likely to shift between voting and abstention, who are less well educated, little interested in politics, without strong partisan convictions, and therefore potentially available for mobilisation by either of the two main coalitions.

Plan of the book

The interpretations discussed above and in the following chapters all reflect a desire to repeat the task, for the 2006 election, that the contributors to this volume's 'predecessor' publication, *The Italian General Election of 2001* (Newell, 2002), collectively sought to perform in relation to that election – that is, to take an 'intellectual photograph' of the contest by providing an account of it as a discrete event, an account that would also allow an appreciation of its broader historical and political significance. That remains the aim here; but photographs, as we know, can capture the same object from several different angles giving rise to several different interpretations. It will therefore necessarily be left to the reader to decide which of these he or she finds most convincing.

As in the case of the previous volume, this one begins with a consideration of the context in which the election took place. As before, there are chapters on the political and on the economic contexts by Gianfranco Pasquino and Michele Capriati respectively; while, out of recognition of the increasing difficulty of understanding the politics of European countries without reference to the EU and international contexts, a chapter – by Giovanna Antonia Fois – has been added on this topic.

The section that follows – 'The run-up to the election' – focuses specifically on the main party and coalition protagonists of the campaign. Just as before, the starting point for the section is the recognition that though Italian elections are increasingly competitions between two powerful coalitions of the centre left and centre right, the composition of these coalitions remains fluid. The authors of the chapters in this section were therefore asked to examine the tactical and strategic considerations exercising the minds of leading politicians in the months prior to the election, in order to explain why it was that the constellation of choices that actually faced voters on election day had the specific profile that it did have.

With that established, the three chapters in the section that follows each analyse the campaign itself from various angles, while the chapters in the last section look at the outcome of the campaign in terms of the electoral performances of the competing line-ups, and the characteristics of the new Parliament that resulted from these performances.

Throughout the volume, the intention has been to retain, with minor modifications, the structure and themes of the 2001 volume – the purpose being to give authors an opportunity to draw on, and develop further, lines of investigation initiated on the earlier occasion, while giving readers the 'added value' of a volume allowing direct comparison of the 2006 election with the previous one. As readers will discover, there were many similarities between the two contests – but also a number of surprising novelties!

Notes

1 FI's vote declined from the 29.5 per cent it had won in 2001 to 21.0 per cent, while both the UDC and the League saw their vote shares rise (to 5.0 and 5.9 per cent respectively). Meanwhile, the parties of the centre left made only modest gains to take 46.1 per cent in 2004.
2 Those elections were a disaster for the Cdl: the governing coalition emerged the loser in twelve of the fourteen regions where voting took place; took 12,220,858 votes (43.9 per cent) as against the centre left's 14,632,412 (52.6 per cent), and lost control of six of the eight regions it had won in 2000.
3 For a more detailed analysis of the hoped-for – and actual – effects of the new electoral law see Chiaramonte (Chapter 10, this volume) and Pasquino (2006).
4 In February, the Minister for Institutional Reform, the Northern League's Roberto Calderoli, was forced to resign after appearing on television sporting a tee-shirt showing an anti-Islamic cartoon, an incident that provoked violent protests outside the Italian consulate in Bengasi leaving eleven people dead. Less than a month later, in March, the Minister of Health, Francesco Storace, resigned, following suggestions that he may

have been involved in spying and hacking activities designed to damage his opponents in the regional elections the year before.
5   It won in terms of seats in 1996 only because the centre right's vote was split by the independent stance adopted at that election by the Northern League.

References

Mannheimer, R. (2006), 'La campagna elettorale del 2006 e la mobilitazione della «terza Italia» politica', in R. Mannheimer and P. Natale (eds), *L'Italia a metà: Dentro il voto del paese diviso*, Milan, Cairo editore.

Mannheimer, R. and Natale, P. (2006), 'Introduzione', in R. Mannheimer and P. Natale (eds), *L'Italia a metà: Dentro il voto del paese diviso*, Milan, Cairo editore.

Newell, J. L. (ed.) (2002), *The Italian General Election of 2001: Berlusconi's Victory,* Manchester and New York, Manchester University Press.

Newell, J. L. (2006), 'The Italian Election of 2006: Myths and Realities', *West European Politics*, 29:4, 802–813.

Pasquino, G. (2006), 'Conclusions' in J. O. Frosini and G. Pasquino (eds), *For a Fistful of Votes: The 2006 Italian Elections*, Bologna, CLUEB.

Segatti, P. (2006), 'Cattolici e voto', in R. Mannheimer and P. Natale (eds), *L'Italia a metà: Dentro il voto del paese diviso*, Milan, Cairo editore.

I
The context

1

The political context, 2001–2006

Gianfranco Pasquino

Introduction

One of the most notable features of the 2001–2006 legislature was Silvio Berlusconi's exclusive, though technically not uninterrupted, tenure of the office of Prime Minister. Following the heavy defeat of the Cdl in the April 2005 regional elections, Berlusconi was obliged by his allies – and, more precisely, by pressure from the UDC – to resign and to create a second government through a rapid cabinet reshuffle (the crisis itself lasting only 67 hours).[1] Nevertheless, Berlusconi achieved at least one extremely coveted record, leading – from 11 June 2001 to 23 April 2005: 1,413 days – the longest-lasting government of the Italian Republic. In the process, he even beat the achievement of his friend Bettino Craxi (whose first government, between August 1983 and April 1987, lasted 1,058 days) because his two successive governments completed the entire parliamentary term. Much to his hidden disappointment, the numerical performance was not matched by an equally stunning political or economic performance.

Political stability, but ministerial reshuffles

To start with, beneath the persistence in office of the Prime Minister and coalition, many important changes took place. In addition to the turnover of quite a number of undersecretaries, several important ministries changed hands. For example, the Ministry of Foreign Affairs went from Renato Ruggiero to Berlusconi, and then, following the latter's nine months' interim tenure, to Franco Frattini and, finally, to Gianfranco Fini; the Ministry of Home Affairs shifted from Claudio Scajola to Giuseppe Pisanu; the Ministry of the Economy went from Giulio Tremonti to Domenico Siniscalco and back to Tremonti; the Ministry of Institutional Reforms went from Umberto Bossi to Roberto Calderoli; the Ministry of Cultural Affairs went from

Giuliano Urbani to Rocco Buttiglione (who was later obliged by the European Parliament to withdraw his candidacy for the post of Commissioner). And this list is not exhaustive. Even the deputy prime ministers were reshuffled, with the appointment first and the resignation next[2] of the UDC's Marco Follini, and with the appointment of Giulio Tremonti following his resignation as Minister for the Economy. Only Fini occupied his post as Deputy Prime Minister without interruption.

Though clearly the result of continuous and in no sense minor controversies none of these reshuffles apparently weakened the Government. However, some of them indicated that the latter was unable to find an agreed policy line and to stick to it with determination. More precisely, the replacement of the Minister of Foreign Affairs, Renato Ruggiero – whose appointment, because of his excellent European credentials, had been strongly backed both by the President of the Republic, Carlo Azeglio Ciampi, and by the President of Fiat, the late Gianni Agnelli – meant precisely that Berlusconi wanted to pursue a different, less European-Union-oriented, foreign policy. He never succeeded in designing a precise alternative; though much to the dismay of most European partners, he claimed a special relationship both with the President of Russia, Vladimir Putin, and with the President of the US, George W. Bush. In the end, a better balanced foreign policy was, to a degree, implemented by Gianfranco Fini. In his persistent search for the full legitimation both of his party and of himself as a potential future leader of the centre right, Fini played a constructive role in relation to the European Constitution while pursuing a more positive policy towards the European Union in general. The replacement and the surprising reappointment of Giulio Tremonti to the office of Minister of the Economy indicates that the coalition also had significant differences of opinion on the economic policies to be followed, especially in the vital area of taxation. Berlusconi had promised significant cuts in the State budget (see below), but the UDC was more interested in obtaining benefits for families and for the South, where the former Christian Democrats think most of their political support lies. In short, one can say that political stability between 2001 and 2006 was provided essentially by continuation in office of the same coalition and not by steadfast policies.

The partners of the Cdl were aware that their often diverging policies and goals were producing significant levels of disappointment in the electorate. However, precisely because of this, at no point did Berlusconi feel sufficiently confident that an early dissolution of

Parliament would return him and his coalition to office as to be able to use it as a threat against his bickering allies. And, since all his partners shared Berlusconi's fears, the 2001–2006 Parliament arrived at the end of its constitutional term. Indeed, Berlusconi was even successful in persuading the President of the Republic to dissolve Parliament on the very last possible date: 11 February 2006. The request was officially justified in terms of the need to obtain parliamentary approval of some important pieces of legislation. Shrewdly, though not unexpectedly, Berlusconi exploited the two additional weeks he thus gained by going on TV as much as possible; for only once Parliament is dissolved does the so-called *par condicio* law take effect. This imposes stringent controls over the TV time that is allocated to parties and political leaders.

Berlusconi's television bombardment, though consciously running the risk of overexposure, was ostensibly aimed at explaining and defending his government's record. In 2001, the centre left's candidate, Francesco Rutelli, had been unable to do this, because he had not been part of the outgoing government.[3] In contrast, Berlusconi decided to exploit what advantage there was in incumbency to the full. This is not the place to provide a detailed assessment of his accomplishments.[4] What is relevant to the analysis of the political context of the 2006 elections are essentially two phenomena. First, there was a visible incumbent. Second, because of the 'Contract with the Italian People'[5] that Berlusconi had spectacularly signed on TV on the eve of the 2001 elections, it was possible fully to evaluate what and how much had been accomplished. Unfortunately, most Italian journalists are either unable or unwilling to acquire the information that would enable them to challenge powerful politicians, let alone the Prime Minister. And opposition leaders did not do any better, preoccupied as they were with other issues and often bickering among themselves.

The challengers

Indeed, the second important element of the political context was represented by what often seemed incredible complacency on the part of the centre-left opposition. In 2001 the centre left had suffered a crushing, not just numerical but also political, defeat. For several years, it remained disunited and fundamentally leaderless. In spite of repeated statements by the leaders of the various centre-left parties that they had a wealth of competent and capable politicians while the centre right was 'owned' and dominated by one master, the fortunes of the centre left seemed to be tied to the return to Italian politics of

President of the European Commission, Romano Prodi. By October 2004, Prodi, who had himself been eagerly awaiting this day, was welcomed with relief by his centre-left supporters. In the meantime, a joint list consisting of the Left Democrats, the Margherita (the 'Daisy') and various minor groups, openly sponsored by his most devoted supporters, had performed rather well in the June 2004 European elections. The most important aspect of these elections, however, was that Forza Italia performed very poorly, losing a significant percentage of votes in comparison with both the 1999 European elections and the 2001 general election.

Once back in Italy, Prodi again found himself without a political party while, at the same time, he did not want to become the leader of any of the existing parties of the centre-left coalition. The Democrats, the party he had founded in the aftermath of his burning parliamentary defeat in October 1998, had joined left-leaning former Christian Democrats (the Popolari) and some other small groups to form the Margherita, which had chosen Francesco Rutelli as its leader. Prodi's principal goal was to be recognised not just as the centre left's prime-ministerial candidate, but as the unique leader of the entire coalition. Understandably, neither the Left Democrats nor the Margherita felt happy with Prodi's claim. Therefore, in order to obtain a robust and undisputable legitimation of his leadership, Prodi asked for primary elections to be held among centre-left supporters. Initially, all the leaders of the centre-left parties expressed reservations clearly stating that there was no doubt that Prodi was indeed the official leader of the coalition. In their opinion, the primaries were neither useful nor necessary.

The second phase of this Italian saga took place in the wake of the April 2005 regional elections. These elections' results can be considered a turning point in exactly the same way that those of the 2000 regional elections were such. At that time, the victory of Berlusconi's coalition in eight regions out of fifteen had indicated that the electoral tide was running strongly in favour of the centre right. Prime Minister Massimo D'Alema had been obliged to resign and the centre-left governing coalition never regained momentum. In April 2005 the centre left won in twelve regions and the centre right retained majorities in only two (in the remaining region the vote was postponed). At that point, Prodi declared somewhat prematurely and optimistically that the results of the regional elections could be interpreted as a sort of 'primary', one that had convincingly legitimated his leadership. He also asked for a strengthening of the relationship between the Left Democrats and the Margherita through the presentation of a joint list to be headed by him. At a stormy meeting of its governing body, the Margherita, much to Prodi's surprise and irritation, rejected the proposal. In reaction, Prodi again put the holding of primaries on the agenda of the centre left, this time irrevocably.

Though the usefulness of primary elections had been debated among centre-left politicians for quite a while, the only significant occasion on which they had been held had been when the centre left had selected its candidate for the office of President of the Puglia Region. Unable to agree on a candidate because Rifondazione Comunista insisted that its candidate had better chances of winning than the one supported by the Margherita and the Left Democrats, centre-left party leaders gave way and accepted the idea of primary elections. Much to their surprise, not only did the quite popular Rifondazione candidate win the primaries, but he also went on, shrewdly repositioning himself, to defeat Forza Italia's incumbent president in the main election.[6]

Though there were, for a variety of reasons, many candidates in the national primaries,[7] there could be no doubt that, officially supported by the Left Democrats and the Margherita, Prodi was the designated winner. However, being the first experiment of this kind, the national primaries raised two important questions: how many voters would participate, and how decisive Prodi's victory had to be. Many bizarre, and especially misguided and uninformed, objections surfaced concerning the possibility that the outcome of the primaries might be decisively influenced by the participation of centre-right voters. Strategically, it was said, they might cast their ballots in favour of Fausto Bertinotti, secretary of Rifondazione Comunista and the candidate who could most easily be defeated by Berlusconi.[8] All of these never especially serious objections can now be permanently put to rest. It remains to stress that even Prodi's supporters proved unable to predict the turnout and the margin of his victory. Given that Prodi had to be prudent, his estimate was for a total participation of between 600,000 and 1 million. He also stressed that the winner had to obtain just one more vote than the other candidates (presumably beyond the 50 per cent threshold).

Much to everybody's surprise, 4,311,149 voters went to the polls on Sunday, 16 October, and 74 per cent of them voted for Prodi.[9] It was not just a significant victory for the professor himself. The spectacularly high turnout was also the product of the mobilisation of the parties of the centre left[10] and of the intense desire of the many social, cultural and professional associations sharing the goals and the ideas (and, most certainly, the ideals as well) of the centre left,[11] forcefully to empower the leader of their favourite coalition. It was an invitation to the leaders of the parties of the centre left to create a more cohesive and less litigious coalition. The high turnout could also be interpreted as a criticism of Berlusconi, whose parliamentary majority had decided, for blatantly partisan motives, to draft a new electoral law (see below).

Prodi's primaries were without doubt a major event for the centre left and, in terms of political participation and political communication, for the Italian political system as a whole. For a very short time, some centre-right politicians entertained the idea of holding primaries for the selection of the leader of their own coalition. An intolerable prospect for Berlusconi (and, in fact, an eventuality that would only have affected negatively his role and prestige), the idea was quickly jettisoned. As for the centre left, it did not really know how fully to exploit the contribution of the primaries to its image or to the task of coalition-building. Instead of asking for primary elections in order to improve the processes of selection of his coalition's parliamentary candidates (something that would have created additional involvement and mobilisation) Prodi re-launched the idea of a new Democratic Party in order to place the Left Democrats, the Margherita, the Democratic Socialists, and the so-called European Republicans all under his leadership. The Margherita replied that a joint list of these parties (the Democratic Socialists soon withdrew) to be presented for the Chamber of Deputies elections was as far as they could go. The Left Democrats dryly remarked that a party congress would have to be called before they could take a step as momentous as the creation of a new party. In any case, the Democratic Party idea never became a means of popular mobilisation during the election campaign.

Moreover, the magic moment of the primaries, in terms of the political enthusiasm they had generated, had passed. It was never to be revived again, even though other successful primaries were held. These included the elections held to select the candidates for the presidency of the Region of Sicily and for the office of mayor of the important city of Milan. Soon, however, party politics resumed at their worst, giving rise to the unregulated selection, reselection and de-selection of parliamentary candidates; bitter disagreements on the programme; tension and conflicts within the centre-left coalition. The leaders of the centre left gave the visible impression of complacency. Taking for granted that they were destined to win the 9–10 April elections, they were already devoting much of their time and energy to the distribution and appropriation of the spoils: governmental (ministerial and undersecretarial positions) and institutional (the offices of president of the

Chamber and Senate and, last, but by no means least, the presidency of the Republic).[12]

The never-ending institutional transition

The most peculiar and disturbing aspect of the 2001–2006 political context was represented by the fact that the Italian political system was still undergoing an institutional transition. I use this term to refer to the ongoing debate on the rules of the game and on the desirability of reform of the representative and governing institutions at all levels. Following the introduction of a new electoral system, made imperative by the 1993 election-law referendum, Italian parties and coalitions and their leaders had been unable to converge on a serious project to revise and update the 1948 Constitution. In spite of being chaired by Massimo D'Alema – General Secretary of the Left Democrats and, at the time, the most powerful politician in Italy – the Bicameral Commission for Institutional Reform (which sat between 1996 and June 1998) was unable to produce an acceptable comprehensive draft. It was doomed by Berlusconi's unwillingness to cooperate with the centre left or, perhaps, as was widely rumoured at the time, by the unwillingness of the centre left to provide Berlusconi with what he was looking for in terms of strict controls on the judiciary and a sort of *passe-partout* for his conflict of interests. Subsequently, Berlusconi was successful in defeating two electoral-law referenda (in 1999 and 2000) the aim of which was to render the electoral system less proportional by abolishing one of the two ballots given to the voters.

At the end of the parliamentary term, in a move designed to meet and pre-empt the demands for devolution being made by the Northern League, the centre left approved a minor redistribution of powers from the central State to regional governments. Perhaps it was an instance of 'too little too late', but in any case the constitutional reform did not make any change to the two institutions really requiring reform, the Government and Parliament, or to their complex and confused relationship. Once in office again as Prime Minister, Berlusconi was pressed by the League to obtain approval of some serious and significant – opponents would say devastating – measures of devolution.

Within the governing coalition of the Cdl there were many different positions as to the desirability and the necessity of a constitutional reform project as ambitious and wide-ranging as the one that was eventually developed. Because of their institutional and political traditions – after all they were the heirs of those who had written the Constitution – former Christian Democrats gave lukewarm support to the idea of incisive reform. Also, because of its tradition and culture, the National Alliance was essentially interested in strengthening the powers and augmenting the prerogatives of the head of government. Above all the Northern League wanted a strong form of devolution as a step towards the granting of full political autonomy to the regions of the north, or what they refer to as 'Padania'. Not famous for his institutional knowledge or preferences, Berlusconi decided, first of all, to give in to the Northern League and appointed their founder and long-standing leader, Umberto Bossi, to the office of Minister for Devolution and Institutional Reform. After Bossi suffered a serious stroke he was replaced by one of his closest collaborators, Roberto Calderoli, whose major asset was not his expertise, but loyalty to his leader.

Divided on almost all institutional and constitutional issues, the centre left could find cohesion only in opposing the complex text[13] that, formulated by four Cdl experts, was submitted to Parliament. After some internal bickering, and subject to constant prodding by the Northern League (supported by Berlusconi himself who did not want to risk losing the League's participation in the Government), the Cdl steered its constitutional reform through the necessary four parliamentary readings. Throughout this long process, the centre left repeated its intention of calling a referendum so that Italian citizens could defeat the 'dangerous and anti-democratic' reform.[14]

The follow-up to the centre left's parliamentary battle was thus the formal declaration that a referendum would be called against the constitutional reform. For some time there was a sort of subterranean mobilisation of the centre left. Though the conditions required for the holding of a referendum – that is, the request of one-fifth of the members of Parliament or of five regional councils – were both quickly fulfilled, the centre left also established a network of citizens' committees, entitled 'Let's Save the Constitution', in order actively to involve voters, to inform them, and above all to collect, as a sign of strength, 500,000 signatures – the alternative means by which a referendum of this kind can be invoked.[15] By the end of February, this effort was crowned with success since almost one million signatures were sent to the Court of Cassation to be validated.

The existence of an ambitious and, some would say, highly dangerous text reforming the Constitution was certainly an important aspect of the 'political context' of the pre-campaign period; but, with the exception of the Northern League, which based its campaign on its great devolution achievement, none of the parties chose to campaign on the issue or to stress the positive or negative aspects of the constitutional reform. The centre left's superior mobilising capacity and the fact that constitutional referenda (unlike referenda invoked with the aim of striking down ordinary laws) do not require the participation of at least 50 per cent of the electorate in order to be valid, meant that the outcome of the referendum was never in doubt. This, in turn, meant two things: first, that the Italian political–institutional transition would not come to an end; second, that institutional and constitutional issues would continue to affect inter- and intra-coalition relationships throughout the 2006–2011 parliament.

Critics of the centre left quickly pointed out, and rightly so, that centre-left leaders were united in opposing the proposals, but quite unable to find any common alternative platform. They revealed themselves to be what most of them always had been: 'constitutional conservatives'. This observation leads naturally to a discussion of the new electoral law approved by the centre-right parliamentary majority.

A new electoral law

Many commentators have credited Berlusconi with a major institutional achievement, and that is the establishment of the bi-polar political competition that had eluded Italian politics for the whole of the first long period of the Republic's existence between 1946 and 1992. Had he not 'taken to the field' in 1994, so the argument goes, the centre right would have remained a sparse collection of rather small parties and of many not especially strong personalities. In 1994, the government of Italy would have been easy prey for a centre left dominated by the former Communists. Under the then existing conditions, no government of the left would have encountered any significant opposition – with extremely negative consequences for the political system. It is my opinion that this interpretation, though widely entertained, is only partially correct or, more likely, substantially wrong.

I would stress that Berlusconi did indeed save the centre right (its voters, their interests and their preferences); but bi-polar competition was simply a by-product, a side effect, of his desire and ability to oppose the (centre-)left coalition for his own personal (rather than for political) ends. In other words, bi-polar competition was in no sense an objective pursued by Berlusconi in order to construct a new political system. After all, he had thrived under the so-called First Republic governed by friendly Christian Democratic and Socialist politicians.

It is also true that Berlusconi claimed to be a 'majoritarian'.

However, proof that he had been so only out of political expediency came when, as I have indicated above, he in fact successfully *opposed* the two referenda (in 1999 and 2000) that were meant to strengthen the majoritarian component of the electoral system that had been dubbed the 'Mattarellum'.[16] By calling on electors to abstain, he ensured that both referenda failed to reach the necessary quorum. In short, Berlusconi's institutional ideas were highly flexible, if not volatile. Moreover, within his coalition, notwithstanding the significant gains in terms of seats that the Mattarellum had provided them with, both the Northern League and the UDC were as a matter of principle definitely willing to advocate, support and approve a proportional electoral law. Moreover, not only did Berlusconi himself think that, as a party, Forza Italia had something to gain from such an electoral system, but most centre-left parties had never hidden their preference for a proportional law either. To put it in somewhat rhetorical and philosophical terms: subject to the Rawlsian 'veil of ignorance' – that is, unable to calculate in advance their gains and losses – a very large majority of Italian parliamentarians preferred (and continue to prefer) a proportional electoral law.

Here, I will not enter into the technical details of the new law whose discussion has been intensely partisan, acrimonious, and often plainly wrong. I will confine myself to a few specific observations. It is my opinion that, at least in consolidated democratic regimes, electoral laws can legitimately be changed at any point in time. In Italy, there is no legal obstacle preventing a parliamentary majority from changing the electoral law. Whenever the President of the Republic finds aspects of a law to be unconstitutional, he has the power to return it to Parliament. In this case, he did not do so. Electoral laws may be changed both for systemic and for partisan purposes. In the first case, the purpose is to improve the working of the political system. No doubt the sponsors of the 1991 and 1993 electoral referenda wanted both to construct better relationships between the voters and their representatives, and to give more power to voters in government formation. To some extent, these systemic goals were achieved. The case of partisan reforms makes its appearance when a parliamentary majority drafts a law that pursues some purpose specifically related to its own role and power.[17] This was the overriding and unacknowledged goal of the electoral reformers of the centre right.

From the very beginning of the discussion of the proposed electoral reform, the partisan purposes of the Cdl were crystal clear. First, the law was drafted in such a way as to prevent the coalition that was to win in 2006, and which at the time looked most likely to be the centre left, from obtaining more than 340 seats in the Chamber of Deputies (the absolute majority being 316). Second, the law was also meant to minimise the numerical consequences of a probable centre-right defeat. The move from (what was largely) a plurality to a substantially proportional electoral law was meant to achieve both results. On the positive side, the Cdl pointed to the fact that bipolar competition would be saved by the existence of a majority bonus to be given to the coalition receiving the largest number of votes. The bonus in seats is certainly a significant encouragement to the formation of large coalitions. The Cdl also stressed that, on the one hand, the vote thresholds that were envisaged for access to the distribution of seats would discourage minor parties, and, potentially, reduce the fragmentation of the party system. On the other hand, because of the reintroduction of a proportional formula, the parties could at last satisfactorily estimate their true electoral strength.

On the negative side, the Cdl did not redesign the constituencies – with the consequence that the existence of long multi-candidate blocked lists makes it impossible to establish any significant connection between the voters and 'their' representative(s). Moreover, though preference voting was rejected for a variety of good reasons (such as skyrocketing campaign costs, exposure to corrupt dealings and party in-fighting), the dreadful consequence is that the voters will have and have had no influence whatsoever on who is elected to Parliament. As for the candidates, for contrasting reasons, none of them have any incentive to campaign. The best placed of them have no need to do so, for they will be elected anyway. With the exception of those noble personalities who have a passion for politics, the worst-placed candidates have no incentive to waste their time, money and energy. Once in Parliament, observance of even the most minor corollaries of accountability to the voters (as opposed to the party leaders) will be left to the good will of parliamentarians, rather than, as should be the case, to the constraining power of institutional and electoral mechanisms.

The triumph of *partitocrazia* and of the 'partycrats' has been assured and sombrely celebrated because the ranking of candidates on the various party lists is bound to determine, with only very minor variations (due to the votes received by each party) the chances of being elected to Parliament. It was not surprising that the leaders of the centre-right parties had no objection to the closed list system. Forza Italia candidates had always been selected directly by Berlusconi or with his decisive approval (and their behaviour had always revealed their full awareness of their situation). The Northern League's parliamentarians had all been chosen by Bossi and been totally loyal to him.

The new system made it possible for Fini to deal harshly with any disloyal 'lieutenants' and, if necessary, severely punish them. As for the UDC, the new electoral system coupled with the party's promising poll ratings suggested that all incumbent parliamentarians would retain their seats and that a few newcomers could be carefully recruited. The protests of the centre left were loud and vociferous, but, understandably, quite short lived. The large parties, and especially the Left Democrats, were indeed visibly happy because they no longer had to make room for the candidates of minor parties. Small parties could now run on their own and then ask for governmental spoils with reference to the size of their vote. The only problem was that the reform involved a redistribution of seats from the red regions, where the plurality system had given the centre left sweeping victories, to some northern regions (and Sicily) where the centre right had enjoyed a similar predominance.

What to a limited extent disturbed the centre left was that the proportional electoral system clashed frontally with a project that some of their leaders, above all Prodi, were entertaining or, perhaps, only debating: the creation of a 'Democratic Party'. Obviously, the creation of such a party – a gift promised, though unenthusiastically by some, to Prodi and his advisors – would have been more likely and more valuable in the context of a plurality system. It would be less necessary, and perhaps even counterproductive, in the presence of a proportional law. This may explain why Prodi was the most outspoken opponent of the proportional law, at times expressing himself in terms that were excessive.[18] If the proof of the pudding is in the eating, then it remains to be seen whether, now that the elections have taken place, the centre left will really find Berlusconi's electoral law as unpalatable and indigestible as they claim. In any case, the decisive test will be represented by the ability of the centre left quickly to prepare a better electoral pudding, one that is neither *antipatriottico*, nor *incostituzionale*, nor *antidemocratico*.[19]

The continuing moral question

Intertwined with the constitutional and electoral proceedings, a new type of moral issue made its appearance in the months preceding the election campaign. It consisted of several threads. First, there were Berlusconi's repeated and successful attempts to block the legal proceedings against him, to delay them, and to prevent the execution of any sentences handed down against him (much important material is presented by Newell, 2005). Second, there was the shameful trajectory of Antonio Fazio, Governor of the Bank of Italy, who in the name of *Italianità* had become the protector of certain unscrupulous bankers, raiders and financiers who were opposing the attempts made by a Dutch and a Basque institution to acquire two important Italian banks. In so doing, the speculators involved violated several laws and were later indicted. In the end, and after a long and depressing tug-of-war (during which even Camillo Ruini, the Cardinal President of the Italian Conference of Bishops, expressed support for Fazio) the Governor was obliged to resign.

Even the large insurance company, Unipol, owned by the (left-wing) League of Cooperatives, fell into the complex web of confused and not fully transparent financial activities. What is more relevant, intercepted telephone conversations between Unipol's Chief Executive Officer, and Piero Fassino, General Secretary of the Left Democrats, allowed Berlusconi to attack the 'red' cooperatives (which enjoy certain constitutionally protected tax privileges) and to declare that the real conflict of interests was not his own, but rather the one concerning the former Communists and their collateral organisations. Much to the surprise of many, Italy's wealthiest entrepreneur declared that he was living proof of the separation of business from politics. Not really isolated episodes, the financial scandals of the summer of 2005 cannot be interpreted as the reappearance of a moral question involving many politicians. On the one hand, it is true that a not-so-modest dose of political corruption has never been absent from the Italian political system. On the other hand, the episodes seemed to be circumscribed rather than of systemic quality. However, Berlusconi exploited them in order to cast a shadow over the integrity of the centre left and to challenge its claims to moral superiority.

Television and the *par condicio* law

One additional issue formed a significant part of the political context in which the election campaign took place. This was the issue of how advantageous it is to have disproportionate access to television and how fair access was in practice. The law regulating television access is known as the *par condicio* (meaning 'equal' or 'fair condition') law and it comes into force at the very beginning of election campaigns. It has represented a traditional punching ball for Berlusconi. He has constantly insisted that a situation in which very small parties are given almost the same amount of air time as large parties such as Forza Italia cannot be considered democratic. In order to redress this disadvantage, Berlusconi massively exploited the period preceding the enforcement of *par condicio* by making lengthy TV appearances on a wide range of programmes where he was hosted, interviewed and complimented by friendly journalists. The centre left found it difficult to counteract this for two main reasons. The first is that some of the centre left's leaders, including Prodi, snobbishly believe that television is not a good vehicle for the communication of political ideas. It is preferable, they believe, to confine exploitation of the medium to a few selected appearances. The second reason is the classic one: centre-left leaders are unable consistently to communicate single, precise and shared messages. Hence, their television interviews often communicated messages that were at odds with themselves. The problem, of course, lies precisely in the fact that those messages faithfully represented the differences and divergences of opinion and positions existing within the centre left. However, Prodi's performances in his two TV duels with Berlusconi were, perhaps because the expectations of both his supporters and opponents were rather low, surprisingly positive.

The decline of Italy

All over Europe there has been a generational renewal of political and governmental leaders, Jacques Chirac being the only remaining leader of the old generation. For a variety of reasons, most important among them being the lack of alternation,[20] the Italian political class has traditionally enjoyed a fair amount of longevity. In a more or less traumatic way, Mani Pulite engineered quite a turnover of politicians and facilitated the appearance of several new political faces. Still, the losers of competitive elections – Berlusconi in 1996, Prodi in 1998, D'Alema in 2000, Rutelli in 2001 – have not, as would be customary in other European democracies, abandoned the political scene. The outcome of this unhealthy state of affairs is that the 2006 election, under the supervision of the outgoing 86-year-old President of the Republic, was a replay of the competition that had taken place between Silvio Berlusconi (who turned 70 in September) and Romano Prodi (67 in August) that had taken place ten years before. Both have already won and lost the office of Prime Minister. In no European political system have leaders of a comparable age recently run for the highest offices. The fact is that in Italy politics represents, in a rather faithful way, the state of the country. For better, but also for worse, Italy has the most rapidly aging population in Europe and one of the lowest birth rates. Its indigenous population is shrinking. The two old men running for office were not especially noted for the wisdom they had acquired. On the contrary, they were the most visible indicators of a country unable to revitalise itself, and perhaps declining.

Acknowledgements

This chapter was written in Washington, DC, in the period between January and April 2006, when I was Affiliated Scholar at the Brookings Institution's Center on the United States and Europe, whose sponsorship I gratefully acknowledge.

Notes

1 For an excellent discussion of the governmental crisis and its 'solution' see Hine and Hanretty (2006). In the curious Italian political jargon, the new government, though consisting mainly of 'old' faces, was supposed to send the voters an appreciable and convincing signal of *discontinuity*.
2 Because of his unhappiness with Berlusconi's policy, personality, and style of leadership.
3 I have argued this point in my analysis of the 2001 political context (Pasquino, 2002). It is fair to add that my evaluation remains somewhat controversial, but the alternative explanations do not appear persuasive.
4 An early, useful and interesting attempt was provided by Luca Ricolfi (2005), and repeated and concluded in Ricolfi (2006). The financial newspaper *Il Sole 24 Ore*, offered a detailed investigation of each of the five points in Berlusconi's famous 'Contract with the Italian People'. A summary of the results was published in the 15 January 2006 issue, p. 11. It is balanced, though nonetheless rather critical.
5 The five promises concerned pensions, taxes, law and order, employment and infrastructural projects. According to the sources quoted above the only promise to be almost fully achieved was the one concerning pensions. As for the other four promises, achievements did not exceed the threshold of 50 per cent.
6 For an analysis of Puglia's primary elections and those of Prodi, see Valbruzzi (2005).
7 To be precise, there were six candidates: Fausto Bertinotti (Rifondazione Comunista), Clemente Mastella (UDEUR), Alfonso Pecoraro Scanio (Greens), Antonio Di Pietro (Italia dei Valori), Ivan Scalfarotto (a young manager living and working in London) and Simona Panzino (an anti-globalisation activist).
8 The centre-left primaries were 'open' – that is, there were no registration requirements, nor any requirement to be affiliated in some way with any of the centre-left parties. Voters were simply asked to identify themselves, to sign a pledge to support the coalition and to donate a minimum of €1 to cover the costs of holding the primaries. Many voters gave much more

and the total sum raised by the primaries was an almost unbelievable €7.5 million. As for the likelihood that centre-right voters would take part in the centre-left primaries, two factors militated against it. First, it is well known that the centre-right electorate is less interested in politics, less informed about politics, and less inclined to participate than the electorate as a whole. Hence a strategic vote would have had to be deliberately organised. Excluding the encouragement given by *Il Giornale*, the daily newspaper owned by Silvio Berlusconi's brother Paolo, no centre-right politician made the attempt. Second, in most areas of Italy, voters are aware of each other's political views and electoral preferences. Few of them would risk the loss of face involved in voting in a contest organised by the opposing coalition unless they wanted to send the message that they were indeed crossing, so to speak, the coalition lines.

 9 The distribution of votes was as follows: Prodi 3,182,686; Bertinotti (Rifondazione Comunista) 631,592; Mastella (UDEUR) 196,014; Di Pietro (Italia dei Valori) 142,143; Pecoraro Scanio (Greens) 95,388; Scalfarotto (Independent) 26,912; Panzino (anti-globalisation) 19,752.

10 Note, however, that even in terms of the most favourable counting criteria, the combined membership of the parties of the centre left does not exceed 1 million.

11 If one wanted to measure the presence of social capital, then turnout by region would offer a good indicator. Or, to put it in another way, in those regions where the 'volume' of social capital was higher, there would one find higher levels of turnout.

12 Once, following the election, the speakers of the two chambers had been elected, Parliament had to be reconvened to elect the President of the Republic, who then appointed the Prime Minister. Presidents are elected by an assembly consisting of the members of the two chambers plus three representatives from nineteen of the twenty regions and one representative from the Valle d'Aosta region. Since, following the first two ballots (at which a two-thirds majority is required) a president can be elected by an absolute majority of the assembly, the winning coalition was able reasonably to expect to succeed in electing one of its parliamentarians to the Presidency.

13 Ironically, some of the centre right's proposals, especially those concerning the strengthening of the powers of the Prime Minister vis-à-vis Parliament and the President of the Republic, were strikingly similar to proposals that had been presented by centre-left parliamentarians. When it comes to institutional matters, there was and remains a fair amount of political expediency within the centre left. This does not bode well for the future of institutional and constitutional reforms in Italy. A panoply of criticisms, some of then contradicting each other, can be found in ASTRID (2004). A scathing assessment of the centre right's reform proposals is offered by Giovanni Sartori (2006).

14 A more sober, less demonising, and balanced assessment would be that the centre right's constitutional reform proposals were, above all, confused in

terms of their goals and the instruments chosen to achieve them. Hence, it can be said that they would probably have produced several inter-institutional conflicts (centre versus periphery; Prime Minister versus President of the Republic; Prime Minister versus his parliamentary majority). Finally, though the ostensible aim of the reform was to give more power to the Prime Minister and to make him a sort of Weberian 'dictator of the parliamentary battlefield', the proposals also embodied the risk that prime ministers could become prisoners of their own parliamentary majorities.

15 The centre right's constitutional reform proposals are usually identified with only one specific aspect, and that is, devolution, or the transfer of significant powers and tasks from central government to the regions. This is mistaken. The text approved by Parliament also contained measures to establish asymmetric bicameralism, to reduce the number of parliamentarians, to give more power to the Prime Minister, mostly at the expense of the President of the Republic, but also of Parliament (on some of these changes the centre left had formulated very similar proposals), and to change the composition of the Constitutional Court.

16 The name of the (former Christian Democratic) deputy who drafted the electoral law is Sergio Mattarella. Severely criticising the outcome, Giovanni Sartori jokingly dubbed it 'Mattarellum' ('rather crazy'). I share Sartori's evaluations. I totally reject the allegations of some politicians and a few political scientists that those, such as Sartori and myself, who have criticised the Mattarellum are responsible for paving the way to a proportional law. Incidentally, both of us have repeatedly argued the case for the French run-off majority system. For the record, I have reconstructed the usage and meaning of the Mattarellum, and presented a critique, in Pasquino (2001).

17 In 1985 the French President, socialist Francois Mitterrand, (re-)introduced proportional representation in order to make it difficult for the centre right to win the 1986 parliamentary elections and, in any case, to limit the size of its victory. He failed on both counts and was then obliged to accept cohabitation with Prime Minister Chirac.

18 In his scathing criticisms, never focused on the technicalities, he even used adjectives largely out of place and devoid of content such as: *antipatriottica, incostituzionale, antidemocratica*. Since the new electoral law had already been duly countersigned by the President of the Republic, Prodi's utterances seemed implicitly and inappropriately directed at the actions of the President whose task is to represent the nation (the motherland, *patria*), to protect the constitution, to guarantee the democratic framework. The last thing the centre left needed to do was to provoke tensions and conflicts with the Quirinale!

19 Reform of the electoral reform is an unlikely prospect. The centre left's programme argues that electoral laws should be changed only with the support of a two-thirds majority – and that is something that can be achieved exclusively through negotiations with the Cdl. Since, as I have indicated, most leaders and parliamentarians belonging to the Cdl are in

favour of proportionality on principle, no agreement could possibly be obtained for a reform abolishing this feature. However, this would give the centre left an easy scapegoat! To leave nothing unsaid, my point here is that on this (as well as in relation to many other elements of their platform, incidentally, 281 pages) the leaders of the centre left were in a position to offer a united front exclusively when opposing Berlusconi's proposals and laws. Their inability to achieve cohesion when it was their turn to offer proposals was shown by the acrimonious discussion that filled many pages of the Italian dailies, between 18 and 22 February, following the presentation of what was supposed to be their platform.

20 The perpetual election winners, the Christian Democrats and their allies, could not be displaced, while the losers, especially the Communists, were able to disclaim responsibility for election defeats by pointing to the existence of the *conventio ad excludendum*, an unwritten agreement of the centrist parties allegedly to discriminate against the Communists by preventing them from participating in government.

References

ASTRID [Associazione per gli Studi e le ricerche sulla Riforma delle Istituzioni Democratiche] (2004), *Costituzione: una riforma sbagliata*, Florence, Passigli.

Hine, D. and Hanretty, C. (2006), '"Così fanno le democrazie avanzate": la coalizione e la crisi di governo in aprile', in G. Amyot and L. Verzichelli (eds), *Politica in Italia 2006 edition*, Bologna, Il Mulino.

Newell, J. L. (2005), 'Corruption-mitigating policies: the case of Italy', *Modern Italy*, 10:2, 163–186.

Pasquino, G. (2001), *La transizione a parole*, Bologna, Il Mulino.

Pasquino, G. (2002), 'The political context 1996–2001', in J. L. Newell (ed.), *The Italian General Election of 2001: Berlusconi's Victory*, Manchester and New York, Manchester University Press.

Ricolfi, L. (2005), *Dossier Italia. A che punto è il 'Contratto con gli italiani'*, Bologna, Il Mulino.

Ricolfi, L. (2006), *Tempo scaduto. Il 'Contratto con gli italiani' alla prova dei fatti*, Bologna, Il Mulino.

Sartori, G. (2006), *Mala Costituzione e altri malanni*, Rome and Bari, Laterza.

Valbruzzi, M. (2005), *Primarie. Partecipazione e leadership*, Bologna, Bononia University Press.

2

The economic context

Michele Capriati

Introduction

The issues at the centre of public debate on the economy between 2001 and 2006 were essentially two in number: the possibility that the country was in a state of economic decline, and loss-making public accounts. The root of these problems goes back many years; but for the first time in Italian history, a cabinet – that is, the Berlusconi government – had been in office for a full term, and it also benefited from a large parliamentary majority. It was therefore in a favourable position to implement wide-ranging long-term policies that could bring about profound changes. In this chapter I will show that these changes did not occur. In order to do this I will: provide a five-year overview of the most important macroeconomic variables; examine the main economic policy measures implemented during the centre-right legislature; summarise the two major coalitions' manifestos; and, finally, focus on the economic issues at the centre of the election campaign and put forward hypotheses on Silvio Berlusconi's 'partial defeat'.

An overview

During the parliamentary debate of 15 June 2006, the new Economy and Finance Minister, Tommaso Padoa Schioppa, defined the state of the Italian economy as 'very serious', saying that the public accounts were in a 'critical' condition. The country, concluded the minister, was running many risks, with a budget deficit close to 5 per cent. 'In many respects the current situation is worse than in 1992, when economic indicators such as the primary budget surplus or the public debt/GDP ratio were in better shape than today'. The latter ratio in particular was worrying: 'it is necessary to reduce it. Until this ratio is reduced we can say whatever we like, but we will not convince the market, which feels invigorated when it smells blood'.[1]

Those who know Padoa Schioppa[2] are well aware of his discreet, cautious approach and his tendency to seek to calm passions in debate. What led a person of such stature to speak so bluntly? In the following section I show that the minister's dramatic tone is largely justified.

Production and prices

In the first five years of the new millennium the Italian economy suffered a severe setback. Between 2001 and 2005, GDP grew on average by 0.6 per cent and its rate of growth was consistently lower than the average for the twelve countries that had joined the euro (see Figure 2.1). After 2001, which recorded growth of 1.8 per cent, near to the levels reached by the other European countries, the increase in GDP was close to zero, except for 2004. The difference with the other countries of the euro zone increased over the entire period, from a minimum of 0.1 per cent in 2001 to a maximum of 1.3 per cent in 2005.

The data on national industrial production point to a phase of prolonged recession. Between 2000 and 2005 production decreased steadily by 4 per cent (6 per cent if one considers only manufacturing output). During the same period of time, industrial production in the euro zone rose by over 4 per cent: 7 per cent in Germany, 4 per cent in Spain, 2 per cent in France, and over 7 per cent in Finland and Sweden.

The output trend in Italy was affected by two main factors: investments and exports (see Figure 2.2). The former gave rise to the growth recorded in 2001 and compensated for the exports collapse in 2002.

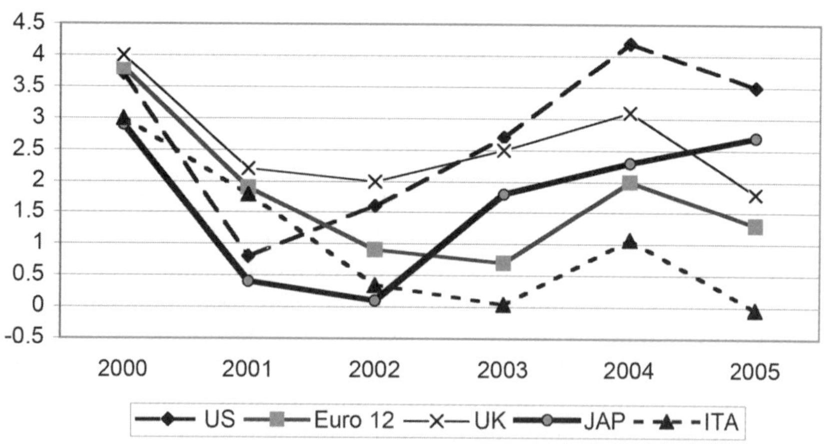

Source: IMF.

Figure 2.1 GDP (% variations over the previous year)

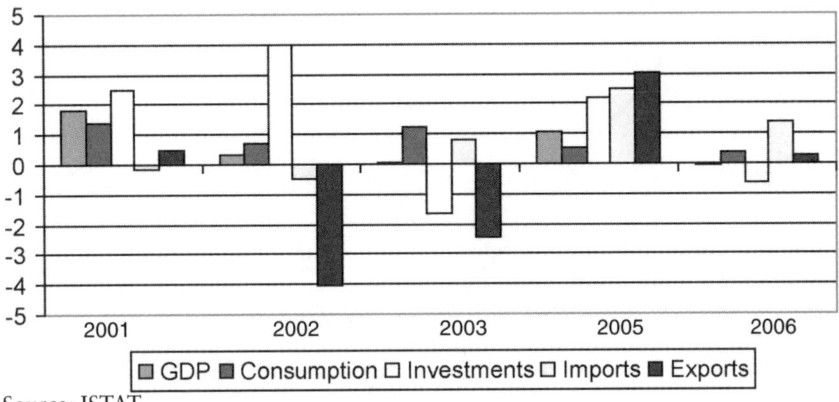

Source: ISTAT.

Figure 2.2 GDP, consumption, investments, imports and exports
(% variations over the previous year)

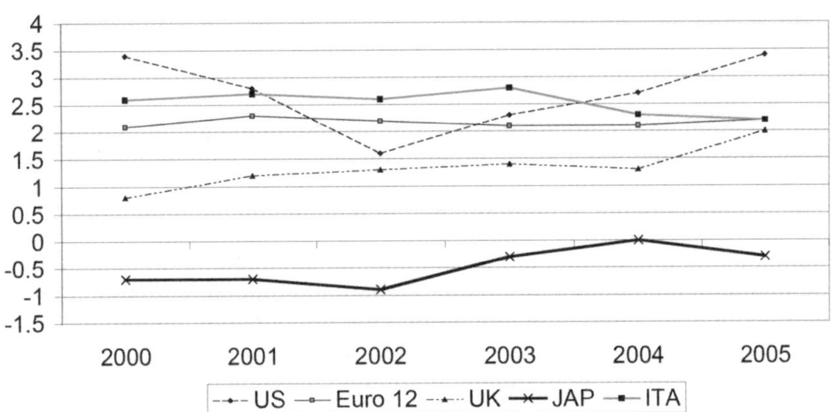

Source: IMF.

Figure 2.3 Harmonised consumer prices indices
(% variations over the previous year)

The latter had a negative influence in 2002 and 2003 and a positive
one on the modest recovery in 2004. The consumption trend was not
particularly healthy over the entire period, while the increase in
imports over the last three years was related to the sharp increase in
the cost of raw materials, particularly that of oil.

Increases in the prices of consumer goods remained above the
average for the countries joining the single European currency (see
Figure 2.3). Interestingly though, they converged towards this average
during 2003–2005. It is worth pointing out that the price increases

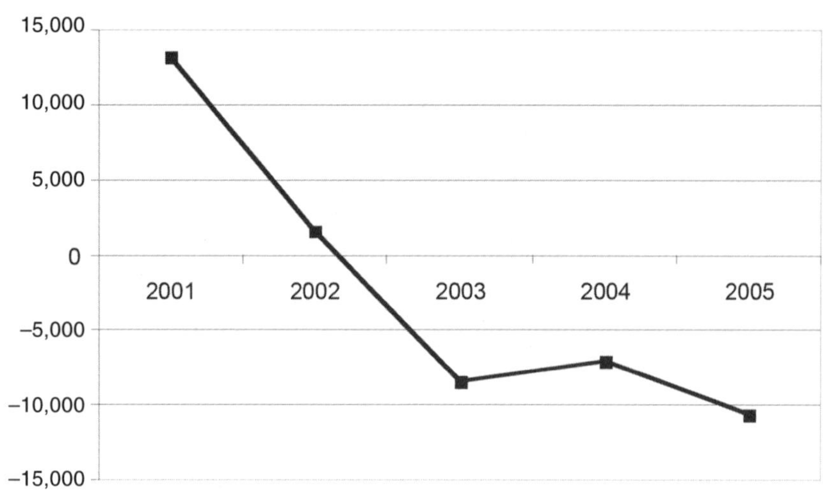

Source: ISTAT.

Figure 2.4 Foreign trade balance (millions of Euro)

recorded for the United Kingdom, unlike those for Italy, were consistently lower than the European average.

Balance of trade

Over the same period of time the competitiveness of the Italian economy declined progressively. Italian exports as a proportion of world trade at constant prices fell from 4.5 per cent in 1996, to 3.5 per cent in 2000 and 2.9 per cent in 2004. After being in surplus for over ten years, the balance of trade went into deficit in 2003 and in the following two years (see Figure 2.4).

Analysis of the structure of the balance of trade highlights two phenomena characterising the trend of the last few years: a deterioration in the balance accounted for by energy expenditure, which, owing to the jump in oil prices, recorded an increase in the deficit of more than €12 billion, rising from –€26 billion in 2001 to –€38 billion in 2005; and a steady reduction in the surplus in the trade in manufactured products, particularly consumer goods, which declined by 35 per cent from +€27 billion in 2001 to the current +€18 billion. The only improvement concerns machine tools with a current surplus of €15 billion compared to €12 billion in 2001.

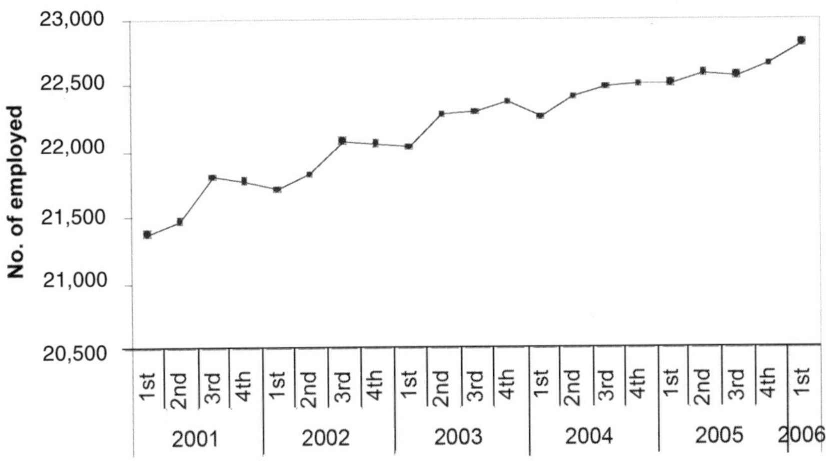

Source: ISTAT.

Figure 2.5 Italy, employment (absolute values, 000s)

Labour market

The trend in the macroeconomic indicators describing the labour market runs in the opposite direction. Between the first quarter of 2001 and the first quarter of 2006, employment grew by 1.5 million (see Figure 2.5) whereas unemployment decreased from 9.1 per cent in 2001 to 7.7 per cent in 2005 (see Figure 2.6).

If employment figures are calculated by referring to standard labour units,[3] one notes first a net slowdown in the rate of growth from 2002, then, from 2004, a reduction in the amount of labour effectively produced by the Italian economy (see Figure 2.7).

We have already seen that between 2001 and 2005 employment increased and the rate of unemployment decreased. However, recent studies have highlighted some peculiarities that are worth considering. First of all, as shown by an investigation carried out by the Bank of Italy (Bank of Italy, 2005; and Istat, 2006a) one ought to subtract from the increase of 1.5 million employed, 641,000 immigrant workers whose positions were regularised thanks to the Bossi–Fini law,[4] which thus added to the statistics a number of employed persons previously excluded but which existed already. At the same time, inclusion of these immigrants in the figures for the number of residents and for the numbers in employment explains why the ratio of those in employment to the resident population (the employment rate)

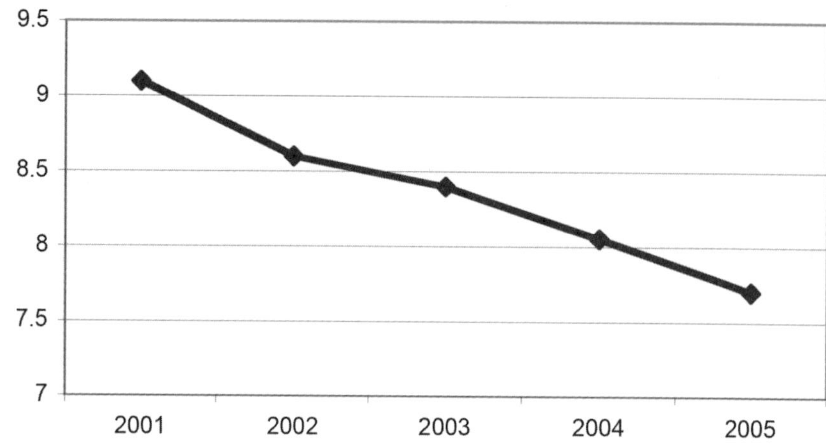

Source: ISTAT.

Figure 2.6 Rate of unemployment (%)

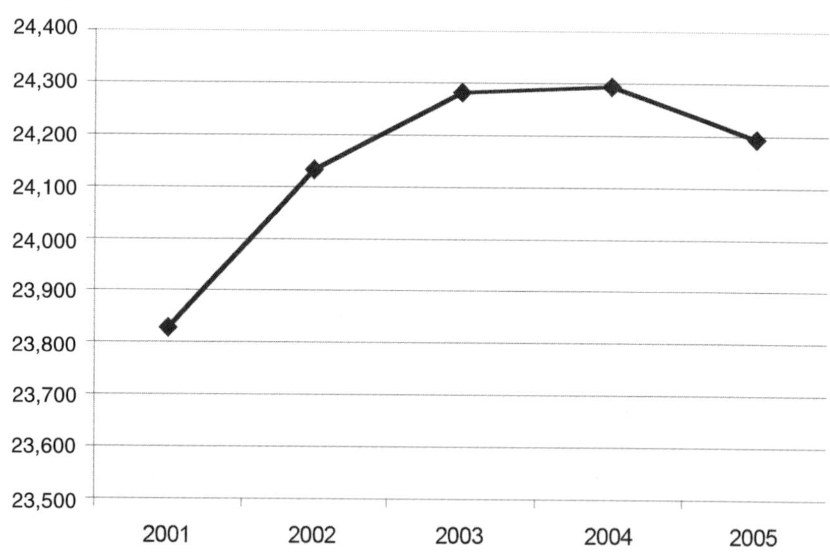

Source: ISTAT.

Figure 2.7 Standard labour units (absolute values, 000s)

remained constant, despite the apparent increase in employment. By considering this accounting effect, the Bulletin of the Bank of Italy (2005) has highlighted how employment stopped growing from the end of 2003 onwards.

Moreover, the reduction in the rate of unemployment is connected with a steady abandonment of the search for work, particularly by the female unemployed in the south. In the last three years in the Mezzogiorno the reduction in the unemployment rate, from 16.8 per cent in the first quarter of 2003 to 14.5 per cent in October 2005, was in reality due to the fact that many people in the south stopped looking for work because of their perceptions of the limited chances of finding it. In fact, despite the reduction in employment, the number of job-seekers decreased by 120,000 (Istat, 2006b).

Public accounts

In 2005 Italy's public debt (see Table 2.1) was 106.4 per cent of GDP, the highest in the euro zone after Greece's (107.5 per cent); the budget deficit was 4.1 per cent, well over the 3 per cent limit established by the Maastricht Treaty, lower only than the deficits for Greece (4.5 per cent) and Portugal (5 per cent).

The ratio of public debt to GDP (see Table 2.2 and Figure 2.8) began to rise in 2005 after a steady ten-year fall, which slowed down considerably in the last few years. The ratio was reduced by 11.9 points between 1996 and 2001 and by 4.8 points from 2001 to 2004; it then increased by 2.5 points and reached a level of 106.4 in 2005. In the latter year the deficit exceeded 4 per cent of GDP despite a constant

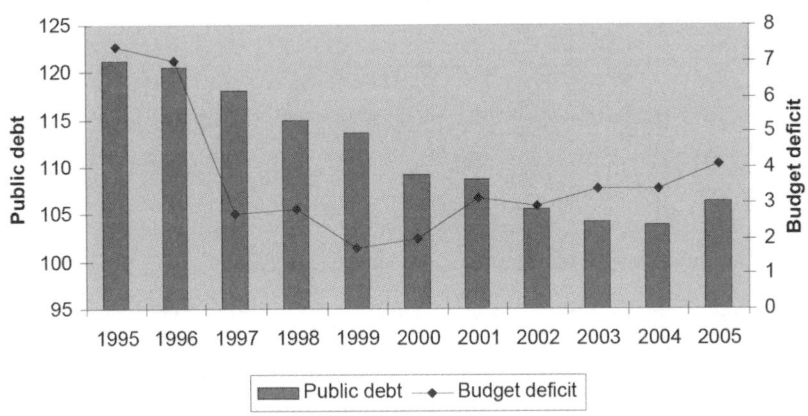

Source: ISTAT.

Figure 2.8 Budget deficit and public debt (% of GDP)

Table 2.1 Budget deficit and public debt in the countries of the euro zone (% of GDP)

Country	Budget deficit				Public debt			
	2002	2003	2004	2005	2002	2003	2004	2005
Germany	3.7	4	3.7	3.3	6.3	63.8	65.5	67.7
France	3.2	4.2	3.7	2.9	58.2	62.4	64.4	66.8
Italy	2.9	3.4	3.4	4.1	105.5	104.3	103.9	106.4
Spain	0.3	0	0.1	−1.1	52.5	48.9	45.4	43.2
Holland	2	3.1	1.9	0.3	50.5	51.9	52.8	52.9
Belgium	0	−0.1	0	−0.1	103.2	98.5	94.7	93.3
Austria	0.5	1.5	1.1	1.5	66	64.4	63.6	62.9
Greece	4.9	5.8	6.9	4.5	110.7	107.8	108.5	107.5
Finland	−4.1	−2.5	−2.3	−2.5	41.3	44.3	44.3	41.1
Ireland	0.4	−0.2	−1.5	−1	32.1	31.1	29.4	27.6
Portugal	2.9	2.9	3.2	5	55.5	57	58.7	63.9
Luxembourg	−2	−0.2	1.1	1.9	6.5	6.3	6.6	6.2
Euro zone	2.5	3	2.8	2.4	68.1	69.3	69.8	70.8

Source: Bank of Italy.

Table 2.2 Principal budget indicators for Italy 1995–2005 (% of GDP)

	1995	1996	1997	1998	1999	2000	2001	2002	2003	2004	2005
Revenue	45.3	45.7	47.7	46.2	46.4	45.4	45.0	44.5	45.1	44.6	44.4
Expenditure	52.7	52.6	50.3	49.0	48.1	47.4	48.1	47.4	48.5	48.0	48.5
of which: interest payments	11.6	11.5	9.3	7.9	6.6	6.3	6.3	5.5	5.1	4.7	4.6
Primary surplus	4.2	4.6	6.6	5.1	4.9	4.3	3.2	2.7	1.7	1.3	0.4
Net deficit	7.4	7.0	2.7	2.8	1.7	2.0	3.1	2.9	3.4	3.4	4.1
Debt	121.2	120.6	118.1	114.9	113.7	109.2	108.7	105.5	104.3	103.9	106.4

Source: Bank of Italy.

reduction (which then came to a halt) in interest costs. Net public spending (total expenditure less interest payments) rose by 2 per cent of GDP, from 41.9 per cent in 2001 to 43.9 per cent in 2005. The primary budget surplus, which was 3.2 per cent of GDP in 2001, fell to 0.4 per cent in 2005.

The latter result summarises the difference between the budgetary policy implemented by the Berlusconi government and the previous one. In the 1996–2001 period the centre-left government aimed to achieve a substantial primary surplus through a tax revenue policy, which, except for 1997 when a great deal of effort was put into meeting the parameters laid down by the Maastricht Treaty for joining the euro, stabilised tax revenue at 45 and 46 per cent of GDP (see Table 2.2), while net public spending was kept stable at 41–42 per cent. This meant being able to generate an average primary surplus of around 5 per cent, a result which helped to reduce the public debt by the significant proportion of 12 per cent of GDP.

The centre right's budgetary policy kept tax revenue between 44 and 45 per cent of GDP, therefore without substantial variations compared with the previous five years, but it steadily increased primary expenditure which came close to 44 per cent in 2005, nullifying the benefit of the primary surplus almost completely. If the Berlusconi government, by maintaining the balance already achieved by 2001 between tax revenue and public spending, had kept constant the difference between net spending and tax revenue in relation to GDP, the budget deficit in 2005 would have been 1.4 per cent of GDP rather than 4.1 per cent.

Is the Italian economy declining?

Such a poor economic performance has led to what has become almost a commonplace (Nardozzi, 2004; Toniolo and Visco, 2004; Boeri *et al.*, 2005): the Italian economy is declining steadily. The most significant facts used to justify this opinion are three:

- limited growth from 1995 to 2005;
- strong decline in the rate of growth of productivity, which became negative in the last few years;
- steady reduction in Italy's shares of world export markets.

All the above processes have been the object of contrasting interpretations which have downplayed their importance. It has been pointed out (Ciocca, 2003; Faini, 2004), in fact, that the reduction in GDP growth is to a great extent to be explained by the low population growth and the changes that have occurred in the age structure of the population, which significantly worsened over the ten-year period, owing to laws restricting immigration.

On the other hand, the marked reduction in productivity can be adequately explained by the profound changes implemented in the regulation of the labour market since 1995. The new laws on employment contracts – especially the *pacchetto Treu*, facilitating the deployment of so-called atypical forms of labour, described below (p. 47) – have permitted an increase in employment despite low GDP growth (Sestito, 2004; Capriati, 2005). One can therefore suggest that they may have encouraged employers to take on unskilled labour, thus causing an overall decrease in labour productivity.

Finally, the reduction in Italian exports as a proportion of world trade is mainly due to the spectacular growth of Asian exports and the exports of China in particular. It is entirely to be expected that the growth of such a large country would bring relative reverses for developed countries, in particular those which, like Italy, specialise in traditional sectors (clothing, footwear, furniture). However, these prolonged difficulties highlight a weakness in the Italian economy which can no longer be explained only by conjunctural factors but needs to be addressed by a substantial restructuring of the production system.

Economic policy measures

Public finances

The critical state of public finances during the last legislature arises from a monumental error contained in the programme of the Berlusconi government right from the outset (Capriati, 2005): that is, the assumption that strong, sustained growth would generate a spontaneous increase in revenue. The trend in 2005, which is out of line with the economic forecast of the Berlusconi government, has been explained by the fact that growth came to a standstill as a result of unpredictable events, such as widespread terrorism, Chinese competition, over-valuation of the euro and a jump in oil prices. In actual fact, the growth forecast had started to be reappraised from the end of 2000, but this was ignored by the centre right, which insisted on drawing up the budget on the basis of envisaged GDP increases greater than 3 per cent a year for all of the subsequent years, thus assuming that greater revenues would cover the main categories of expenditure and some tax cuts. The international explanations did not stand up to the facts, which show that other industrialised countries, as we saw earlier, experienced less difficulty compared to the Italian economy which, in contrast, lost ground to the partners of the euro zone.

In the last legislature the envisaged revenue increases did not materialise, this causing a progressive deterioration in the public accounts, particularly in the primary surplus. Despite the growing imbalances, the Minister of the Economy and Finance failed to exert strict control over public spending, preferring to adopt temporary short-term measures such as tax and contribution amnesties and an amnesty for infringements of building regulations, which produced occasional tax receipts even while the underlying trend in public finances was increasingly negative. In this way the minister shifted the burden of structural reorganisation onto younger generations and future ministers (Capriati, 2005).

The deterioration in the public accounts did not lead to serious difficulties with the partners of the euro zone thanks to the relaxation, promoted by the Italian government itself, in the parameters laid down by the Growth and Stability Pact, which resulted in an increase, from one to two years, in the amount of time countries would have to correct excessive deficits before the infringement procedures would be applied (see chapter 3).

Fiscal policy

The fiscal policy of the centre-right government envisaged a substantial reduction in the Imposta sul Reddito delle Persone Fisiche (Personal Income Tax; IRPEF), a reduction in the tax rate on business incomes, and abolition of the Imposta Regionale sulle Attività Produttive (Regional Business Tax; IRAP) and the inheritance and capital transfer tax (Bosi and Guerra, 2005; Guerra and Zanardi, 2006).

This package of proposals was criticised from the outset both for its likely effects on the public accounts and for the risk it carried of distorting the tax system (Capriati, 2002). In fact, the Personal Income Tax reductions were to be achieved by reducing to only two the number of rates – the first, of 23 per cent, to be imposed on incomes up to 200 million lire (€103,291.38); the second, of 33 per cent, to be imposed on incomes above that amount – thus considerably reducing the progressivity of the tax, particularly if one considers that the second income band concerned only 0.5 per cent of taxpayers.

The entire fiscal reform project was based on the expectation of high growth rates and the idea that tax reductions themselves generate higher revenue as a result of the higher growth deriving from them. On the basis of these assumptions – which, incidentally, are not confirmed either by theory or by empirical evidence – the government considered it superfluous to provide the necessary financial resources to cover tax cuts. The government's fiscal policy was soon translated into a complex law of delegation[5] whose provisions were therefore implemented almost entirely through legislative decrees. The inheritance and capital transfer tax was abolished almost as soon as the government took office[6] and the so-called 'first module' of the reform was then introduced in order to cut taxes, particularly for those on low and medium incomes, by a total of €6 billion. Three years later, in 2004, the 'second module' was passed with the aim of cutting taxes by a further €6 billion, this time on the highest incomes in particular. In the meantime, the tax on business incomes was reduced to 33 per cent while abolition of IRAP was shelved.

While these cuts were coming into effect, other measures were being implemented to neutralise substantially the drop in revenue and in many cases increase the total levy. Passage of the 'first module' of the fiscal reform simultaneously abolished the legislation of the previous government, which had reduced IRPEF. Compensation for fiscal drag (amounting to about €6 billion, which thus reduced by half the impact of the reduction of IRPEF) was denied; incentives to investments and employment in the south were cut; tax credits were made discretionary and more complicated; expenditures on capital account were turned into mortgages; Dual Income Tax, which had allowed reductions in the taxation on business incomes, was abolished.

What were the effects of these interventions on tax revenues? Despite the overall increase in the tax burden, fiscal receipts gradually decreased, except for 2003, when the impact of tax amnesties was greater. The apparent contradiction between an increase in the tax burden and a decrease in tax receipts is explained by the rise in tax evasion, which, far from being opposed during the Berlusconi legislature, was strongly encouraged by the above-mentioned tax and contribution amnesties and the amnesty for infringements of building regulations, introduced in order to present a healthy budget.

The amnesties had a negative effect not only because they encouraged tax evasion (if I evade paying taxes today, tomorrow there will be an amnesty which will allow me to go unpunished) but also because the solution to the problem of balancing the public accounts they provided was temporary. In fact, no sooner had the amnesties expired than the real situation emerged dramatically, forcing the Government to appeal to Brussels for clemency by suspending application of the excessive deficit procedure, which, at that point, could no longer be avoided.

Industrial policy

The stagnation of the Italian economy, highlighted in the introduction to the present chapter, can be largely explained by the crisis of the industrial system, which suffered from a steady reduction in innovative capacity and a permanent loss of competitiveness.

What were the policies implemented by the centre-right government to deal with these difficulties? The interventions of the Berlusconi government in industry were characterised by the absence of any explicit or coherent policy. The only government document (MAP, 2005) that tackled industrial problems in a systematic way was presented by the Industry Minister, Claudio Scajola, in December 2005, two months before the end of the legislature. The content of the document conflicted with the Government's actions during the previous years. In contrast with the claims made until then, the Government admitted that there was a serious industrial crisis of a structural nature and suggested, in clear conflict with its practice of interventions 'across the board', the need for selective interventions that would favour the development of strategic industrial activities. Business concessions were substantially reduced,[7] and were also revised by partially transforming capital-account contributions into concessionary public financing, and by imposing, as a condition for granting concessions, the requirement that matched funding be available. The Government's incentives policy was characterised by growing uncertainty both with regard to the availability of resources and with regard to the incentive mechanism. The main intervention realised by the Berlusconi government to support investments was the Tremonti Law, which cost over €8 billion and financed industrial investments automatically, without applying any selection criteria. The main effect of this intervention was an anomalous growth in investment in 2002 (see Figure 2.2).

During processes of reorganisation of European industry the choices made by the Government in strategic sectors added to uncertainty among large Italian companies. In fact the Berlusconi government refused to sanction Italian participation in the Airbus consortium's project for the construction of military transport aircraft, thus cutting Italian industry off from one of the most important industrial initiatives to have been developed in Europe in recent years. Furthermore, the centre-right government declined to guarantee Italian participation in the Galileo project, whose aim is to realise a European system of satellite positioning that challenges the American GPS monopoly. This decision meant losing the opportunity to host in Rome the project's business headquarters, which were established in Munich instead.

Labour market

The main intervention of the Berlusconi government in the labour market was law no. 30/2003,[8] which, by diversifying the types of employment contract that could be applied 'at the margins' (that is, to new employees), aimed at achieving greater flexibility in relations between employers and employees. The law introduced 'staff leasing', which allows people to be employed through appropriate employment agencies; 'work on call', which allows companies to call on staff to work at any time subject to appropriate payment; 'job-sharing', a system whereby two or more people do a job that would otherwise be done by a single person; 'project contracts', which regulate jobs linked to the execution of temporary, specialised activities.[9] The first Report on law no. 30/2003 carried out by Confindustria (General Confederation of Italian Industry) reveals that the use of job-sharing, work on call and staff leasing is substantially nil or marginal. In fact only 2.2 per cent of the companies investigated had used them. Of the 42 types of job contract, many are scarcely used by businesses, something that probably indicates that the system is excessively flexible. Owing to the consolidated forms of contract, mainly introduced in 1997 by the so-called *pacchetto Treu* (a series of labour-market reforms, named after their sponsor, Tiziano Treu), job insecurity has been on the rise. An investigation carried out by the Confederazione Generale Italiana del Lavoro (General Confederation of Italian Labour; CGIL) shows that the proportion of temporary jobs has increased in all sectors: in 2004, 70 per cent of new employees had temporary jobs. Today in Italy so-called atypical workers amount to over 2.5 million and include those with contracts for: coordinated and ongoing collaboration (1,177,000); occasional collaborators (106,000); collaborators with VAT registration numbers (311,000); people employed on temporary contracts (502,000); and associates in partnership (400,000). If one also takes into account the number of people having temporary contracts with employment agencies (1,599,000), the number of workers with precarious jobs is 4 million. This phenomenon is directly related to the lower productivity of the country's economy – as well as to lower household consumption, declining investment and stagnant birth rates.

The Mezzogiorno

According to the Svimez Report (Svimez, 2005), in 2004 the southern economy recorded a rate of growth lower than that for the centre-north for the first time in many years. In 2004, GDP growth in the centre-north was 1.4 per cent (0.2 per cent in 2003), versus 0.8 per cent in the south (0.4 per cent in 2003). The employment indicators too showed a situation of great difficulty. For the second consecutive year the Mezzogiorno lost a large number of employed people (−23,000 units); while, as we saw earlier, a large number of the unemployed were inactive, a sign of disheartenment which discouraged them from looking for a job.

What were the main instruments of regional policy aimed at changing this age-old state of affairs? In the 2001 election programme of the Casa delle libertà (Cdl) a central role in the development of the Mezzogiorno was to be assumed by the so-called *Legge Obiettivo* (Objective Law), eventually passed in December of that year and which planned major public investment projects 'to bring the infrastructure of the south up to the levels of the rest of the country'.[10] According to an estimate provided by Svimez (2005), updated to 30 April 2005, of 86 national projects financed by the *Legge Obiettivo* at a total cost of €52.7 billion, 45 were located in the south at a cost of €14.4 billion (27.4 per cent of the national total). Of these, only eight had had sites found for them. Meanwhile, the funds that had actually been disbursed amounted to only 9.8 per cent of the projects' combined cost (equivalent to 1.5 per cent of the total cost of the projects financed by the *Legge Obiettivo* in the south), thus delaying their progress. The effectiveness of this intervention in the Mezzogiorno was therefore very limited.

Another important intervention in the Mezzogiorno was the creation of the *Fondo Unico per il Sud* (Single Fund for the South), an instrument which facilitated the identification and flexible management of additional resources for the south. It needs to be pointed out, however, that despite adequate funding, the way in which the cash flow was managed prevented an effective use of the available resources.

The above-mentioned incentives reform, the Tremonti Law, is still incomplete and places a series of obstacles in the way of access to concessionary financing intended for small and start-up businesses. Law no. 488/1992, which was the main instrument of concessionary financing for disadvantaged regions, did not reform the general organisation of such financing and does not appear to have influenced investors' strategies or adequately stimulated production and organisational innovation. This created a climate of uncertainty among investors which did not help business development in the Mezzogiorno.

Sviluppo Italia, the development agency owned entirely by Ministry of the Economy and Finance, was given the task of attracting investment. However, the new 'localisation contract', which was supposed to encourage and attract foreign investment in a more rapid and flexible way, was not effectively realised – shown by the fact that only two contracts got off the ground in 2005.

More recently the centre right's policies have favoured the privatisation of social wealth. The 2006 Finance Act introduced the measure that provides for the building of large tourist settlements along the coast to increase public revenue.[11]

The economic proposals of the two coalitions

As often happens at election time, the programmes ended up staying in the background of political debate, which focused instead on a few, effective slogans intended to capture the electors' attention. However, the rundown state of the Italian economy described earlier forced the two coalitions to respond in an appropriate, constructive way. They reacted to this imperative through their official political programmes rather than through the debate that took place during the election campaign.

The programme of the centre-right coalition

The initial sections of the centre right's programme focused on the results achieved during the five-year Berlusconi government and on the external factors that had supposedly prevented the achievement of better economic results: the terrorist attack on the Twin Towers, competition from Asian countries (particularly China), the increase in oil prices, the euro and globalisation. The programme listed the 'thirty-six great reforms of the Berlusconi government', and included among them: the labour-market reform (law no. 30/2003), the fiscal reform, the *Legge Obiettivo*, the Single Fund for the South and the incentives reform. After the section on the coalition's values (peace and freedom; international dialogue; Europeanism and Atlanticism; the maintenance of 'our' identity and traditions; the defence of religious values, the family, and the Christian Judaic origins of Europe) the programme moved on to outlining what would be accomplished in case of victory. This part of the programme was made up of ten parts, eight of which began with the phrase 'we will continue . . .' – thus indicating a strong desire to insist on continuity with the programme of the previous legislature, not entirely carried out. With particular reference to economic issues, the programme reaffirmed the intention to increase job opportunities for women and young people; to implement the ten-year plan for major works; to support business and Italian manufacturing; and to launch a special housing plan and reduce public spending in order to reduce taxation. Of course, each of these points contains a detailed account of the concessionary or expenditure measures that are to be implemented in order achieve them. On the whole, unlike the 2001 programme of the Cdl, the 2006 programme omitted philosophical considerations about economic growth, which found their inspiration in the economic policies of the Conservative governments of the 1980s in the UK, and provided a pragmatic list of single initiatives aimed at completing the transformation of the economy and the state.

The programme of the centre-left coalition

The approach and objectives of the centre left's programme were different. Resulting from the necessity to tie down the nine coalition parties to a common programme for government, it was less succinct than the centre right's programme (which was only 21 pages long) and, at 281 pages, was structured in greater detail. The centre left's programme was made up of thirteen sections. The first five were devoted respectively to institutional problems, the quality of public administration, justice, security, and international politics. The following four were devoted instead to economic issues: a new strategy to overcome the industrial crisis and sort out public finances; the Mezzogiorno; education; and training and research. The remaining four sections concerned Italians living abroad, immigration, information and culture.

As for the economy, the centre left's programme identified the main orientations of future government policy. To resolve the deep industrial crisis, it adopted the 'Lisbon strategy' (Consiglio Europeo, 2000), which rests the possibilities of recovery of the European economy on technological innovation together with the valorisation of human capital. It also implements policies that strengthen education, training and research. To this end it proposed an effective policy of liberalisation of the market economy: more transparency and more competitiveness, to the advantage of savers and consumers (Amendola *et al.*, 2005; Costi and Messori, 2005). With regard to work and welfare the centre left's programme found its inspiration in the European model, which aims to combine employment growth with a social security system that is just, comprehensive and effective (Giannini and Onofri, 2005).

The strategy to improve the state of public finances aimed to achieve a fairer tax system, fight tax evasion and reduce the cost of labour. For the Mezzogiorno it aimed to create infrastructures able to include this part of the country in the new flow of goods and capital that is affecting the Mediterranean (Rossi, 2005; Barca, 2006). It also formulated a new industrial policy based on selective incentives and greater social inclusion of the southern citizens, who are socially and economically weaker.

Comparing the economic effects of the two programmes

By their very nature, election programmes are rather vague when it comes to costing proposed measures, since they are primarily intended to reflect rather than challenge the viewpoints of potential voters in order to achieve the maximum possible support. Even an approximate estimate of the costing of the proposed initiatives would have to indicate how to finance them, hence specify the inevitable tax increases and/or reductions in public spending. These themes are notoriously unpopular and do not generate support.

Thanks to the work of a group of economists (La Redazione de lavoce, 2006), the two coalitions' programmes have been compared and contrasted, and an estimate of the minimum and maximum costs of the proposed initiatives has been provided (see Table 2.3).

Table 2.3 The yearly cost of the main undertakings of the two coalitions (billion Euros)

	Casa delle libertà		Unione	
Undertakings	min	max	min	max
reduction of *cuneo fiscale*	6	6	10	10
minimum pensions	5	30		
tax cuts for large families	3	18		
reorganisation of child allowance & tax cuts			1	2
crèche facilities and minimum incomes			4	6
reform of social safety net			2.5	3.5
third phase of the IRE-IRPEF reform	10	12		
fiscal drag repayments			2	2
tax cuts for re-invested profits	5	5		
gradual reduction of IRAP	2.5	25		
abolition of ICI for first-time home buyers	2.5	3		
tax rate reduction on bank deposits	1.9	1.9	0.9	0.9
Total	35.9	100.9	20.4	24.4

Source: www.lavoce.info

The programme of the Cdl was found to be the more expensive, the cost of its proposed measures amounting to a minimum of €36 billion and a maximum of €101 billion a year, between 2.5 and 7 per cent of GDP. The cost of the measures proposed by the Unione is significantly lower, ranging from €20 billion to €24 billion, between 1.4 and 1.7 per cent of GDP. The most significant differences between the two programmes concerned three measures: minimum pensions, tax cuts for large families and the reduction in IRAP. In the case of these three initiatives the large differences between the minimum and maximum values can be explained by the fact that neither of the programmes revealed many of the important details that would be needed to estimate the costs of the measures accurately. The Cdl provided only vague information on the financial resources to be used to meet the costs, such as measures to reduce tax evasion, the beneficial effects of growth on tax revenues, and the sale of public assets (the latter, however, has a direct impact on the public debt rather than the deficit). The Unione proposed to raise about €7 billion by increasing income tax and social security contributions by the self-employed, and by reintroducing inheritance tax for the largest estates. Therefore about a third of the Unione's commitments are credible.

How did Berlusconi almost manage to win?

To summarise the present discussion one can safely affirm that the Berlusconi government:

1. held office during a downward phase of the Italian economy;
2. failed to implement effective policies to deal with the critical state of the economy; and
3. seriously compromised the balance and future sustainability of the public accounts.

These and other circumstances[12] caused the centre right to be at a distinct disadvantage in these elections. Less than a month before the elections, the gap between the two coalitions was estimated at 4–5 percentage points.

During the last few weeks of the election campaign the strategy employed by Berlusconi to offset this disadvantage was based on his constant presence in the media and his insistence on three issues: the communist threat, the accomplishments of his government and fiscal reform. I have already discussed the second issue by analysing the macroeconomic results of the Berlusconi government and delving into some of the policies implemented during Berlusconi's five-year term of office.

I will now examine the fiscal issue. This theme was deployed in the election campaign according to the classic tenets of populist strategy (Berselli and Cartocci, 2006): first there is the presentation of an all-embracing election programme, then the selection of the themes that are most likely to impress the electorate, and finally an obsessive election campaign centred around these central themes. In this way the most controversial issues were kept in the background and conveniently forgotten, thus avoiding any serious debate on the real state of transport, education, health, business competitiveness, and other important areas of social and economic life after five years of centre-right government.

The tax issue was in turn used as a weapon against the centre left by claiming that a Prodi government would increase total revenue by imposing taxes on gilt-edged securities, home ownership, high incomes, capital transfers and inheritances. To these attacks the centre left responded in a rather general, imprecise way, as was the case with the issue of reintroduction of inheritance and capital transfer tax, which, according to some exponents of the radical left, would involve small and medium-sized estates, while Romano Prodi talked rather generally of estates worth 'over several million euros'.

The key points made by the centre right in the economic area took the shape of a long list of tax reductions: a 40 per cent reduction in the tax burden, tax reductions for large families, and so forth.[13] Towards the end of the election campaign these promises followed each other with perfect timing, in a flawless 'Rossini crescendo'. During the face-to-face debate on 3 April, the final speech by Berlusconi, which could not be challenged by Prodi, ended with the promise to abolish the Imposta comunale sugli immobili (Local Property Tax, ICI). Of Italian families, 87 per cent own a house. The cost of abolishing the tax has been estimated at €2.5 billion. The day after, at a trade conference, Berlusconi proposed to abolish IRAP for small and medium-sized enterprises (minimum cost: €2.5 billion, maximum cost: €25 billion). The following day, the last of the election campaign, he promised to abolish the Tassa per lo smaltimento dei Rifiuti Solidi Urbani (Solid Waste Management Tax; TARSU) (cost: €4.3 billion).

The centre left also tried to simplify its tax proposals by focusing the election campaign on one point: a 5 per cent reduction in the gap between net salaries and employers' labour expenditures (the so-called *cuneo fiscale*) at a cost of €10 billion. As Prodi later explained on television, 'this means that the average employee will have their wage packet increased by €600 a year and a craft business will save about €12,000'. The aim of the proposal was to help businesses, to increase net salaries and to stimulate household consumption. The financial resources for the measure were to come from additional revenue deriving from measures against tax evasion, the introduction of a single tax rate on unearned income and the reintroduction of inheritance tax.[14]

Berlusconi's objective was to present his coalition as the only one capable of reducing the tax burden on citizens,[15] while at the same time presenting the opposing coalition as the advocate of greater financial sacrifices. This contraposition enabled Berlusconi to unite the part of Italy that is intolerant of rules and regulations and is made up of owners of small and very small businesses who miss the good old days of competitive devaluations and are terribly frightened of the Chinese. This part of Italy also includes many citizens in northern Italy who feel defrauded by the State, perceiving it as incapable of offering adequate services despite high taxation. Many tax-evaders who fear the tighter controls announced by the centre left also belong to this part of Italy, as do those among the most fortunate in Italian society, who fear they might lose their privileges (and perceive their sons and daughters as being overtaken by the children of ordinary workers[16]). This part of Italy is also disproportionately made up of the less well-educated – of people who, thanks to television, see Berlusconi as the symbol of success, one who expresses all the unfulfilled wishes of an Italy aspiring to increased material wealth that includes property, cars, mobile phones and holidays. In the last few years this contraposition has also been fuelled by widespread social unrest generated by the crisis suffered by some traditional sectors of the Italian economy, which has provided fertile ground for fear and uncertainty.

In a country where for many decades the State has been unable to guarantee efficient public services equally distributed over the national territory (Svimez, 2006), and where only a section of the population contributes to the cost of public expenditure, people believe that it is right not to pay taxes (Guerra and Zanardi, 2006). In the 2006 campaign, the bet on attempting to harness widespread selfishness thus proved to be (almost) a winner.

Notes

1 See the report on the parliamentary debate in *La Repubblica*, 15 June 2006.

2 Tommaso Padoa Schioppa was a member of the Executive Committee of the European Central Bank between 1998 and 2005, Chairman of the

Commissione Nazionale per le Società e la Borsa (Securities and Exchange Commission, CONSOB) between 1997 and 1998, Deputy General Manager of the Bank of Italy from 1984 to 1997, and head of the European Commission's Directorate General for Economic and Financial Affairs from 1979 to 1983.

3 Standard labour units may refer either to the amount of labour of a full-time worker or to the equivalent amount of labour of part-time workers or of workers with more than one job, net of wage supplementation fund workers. In other words, ISTAT (Italian National Institute for Statistics) calculates employment by taking into account the fact that many employment contracts are not full-time and, therefore, that they must be given less weight in the total estimate compared to permanent posts.

4 Named after its principal sponsors – the Northern League's Umberto Bossi, and National Alliance leader, Gianfranco Fini – the law was introduced in 2002. It aimed, among other things, to restrict immigration by means of the stipulation that numbers were to be fixed, each year, by means of executive regulation. At the same time it offered certain categories of immigrant lacking regularly issued residence permits the opportunity to legalise their positions.

5 A 'law of delegation' is a law that, in accordance with article 76 of the Constitution, gives the Government authority to issue decrees having the force of law. Laws of delegation can only be enacted for specific, explicitly stated, purposes; they must specify time limits within which the decrees are to be promulgated, and they must set out the principles and guidelines to which the decrees are to adhere.

6 The previous centre-left government had already abolished the tax on inheritances below €175,000 per beneficiary.

7 Public funding for businesses was cut from €6.5 billion in 2002 to €5.0 billion in 2004, representing a reduction of almost 25 per cent. The reduction in available resources led to a fall in investment, which went from €40 billion in 2001 to €27 billion in 2004 (Brancati, 2005).

8 Another measure that was announced but never actually implemented – this owing to the strong opposition it aroused – was reform of the 1970 Workers' Statute (Capriati, 2005).

9 In the last few years the diversification of contracts has been significant. Since the 1970s, when the main type of contract, to which there were very few exceptions, was one offering permanent employment, we have moved to a situation in which there are now, according to ISTAT, no fewer than 42 types of contract.

10 See the 'Patto per l'Italia' (Pact for Italy) signed by the trade union confederations CISL (Italian Confederation of Workers' Trade Unions) and UIL (Union of Italian Workers), and by business organisations, on 5 July 2002.

11 With the end result of selling off part of the natural heritage for the benefit of a few and defacing some beautiful stretches of unspoilt coastline, mainly in the southern regions.

12 On the national and international political circumstances that caused a loss of credibility of the Berlusconi government, see chapters 1, 3 and 10 in this volume.
13 See the partial list in Table 2.3.
14 For an interesting debate on the usefulness of the proposal and its area of application see Richiardi and Leombruni (2006); Giannini and Guerra (2006a, 2006b).
15 Even if the fiscal burden during the five years of the centre-right government did not decrease significantly.
16 During the televised debate with Prodi, Berlusconi said explicitly that this was regarded as an 'injustice' by his coalition.

References

Amendola, M., Antonelli, C. and Trigilia, C. (2005) (eds), *Per lo sviluppo. Processi innovativi e contesti territoriali*, Bologna, Il Mulino.

Bank of Italy (2005), 'L'impatto della regolarizzazione dei lavoratori immigrati sulla crescita dell'occupazione nella Rilevazione sulle forze di lavoro', *Bollettino Economico*, no. 45, November.

Barca, F. (2006), *Italia frenata. Paradossi e lezioni della politica per lo sviluppo*, Rome, Donzelli editore.

Berselli, E. and Cartocci, R. (2006), 'Due Italie, forse. A proposito delle elezioni del 9–10 aprile', *Il Mulino*, no. 2. March–April, pp. 243–252.

Boeri, T., Faini, R., Ichino, A., Pisauro, G. and Scarpa, C. (2005) (eds), *Oltre il declino*, Bologna, Il Mulino.

Bosi, P. and Guerra, M. C. (2005) (eds), *I tributi nell'economia italiana*, Bologna, Il Mulino.

Brancati, R. (2005) (ed.), *Le politiche per la competitività delle imprese. Rapporto MET 2005*, Rome, Donzelli editore.

Capriati, M. (2002), 'The economic context 1996–2001', in Newell, J. L. (ed.), *The Italian general election of 2001: Berlusconi's victory*, Manchester and New York, Manchester University Press.

Capriati, M. (2005), 'The Italian economy, 2001–03', *Modern Italy*, 10:1, 37–57.

Ciocca, P. (2003), 'L'economia italiana: un problema di crescita', *Bollettino Economico*, no. 41, Bank of Italy.

Consiglio Europeo (2000), *Conclusioni della Presidenza al Consiglio europeo del 23–24 marzo*, Brussels.

Costi, R. and Messori, M. (2005) (eds), *Per lo sviluppo. Un capitalismo senza rendite e con capitale*, Bologna, Il Mulino.

Faini, R. (2004), 'Fu vero declino? L'Italia negli anni '90', in G. Toniolo and V. Visco (eds), *Il declino economico dell'Italia. Cause e rimedi*, Milan, Bruno Mondadori.

Giannini, S. and Guerra, M. C. (2006a), 'Un cuneo da tagliare. Con cautela', www.lavoce.info, 15 May.

Giannini, S. and Guerra, M. C. (2006b), 'Il cuneo visto da vicino', www
.lavoce.info, 16 June.

Giannini, S. and Onofri, P. (2005) (eds), *Per lo sviluppo. Fisco e Welfare*,
Bologna, Il Mulino.

Guerra, M. C. and Zanardi, A. (2006) (eds), *La finanza pubblica italiana.
Rapporto 2006*, Bologna, Il Mulino.

ISTAT (2006a), 'Gli stranieri nella rilevazione sulle forze di lavoro', *Metodi e
Norme*, no. 27.

ISTAT (2006b), *Rilevazione delle forze di lavoro, I trimestre 2006*, 20 June.

La Redazione de lavoce (2006), 'Doppio sguardo prima del voto', www
.lavoce.info, 6 April.

MAP [Ministero delle Attività Produttive] (2005), *Programma triennale di
politica industriale*, Rome.

Nardozzi, G. (2004), *Miracolo e declino. L'Italia tra concorrenza e
protezione*, Rome and Bari, Laterza.

Richiardi, M. and Leombruni, M. (2006), 'Toglietemi tutto, ma non il cuneo
fiscale', www.lavoce.info, 16 June.

Rossi, N. (2005), *Mediterraneo del Nord. Un'altra idea del Mezzogiorno*,
Rome and Bari, Laterza.

Sestito, P. (2004), 'Dalla crescita senza occupazione all'occupazione senza
crescita: di cosa occorre preoccuparsi?', in Unioncamere, *Rapporto Italia
2004*, Rome.

Svimez (2005), *Rapporto 2005 sull'economia del Mezzogiorno*, Bologna, Il
Mulino.

Svimez (2006), *Rapporto 2006 sull'economia del Mezzogiorno*, Bologna, Il
Mulino.

Toniolo, G. and Visco, V. (2004) (eds), *Il declino economico dell'Italia. Cause
e rimedi*, Milan, Bruno Mondatori.

3

The EU and international contexts

Giovanna Antonia Fois

Introduction

Foreign-policy issues were not salient in the campaign. For example, during the TV debates between Silvio Berlusconi and Romano Prodi, little was said by either contender and in most cases a bi-partisan tone prevailed. Nevertheless, the campaign was very frequently punctuated by foreign-policy issues and the competing elites were not slow to exploit them for partisan advantage. For example, a few weeks before election day Berlusconi went to Washington, where his very friendly personal relationship with President Bush and his speech to Congress were presented as symbols of the great respect that had been acquired in American circles by the centre-right government. Prodi launched his election campaign in Brussels, where, greeted as a former president of the European Commission, he stressed the faults in the Government's European policy, while former German Chancellor Helmut Kohl was a special guest at the rally to launch the centre left's election campaign.

Moreover, foreign policy was always 'there', in the background of the campaign, since the external arena is a source of constraints and opportunities for political elites everywhere. If such constraints limit the availability of economic and other resources, then elites become unable to satisfy their voters' demands and risk losing support to alternative elites offering different strategies and agendas (Cotta, 1998; 2005). Alternatively, political elites can try to recover, in the external arena, prestige and power lost in the internal one, or else can use external constraints as a tool to gain and maintain support for their policies and as a scapegoat for policy failures. Thus, the international context must be central to the competition between an incumbent government and its opposition (Cotta, Isernia and Verzichelli, 2005).

Finally, the international and domestic arenas have traditionally been, in the Italian case, especially tightly interwoven. After World

War II, Italian political parties had fundamentally opposing attitudes towards the Eastern and Western geo-political blocks and to the international alliances arising therefrom, and this was a basic determinant of their acceptability or otherwise as potential government partners (Romano, 2002). In other words, the international situation was 'internalised' by the governing parties, in particular the Christian Democrats, in order to guarantee the stability of their hold on power. At the same time, internal weaknesses and instabilities were 'externalised' in order to obtain resources and support, mainly from the US but also from the European Community (EC) (Isernia, 1996). In the Cold War era what was called a 'low-profile' foreign policy was, rather, a 'low-cost' policy whereby Italy's political elites were able to maximise security and the prospects for economic development thanks to the guarantees that came with membership of NATO and the EC (Andreatta, 2004). Since the end of the Cold War, the term *vincolo esterno* ('external constraint') has been widely used in Italian political parlance to describe the way in which international influences impinge on the domestic political agenda by setting policy goals and tying the hands of political elites. It was, for example, widely used as a metaphor to describe the choices made by Italy's political elites on the path that would lead to Economic and Monetary Union (EMU). During the crisis of the 'First Republic', governing parties of the 1990s linked incisive reform of public expenditure and reduction of the public debt to the likelihood of success in meeting the convergence criteria that had to be satisfied in order to be considered eligible for entry to the third phase of monetary union (Dyson and Featherstone, 1999). In order to free these issues from the vetoes and demands of political parties and interest groups, political elites presented their choices as technical rather than political questions.

The remainder of this chapter is divided into six sections. The four that follow consider the principal foreign policy developments to make their effects felt on the campaign: the intervention in Iraq; reactions to development of the nuclear programme in Iran; energy imports and relations with Russia; policy towards the EU. The fifth section compares and contrasts the foreign-policy proposals of the two coalitions. The sixth section draws some conclusions about the relevance of the international context for the 2006 campaign.

Iraq

The appointment as Foreign Minister in May 2001 of Renato Ruggiero – a non-party figure, a former ambassador and World Trade

Organisation president – was taken as a sign of continuity with the traditionally pro-European attitudes of previous Italian governments. However, the Twin Towers attack on 11 September 2001 radically changed the foreign-policy agenda. Terrorism and the Middle East now occupied the most prominent positions, reinforcing the change in emphasis between the twin pillars of Italian foreign policy – commitment to Europe and to the Atlantic alliance – that appeared to have come with the advent of the new government; for Berlusconi's stated intention to reinforce Italy's relationship with the US was accompanied by a seemingly more assertive and less acquiescent stance in defence of Italian interests in the European arena (Aliboni, 2003a; Aliboni, 2003b; Nuti, 2003; Frattini, 2004; Guerrini and Silvestri, 2004; Walston, 2004). In this context the *vincolo esterno* metaphor came to connote less the implementation of reforms and a guarantee of modernisation than a straightjacket, curbing the sovereignty of, and opportunities available to, the nation state.

The most immediate and more specific consequence of the Twin Towers attack was operation Enduring Freedom, the Anglo-American-led intervention in Afghanistan in which Italy participated with an air-naval mission and subsequently with an enhanced contribution to the UN mission. Whereas Enduring Freedom had bipartisan support, the centre left opposed the second mission, in 2002, which reinforced the Italian contribution as requested by the US. If the UN played a role, then this became less and less relevant with the passage of time since it was difficult to reconcile article 2 of the UN Charter, forbidding the use of force, with the position of the US, which wanted to manage the crisis autonomously.

The changed attitude of the US was revealed by US President George W. Bush's preventive defence doctrine, asserting that terrorists should be struck before they threatened the security of the United States. With this it became clear that one of the main targets would be Iraq whose ruler, Saddam Hussein, was accused of having weapons of mass destruction and of supporting terrorism.

President Bush considered neither the results of the United Nations Iraqi weapons inspections nor the caution urged by some of his own advisors, and he refused to continue negotiations with the Iraqi regime. The European Union was unable to adopt a unitary position, division in Europe reaching its height on 2 February 2003 when the leaders of eight European countries (Denmark, the UK, Italy, Poland, Portugal, Spain, the Czech Republic and Hungary) sent a letter to Bush supporting the US position in the Iraqi crisis, while France and Germany flatly refused any participation in the war, arguing for a negotiated solution. The draft UN Security Council resolution against Iraq proposed by the US and the UK was withdrawn in March 2003, after it became clear that it would be blocked by French and Russian vetoes. On 20 March 2003, Anglo-American forces began their attack. After the defeat of Saddam Hussein, President Bush declared the intervention a success and the Italian Parliament approved the financing of a military presence in Southern Iraq (commencing in June 2003) claiming that it was consistent with UN resolution 1483 of 22 May 2003.[1] The ostensible aim of the mission was to bring security and humanitarian aid to the civilian population and logistical support to the newly constituted police force. While a large part of the opposition had supported intervention in Afghanistan, it strongly contested the Italian government's decision to support the new Bush doctrine. The opposition would not accept the idea of Italian participation in an Anglo-American initiative that it regarded as a radical break with the traditional approach of Italian foreign policy, which had sought the peaceful settlement of international disputes through multilateral rather than unilateral action (Baldi and Nesi, 2005; De Guttry and Pagani, 2005).

In light of this, there were at least two reasons for thinking, at the outset of the election campaign, that the war in Iraq might play a salient role. First of all, the end of Saddam Hussein's regime and the holding of democratic elections did not bring peace, and relations among Iraq's various religious and ethnic groups were not normalised by the new Constitution. Security and stability, which had been among the principal official justifications for the war, were not achieved since foreign armies and civilians continued to be the targets of terrorist attacks. The foreign armies were able neither to act as mediators nor to enforce human rights. The Abu Graib prison scandal, involving human rights violations and torture, highlighted the contradiction between the policing methods used by the Anglo-American forces and an intervention whose ostensible aims were to free the Iraqi population from a bloody regime and to bring democracy and freedom. The Italian government did not take a position on any of these issues.[2] Second, the large number of casualties among both civilians and soldiers was an issue with the potential for considerable impact on public opinion. The kidnapping of several Italian journalists and volunteers; the terrorist attack, in November 2003, on the Italian base in Nassirya, causing eighteen deaths; the death, in February 2005, of the military intelligence official Nicola Calipari, killed by an American soldier while escorting to Baghdad Airport a recently released Italian hostage, the journalist Giuliana Sgrena: all these episodes gave the opposition arguments to support a case that they had been correct to oppose the intervention in Iraq, which had revealed itself to be a strategic mistake.

That the issue failed to acquire much prominence in the campaign is probably to be explained by the preventive action taken by the centre right; for the approach of the election put on its agenda the end of the mission and the role of multilateralism. Just prior to his visit to Washington, on 30 October 2005, Berlusconi declared that he had always been against military intervention, a position of which he said he had tried to persuade Bush, in cooperation with the Libyan leader, Colonel Gheddafi. Pierferdinando Casini, UDC leader, suggested that a common point of view could be found between the Government and the opposition on the withdrawal of Italian troops. In his opinion, to remain in Iraq would signify the postponement of a suitable political settlement, and therefore the role of the Italian army should be transitory. The centre left shared this point of view, but positions within the coalition differed with regard to the timing: some were in favour of an immediate withdrawal; others wanted a withdrawal negotiated with the American and Iraqi governments. In November 2005, the Defence Minister, Antonio Martino, declared that the Italian army had been accomplishing a humanitarian task and that withdrawal would be managed with the Iraqi government. This position was confirmed by Berlusconi, who announced that withdrawal would be complete by the end of the 2006.

Iran and the Middle East

The Iranian presidential elections of 17 June 2005 were won by the populist leader Mahmoud Ahmadinejad, who defeated the more centrist candidate, Akbar Hashemi Rafsanjani. They thus brought a halt to the slow and often contradictory evolution of the country towards a more democratic regime and to greater cooperation with Europe, as Iran's foreign policy grew increasingly hostile towards the Western countries. The US government had from time to time claimed that Teheran had connections with terrorism in Iraq, but, in spite of the US position, Italian governments, like those of other European countries, had been working towards improving cooperation and 'critical dialogue', especially with the former president Mohammad Khatami.

The possibilities of cooperation with Europe were limited by the country's nuclear development programme and by Ahmadinejad's declarations, shortly after his election, concerning Israel. In September

2005 Ahmadinejad defended the right of Iran to produce nuclear energy, and later on said that the 'Zionist' identity should be eliminated. European governments had been trying to push Iran's exploitation of nuclear energy in the direction of civil and pacific purposes, while the Bush administration had suggested referring Iran to the Security Council. However, the statements of Ahmadinejad threatening the existence of Israel stopped all negotiations. Berlusconi stated that the Iranian president's aggressive attitude was unacceptable and that his behaviour would not ease the peace process in the Middle East. Following riots and demonstrations in Teheran supporting both the development of nuclear research and the threats to Israel, Iran came to be considered a crucial menace to international stability also because it was suspected of encouraging terrorism (by supporting Hezbollah) and of intervening in Iraq (by inspiring Shiite guerrillas in the South).

In Italy, in November 2005, Ahmadinejad's declarations concerning Israel provoked Giuliano Ferrara, the editor of *Il Foglio*, a newspaper owned by Berlusconi, into instigating a torch-lit procession in support of Israel and into declaring that Iran should be isolated by the international community and by the UN. This initiative acquired great symbolic significance, a spokesman for the Roman Jewish community, Riccardo Pacifici, affirming that those who failed to participate in the procession were to be considered enemies of Israel. In fact the initiative had the aim of embarrassing the centre left – which was accused of being biased towards the interests of the Palestinian people at the expense of Israel – and of exploiting the divisions within its ranks: in fact, while DS leader Piero Fassino declared that he would participate in the procession, RC leader Fausto Bertinotti declared that he would have agreed to participate had the appeal referred, not only to the right of Israel to exist, but also to the right of the Palestinians to an independent state. The initiative was one that would allow any feeble support for Israel to be presented as a manifestation of anti-Semitism. And, as it turned out, it was extraordinarily successful from the Government's point of view, with bi-partisanship being assured by the participation of several leaders of the Margherita and the DS,[3] while the leader of the Unione, Prodi, was induced to meet the Israeli and Iranian ambassadors in order to convey his solidarity with Israel and express his concern about Ahmadinejad's declarations, and to write a letter of solidarity to Israel's prime minister, Ariel Sharon. Meanwhile, Hamas' victory in the Palestinian general election of 25 January 2006 was viewed with great concern by Western countries, which responded by cutting off financial aid to the Palestinian Authority. In Italy, the centre-left coalition, considered the principal heir of the country's traditionally pro-Arab foreign policy in the Middle East, gave out contradictory messages: leader of the Margherita, Francesco Rutelli, declared that Hamas had officially to recognise Israel's right to exist, while DS president Massimo D'Alema claimed that the victory of Hamas was due to the politics of Israel.

As far as the nuclear development programme was concerned, Iran wanted to produce nuclear energy, whereas Western countries, and especially the US, claimed that the real purpose was to produce nuclear weapons. When, in November 2005, an Iranian press agency defined Italy as a Zionist country and sponsored a demonstration at the Italian embassy in Teheran, Foreign Minister Gianfranco Fini declared, on 2 November, that since Iran was a challenge to Israel and to the international community, the board of governors of the International Atomic Energy Agency (IAEA) should deliver its dossier on Iran's nuclear programme to the Security Council, and that sanctions should be adopted. In response, Iran proposed further negotiations with the European Union, while the IAEA decided to acquire more material and to monitor Iranian attitudes towards its inspections. Fini's position was shared by a part of the centre left. For example, Arturo Parisi, president of the Margherita, declared himself in favour of the adoption of political sanctions against Iran, and proposed a more salient role for Europe, in order to help the US to defend Israel and to avoid the risk of a nuclear escalation. Nevertheless, he stressed that article 11 of the Italian Constitution (repudiating recourse to war as a means of resolving international disputes and emphasising the role of international organisations as promoters of peace) should be the benchmark of Italian foreign policy. And even though the centre left condemned the statements of the Iranian president, in Parliament it found it difficult to find a common position, the motion on this issue being subject to lengthy negotiation, since the extreme left did not want sanctions of any kind to be mentioned. Following the decision of the Governor of the IAEA, on 2 of February 2006, to present the Iranian dossier to the UN Security Council, which had a month to decide sanctions against Iran, centre-left divisions were less in evidence than was the degree of bipartisanship on the issue between the two coalitions: in the two TV debates between Berlusconi and Prodi, both declared that the Iranian crisis would have to be resolved through multilateralism and with the intervention of the UN and the EU.

However, attempts at promoting dialogue with the Islamic world did not enjoy unanimous support in the centre-right coalition. The merits of a cooperative attitude were not accepted by the Northern

League or by the President of the Senate, Forza Italia's Marcello Pera, who argued for defence of the West and of Christian values against the supposed Islamic menace. This part of the coalition argued that Islamic countries could not be moderate and that cooperation was impossible. The contrasting sentiments within the coalition came to the surface when cartoons presenting the Prophet Mohammed in a derogatory light were published by a Danish newspaper, provoking violent reactions throughout the Islamic world. On 3 February 2006, in response to a reappearance of the cartoons in French newspapers, an EU agency in Gaza City was assaulted and subsequent days saw violent protests against Europe in Teheran and in the cities of other Islamic countries. On 7 February, the Danish embassy in Teheran was attacked, but protests took place almost everywhere, even in moderate countries like Jordan. In Syria and Lebanon, the Danish and Norwegian embassies were burned; in Pakistan riots provoked the deaths of three people. Worry about rapid escalation of the protests was expressed by many Imams concerned that the cartoons could be used as a pretext for still more violent action by fundamentalists. A wide-ranging debate took place throughout Europe about the basic value of freedom of the press versus the equally fundamental value of respect for religious symbols. It was at this point that the Minister for Institutional Reform, Roberto Calderoli, appeared on television wearing a tee-shirt showing some of the contested cartoons. In spite of protests by the Italian Islamic community and a number of Arab countries, the minister refused to apologise, declaring instead that he felt honoured to be threatened by al Qaeda.[4] Protests and riots grew increasingly serious, the explosion of violence leading to the deaths of fourteen people in Benghazi where, on 17 February, the Italian consulate was attacked. Foreign Minister Fini initially declared that the assaults had been mainly directed against the Libyan government, accused of being too acquiescent towards the West, but was eventually forced to acknowledge that responsibility for what had happened lay with the provocative behaviour of Calderoli. The good relationships Italian governments had established with the Libyan leader seemed to be put in danger and enabled demands for reparations for damages deriving from Italy's colonial past in Libya once more to gain centre stage. The Prime Minister, interviewed by Al Jazeera on 22 February, tried to reduce the tensions by emphasising that Italy had always respected Islam; but the situation was becoming increasingly complex for the Government. Fini on the one hand affirmed that Calderoli should resign, and on the other, asked Colonel Gheddafi to drop the colonial issue. In the end, what amounted to a compromise was reached when Calderoli resigned and the Italian government promised to build a new motorway in Libya. Meanwhile, the European Parliament condemned what it called Calderoli's provocative and xenophobic act and the Northern League was expelled from the European parliamentary group of which it had hitherto been a member, the Independence/Democracy Group.[5]

Energy

Italy is almost entirely dependent for its energy supplies on imports of oil and gas – which account for 85 per cent of its requirements – the main exporters being Norway, Algeria, Russia and Iran. This dependence has not been managed through a national plan for alternative sources of energy such as wind and solar power, while nuclear energy production is precluded by the result of the referendum held in 1987 following the Chernobyl accident, which led to a halt in the construction of nuclear power plants and to closure of the four existing ones. Assuring Italy's energy needs thus rested on exploiting the country's geo-political role in the centre of the Mediterranean – this providing the basis for the Christian Democrats' traditionally pro-Arab foreign policy, through which friendly relationships with the countries concerned would secure gas and oil supplies. As former Prime Minister Giulio Andreotti stated in a recent interview, 'we were the first to have good relationships with the Arabs and with North Africa. This policy, strongly criticised, has now been revisited by all European governments as has been shown by the visit to Gheddafi of Tony Blair' (Arachi, 2005: 5). And the role of Italy in the Mediterranean, and in re-establishing relations between the US and Libya, was stressed by President Bush during Berlusconi's October 2005 visit to Washington.

The friendly relationship of Berlusconi with Russian President Vladimir Putin was, after 2001, crucial to the conclusion of several contracts between Italy's publicly owned energy company, Ente Nazionale Idrocarburi (National Hydrocarbon Corporation; ENI) and the Russian corporation for the extraction and supply of natural gas, Gazprom. Apparently in order to avoid the application against it of antitrust regulations, ENI, at the end of September 2005, surrendered control of a percentage of the Russian imports to Central Energy Italia (CEI), a company owned partly by Bruno Mentasti Granelli, a friend of Berlusconi. Doubts about the appropriateness of this arrangement arose from the questions it raised about a further conflict of interests for the Prime Minister. In fact, the arrangement appeared to be related to the Government's decision to replace Vittorio Mincato with Paolo Scaroni at the head of ENI which, as its part of the deal, got an extension of the existing contracts for gas imports for a further ten years until 2027. Meanwhile, Mentasti had been a close business associate of Berlusconi and 33 per cent of CEI was owned by Gazprom itself.

The very cold winter of 2005–2006 triggered a crisis in gas supplies: Ukraine would not accept new prices set by Moscow, and Russia claimed that Ukraine was stealing gas from the pipes supplying Europe and passing through Ukrainian territory. Thus, in January and February, gas supplies to Europe were severely reduced – in Italy by 25 per cent. In these circumstances, the special relationship between Putin and Berlusconi was overshadowed by European initiatives. Foreign Minister Fini invited Brussels and the Austrian presidency to take united and decisive action to deal with the problem claiming that priority should be given to diplomatic initiatives by the EU as a whole because the consequences of a lack of energy would affect all of the member states and because only Europe had the political strength to induce Kiev and Moscow to resolve their differences. While the EU was negotiating, the government issued a series of regulations designed to conserve gas supplies. Berlusconi and Economy and Finance Minister Giulio Tremonti denied that the shortage of gas imports had brought tensions with Russia and claimed that nuclear power was the only feasible solution to Italy's energy problems. Despite this, Italy did not participate in the summit on energy between Germany, Spain and France that took place in February and the actions of the government and ENI were heavily criticised in Parliament.

Another aspect of the energy problem was the failed attempt of the Italian National Electricity Corporation Enel (Ente nazionale per l'energia elettrica) to gain control of the French energy company Suez. France countered the risk that Enel would succeed in its take-over bid by sponsoring a merger of Suez with Gaz de France, a public company. The French government's actions were strongly criticised in Italy as a form of protectionism contrary to Europe's single-market rules, and the Italian government demanded the intervention of the EU Commission. The case had not been resolved by the time of the election itself and led to bitter polemics between the two coalitions. Prodi declared that if instead of pushing for the appointment of Rocco Buttiglione as a European Commissioner in 2004, the Government had defended the position of Mario Monti as EU Competition Commissioner against the opposition of France and Germany, Italy would not still be 'the soft underbelly of Europe': his Commission, with Monti holding the competition portfolio, had been the only barrier against the creeping renationalisation of the European economy. Fini, for the centre right, replied that Prodi was saying something manifestly unfounded for the sake of conducting an 'internal polemic' (Bussi, 2006).

Europe

Italy's political elites have traditionally been 'Euro-enthusiasts', but after 2001 the tone of political debate about Europe began to change (Cavatorto, 2005; Cavatorto and Fois, 2005). On the one hand, Italy was an active participant in the Convention on the European Constitution, which was signed in Rome and ratified by a large majority in Parliament – thus confirming the traditionally pro-European attitude of Italy's political class and the country's role as part of the 'ceremonial core' of the EU.[6] On the other hand, a number of the specific pronouncements of the Prime Minister and other members of the government (especially Economy and Finance Minister Tremonti) betrayed an attitude towards Europe that was far less unconditional than had been typical of governments until then (Quaglia, 2003; Conti, 2005; Conti and Verzichelli, 2005).

Several aspects of the EU were the targets of criticism. The apparent inability or unwillingness of the EU to do more to protect Italian textiles from the effects of cheap imports from countries such as China were stressed, as was the democratic deficit of European institutions. But above all, objections centred on the rigidity of the economic criteria that had had to be met in order to be part of EMU and that were written into the Growth and Stability Pact (GSP) (Fois, 2005). The euro was considered to be the cause of inflation, while its appreciation against the dollar was held to be responsible for a worsening balance of payments and a declining performance of Italian exports. Finally, dissatisfaction was expressed with the rules of the GSP for their supposedly negative effects on economic growth and development.

Reform of the GSP was not only an Italian concern. During the Italian Presidency, between July and December 2003, the Commission recommended application of the excessive deficit procedure to France and Germany. Italy acted to ensure the adoption of a Council decision to suspend application of the procedures, working out a political declaration that gave France and Germany more time to comply with GSP parameters. The Commission resorted to the European Court of Justice. In annulling the suspension adopted by the Council, the Court opened the doors to a debate on the need to amend and improve the GSP, and Berlusconi sought to take advantage of this. In a letter to the

Dutch Prime Minister (and President of the Council), Jan Peter Balkenende, Berlusconi stressed the economic risks deriving from globalisation and the lack of competitiveness of European exports; he stated, too, that the effects of appreciation of the euro on the Italian economy had been 'dramatic'.[7] The letter to the Dutch Presidency did little to modify the agenda, and the role of the Prime Minister in the reform process was limited, negotiations being led mainly by Economy and Finance Minister Domenico Siniscalco. This meant that the pugnacious tones used in the domestic arena were not echoed in the corridors of the EU, where Siniscalco supported a compromise solution put forward by the Luxembourg Presidency. This aimed to assure flexibility while preserving credibility (Fois, 2006). In the end, the reform that was adopted in March 2005 abolished the GSP stipulation that GDP had to fall by 2 per cent for a country to avoid the excessive deficit procedure under the 'severe economic downturn' criterion. Since the reform, it has been sufficient for a country to experience negative growth of any entity in order to avoid the procedure. In addition, the reform extended the range of 'relevant factors' to which a country could refer to avoid the procedure and extended from one to two years the deadline by which countries had to correct deficits in the event of the procedure being invoked.

The major issue at stake for Italy, however, was the provision concerning levels of public debt. The outcome was the preservation of the status quo, since the matter remains governed by the regulations of 1997. Indeed the reform provided for a reinforced framework of surveillance. Nevertheless, after the reform was adopted, the Government argued that Italian diplomacy had been successful, its arguments recognised by the country's EU partners. This, the Government claimed, confirmed the leadership role of Italy in the international arena.[8] According to the Minister for Communications, AN's Maurizio Gasparri, Brussels had recognised that constraints had to be eased in order to combat unfair competition by Chinese producers and that this showed how mendacious were the complaints of the left, which accused the Italian government of Euro-scepticism: the centre right was the rescuer of European and Italian economies that had been choked by Prodi,[9] first as the prime minister that had led Italy into the euro, then as president of the European Commission. UDC leader Marco Follini argued that increased flexibility was a European as well as an Italian goal, since it would encourage economic development.[10] The centre-left parties considered the outcome of the negotiations 'rather satisfactory', even if there still remained uncertainties surrounding its implementation. In particular, Margherita spokesperson Enrico Letta, thought it positive that Italy had not been penalised by the debt criterion. Prodi argued that the reform went in the right direction, but that its results were of limited relevance to the Italian situation, which still required a drastic debt reduction policy.[11]

Finally, the Italian government played a salient role, in cooperation with France and the UK, in opening EU membership talks to Turkey after a marathon round of negotiations in October 2005 where the main sticking point had been Austrian insistence that Turkey be offered less than full membership. The Prime Minister, Berlusconi, often stressed his personal commitment to the achievement of membership for Turkey with the latter's Prime Minister, Recep Tayyip Erdoğan; while to Foreign Minister Fini Turkish membership would be an asset against fundamentalism. He also considered it a very significant option for the Italian government, since it would shift the EU's centre of gravity towards the Mediterranean and the Middle East, strategic areas for the advancement of Italian interests.[12] Moreover, in his opinion, Turkey was the model of a democratic state, one based on the rule of law and the observance of human rights. To Deputy Prime Minister Follini,[13] the accession of Turkey would be a highly positive event, since the building of an Islamic democracy was the main antidote against fundamentalism. After this clear position the Cdl split when, on 3 October, the European Parliament voted on the issue. Only FI voted for the opening of negotiations. The League was, in fact, opposed to the Italian government's official position of support for Turkish membership (and in 2004 had even organised a street demonstration to emphasise its stance) and thus voted no; while AN, aware of public mistrust of the idea of Turkish membership, abstained.

Programmes

As the four preceding sections make clear, the two main coalitions were far from united in their foreign-policy positions; moreover, their constituent parties were encouraged by the change of electoral system to diversify their offerings on foreign policy as much as on anything else, with the result that given policy goals were shared by political parties across the coalitions. Nevertheless, with regard to foreign policy, the electoral programmes of the two coalitions were very different.

The centre right's programme lacks a section specifically devoted to foreign policy; and where it is mentioned, the international arena is usually presented in dark shades as a factor limiting the effectiveness of government action. Threats to the security and welfare of Italian families and firms are presented mainly as coming from the outside, and the *vincolo esterno* is interpreted not as the external definition of policy goals to be achieved, but as a hindrance to good government performance. In its preface the programme describes how the world has changed dramatically in the previous five years; it underlines the risks generated by terrorism, the heavy losses provoked by the unfair competition of China and Asia, the disadvantages brought by the euro, both in terms of the purchasing power of families and in terms of the competitiveness of domestic firms. The economic crisis was caused by the previous leftist governments, which failed to regulate globalisation, and whose push towards liberalism was driven by their desire to be forgiven for their communism. The second part of the programme presents the achievements of a government which, though being 'forced to fight the continuous crisis inherited from the left', was able to observe EU parameters and to assure economic growth.

Italian foreign policy, the programme continues, has been inspired by the pursuit of peace and freedom, to which tasks have been linked the alliances and missions pursued by the government on the world stage. In this context, Europeanism and Atlanticism remain crucial choices. As far as Europe is concerned, the programme's main point is the need for the construction of a Europe of the people – one inspired by subsidiarity, federalism, the preservation of identities and the strengthening of Christian traditions. Rather than Europe itself, it is the nation states that have the most significant role to play in dealing with the present challenges.

With regard to the future, the programme states that foreign policy will continue to strengthen the role Italy has acquired thanks to its enhanced international credibility, reasserting the commitment to Europe as well as to the alliance with the US and the advancement of freedom and democratic institutions in the world.

The centre left's programme is in almost all respects the opposite of that of the centre right. It has two chapters specifically devoted to foreign policy, the first of which stresses the opportunities – in terms of economic and monetary stability – stemming from membership of the single currency and the European Union. While for the centre right, the emphasis in its programme is on the challenges faced by the nation state as the result of threats coming from outside, for the Unione, Europe is the arena in which problems (such as immigration and citizenship) can be faced and resolved. Thus its programme states that, in contrast with a centre right that juxtaposes Europe to the successful pursuit of Italian interests, the centre left plans to reinforce the European integration process through the re-launching of institutional reforms, enlargement, and the further development of the EU's Common Foreign and Security Policy.

The second chapter devoted to foreign policy reaffirms a commitment to multilateralism, multi-polarity, cooperation and sustainable development as fundamental values in international affairs. It links article 11 of the Italian Constitution with Chapter VII of the UN Charter, both allowing the use of force only as a collective security measure; it stresses its support for a growing role of the General Assembly and of the International Criminal Court in cases of genocide; it emphasises that Italy has a permanent interest in the growing autonomy of the United Nations and in an improvement of its decision-making procedures. The central section of the chapter, devoted to Iraq, argues that the war was a mistake in that it increased rather than solved the problem of security. In this field, it says, the Government should send a strong message to the country and to the international community through the withdrawal of Italian troops in consultation with the Iraqi government. Concrete actions aimed at supporting Iraq's democratic transition are promised. Another section is devoted to the centrality of the Mediterranean to Italian foreign-policy interests. It is necessary, the document says, for the Italian government to foster, in the region, peace, economic stability and democracy along three axes: cultural, economic and political. Two final sections are devoted to the theme of international cooperation for development and to new defence policies (promising action in the areas of European defence and US–EU defence cooperation; the organisation of Italy's military forces; military personnel).

Conclusion

In spite of the emphasis the two coalitions gave to other issues, they were unable to ignore the international context, which was occasionally drawn explicitly into debate even when the latter focused on more 'common' subjects, like taxation or welfare. Four features above others characterised the role of foreign policy in the campaign. First, such debate as there was focussed mainly on the past, while proposals for the future gained very little, if any, hearing. This bias towards the past was particularly evident in the programme of the CdI. The centre left, in its programme, set out a detailed agenda for future action but did not focus attention on it.

Second, despite the expression of different and sometimes inconsistent attitudes on foreign policy by parties belonging to the same coalition, the two coalitions' programmes differed in fundamental ways. Seldom did the centre right refer to the external arena as a resource for the future of Italy, while the *vincolo esterno* was used mainly in order to justify the Government's policy failures. Though emphasising the external origins of crises and emergencies, the programme views nation states as the central actors, giving very little role to multilateralism as a means of solving problems. The centre left's programme, by contrast, is much more oriented to the opportunities deriving from the international context, and, in the emphasis it gives to the role multilateralism and international institutions, appears to want to 'externalise' internal problems.

Third, while Berlusconi stressed what he claimed was the discontinuity of his foreign policy with that of preceding governments, his affirmation could be questioned in several respects. For instance, the more assertive position he claimed for Italy was often confined to the internal arena rather than being actually pursued in the external one, as was apparent from the Calderoli episode. Greater assertiveness was also limited to the domestic level in the case of Europe, notwithstanding the bitter criticism and dissatisfaction expressed by several ministers and which was sometimes interpreted as Euroscepticism. The traditional Europhilia of Italian political parties and elites has indeed been challenged by the threats arising from the economic downturns of recent years, but neither has it been replaced by a diffuse Europhobia, or by an alternative model. The intervention of the European Union was called for on several occasions when energy problems, terrorism, immigration and a revival of protectionism revealed the weaknesses of unilateral action and in particular of the Italian economic system.

Finally, the war in Iraq was perceived by a majority of the public as a mistake and had the potential to make a strong impact on public opinion, though the role of the Italian army was appreciated. Many Italian voters were uncomfortable with the intervention, this feeling extending well beyond the boundaries of the movements for peace inspired by the Catholic Church or the extreme left. Political elites perceived this discomfort, and thus on this issue, the two coalitions ended up taking campaign positions that were very close to one another, both envisaging the withdrawal of troops by the end of 2006. The international context was thus 'present' in the campaign, perhaps to an extent greater than political elites might have desired, with the consequence that, though its electoral impact may be hard to quantify, its relevance can hardly be denied.

Notes

1 This resolution appealed 'to Member States and concerned organizations to assist the people of Iraq in their efforts to reform their institutions and rebuild their country, and to contribute to conditions of stability and security in Iraq'; and called upon 'all Member States in a position to do so to respond immediately to the humanitarian appeals of the United Nations and other international organizations for Iraq and to help meet the humanitarian and other needs of the Iraqi people by providing food, medical supplies, and resources necessary for reconstruction and rehabilitation of Iraq's economic infrastructure'.

2 Unlike other European governments, the Italian government never questioned the US about Abu Graib, Guantanamo or Falluja, the Iraqi town bombed by US troops with phosphorous.

3 Even though the leaders of the Greens, RC and the PdCI announced that they would not participate, many of their supporters did.

4 His name appeared on a website connected to al Qaeda.

5 The group brings together EU critics, Eurosceptics and Eurorealists.

6 The Northern League and RC voted against ratification.

7 *Corriere della Sera*, 19 November 2004.

8 Government press release on the Ecofin final draft, Ansa 21 March 2005.

9 Ansa 21 March 2005. To Isabella Bertolini, deputy leader of the FI group in the Chamber of Deputies, the reform confirmed Italy's leadership role in Europe and represented the victory of good sense against the grey Euro-bureaucrats.

10 Ansa 21 March 2005.

11 Ansa 21 March 2005.

12 European Parliament session 555, 3 December 2004.

13 European Parliament session 572, 20 January 2005.

References

Aliboni, R. (2003a), 'Neo-nationalism and neo-Atlanticism in Italian foreign policy', *The International Spectator*, 48:1, 81–89.

Aliboni, R. (2003b), 'La politica estera del governo Berlusconi', in A. Colombo and N. Ronzitti (eds), *L'Italia e la politica internazionale, Edizione 2003*, Bologna, Il Mulino.

Andreatta, F. (2004), *Alla ricerca dell'ordine mondiale. L'Occidente di fronte alla guerra*, Bologna, Il Mulino.

Arachi, A. (2005), 'Andreotti: un miracolo, i nemici marceranno insieme', *Corriere della Sera*, 2 November.

Baldi, S. and Nesi, G. (eds) (2005), 'L'Italia al palazzo di vetro', Quaderni dell'Università degli studi di Trento.

Bussi, C. (2006), 'Bruxelles: rispettate le regole, non lo spirito Ue', *Il Sole 24 Ore*, 28 February.

Cavatorto S. (2005), 'Attuare Maastricht e la politica delle "rigidità flessibili"', in M. Cotta, P. Isernia and L. Verzichelli (eds), *L'Europa in Italia. Élites, opinione pubblica, decisioni*, Bologna, Il Mulino.

Cavatorto, S. and Fois, G. A. (2005), 'Le elites politiche italiane nelle grandi scelte comunitarie', in M. Cotta, P. Isernia and L. Verzichelli (eds), *L'Europa in Italia. Élites, opinione pubblica, decisioni*, Bologna, Il Mulino.

Conti, N. (2005), 'Party conflict over European integration in Italy: a new dimension of party competition?', paper presented to the 55th Annual Conference of the Political Studies Association, University of Leeds, 5–7 April.

Conti, N. and Verzichelli, L. (2005), 'La dimensione europea nel discorso politico in Italia: un'analisi diacronica delle preferenze partitiche (1950–2001)', in M. Cotta, P. Isernia and L. Verzichelli (eds), *L'Europa in Italia. Élites, opinione pubblica, decisioni*, Bologna, Il Mulino.

Cotta, M. (1998), 'Le élites pubbliche nazionali di fronte all'integrazione', *Il Mulino*, no. 3, pp. 445–456.

Cotta, M. (2005), 'Élite, politiche nazionali e costruzione della *polity* europea. Il caso italiano in prospettiva comparata', in M. Cotta, P. Isernia and L. Verzichelli (eds), *L'Europa in Italia. Élites, opinione pubblica, decisioni*, Bologna, Il Mulino.

Cotta, M., Isernia, P. and Verzichelli, L. (eds) (2005), *L'Europa in Italia. Élites, opinione pubblica, decisioni*, Bologna, Il Mulino.

De Guttry, A. and Pagani, F. (2005), *Le Nazioni Unite*, Bologna, Il Mulino.

Dyson, K. and Featherstone, K. (1999), *The Road to Maastricht, Negotiating Economic and Monetary Union*, Oxford, Oxford University Press.

Fois, G. A. (2005), 'Loyalty to Europe. Italian political elites and the European monetary integration process', paper presented to the 55th Annual Conference of the Political Studies Association, University of Leeds, 5–7 April.

Fois, G. A. (2006), 'Is Europe a threat to Italy? The Euroscepticism in the second Berlusconi government', paper presented to the 56th Annual Conference of the Political Studies Association, University of Reading, 4–6 April.

Frattini, F. (2004), 'The fundamental direction of Italy's foreign policy', *The International Spectator*, 34:1, 95–99.

Guerrieri, P. and Silvestri, S. (2004), 'New alliances, governance of the international system and Italy's foreign policy choices', *The International Spectator*, 39:1, 101–102.

Isernia, P. (1996), 'Bandiera e risorse: la politica estera negli anni '80', in M. Cotta and P. Isernia (eds), *Il gigante dai piedi di argilla*, Bologna, Il Mulino.

Nuti, L. (2003), 'The role of the US in Italy's foreign policy', *The International Spectator*, 48:1, 89–101.

Quaglia, L. (2003), 'Euroscepticism in Italy and centre-right and right wing political parties', Sussex European Institute, SEI working paper no. 60, University of Sussex.

Romano, S. (2002), *Guida alla politica estera italiana. Da Badoglio a Berlusconi*, Milan, Rizzoli.
Walston, J. (2004), 'The shift in Italy's Euro-Atlantic policy. Partisan or Bipartisan?', *The International Spectator*, 39:4, 115–125.

II

The run-up to the election

4

The parties of the centre left

Sarah Rose

Introduction

An examination of the state of the Italian centre left in 2006 might at first sight lead one to conclude that nothing had changed since the general election of a decade earlier. The coalition of 2006 was once again an alliance led by Romano Prodi and made up of a multiplicity of parties with disparate ideological heritages ranging from communism to social liberalism and Christian democracy. Yet within the coalition a number of significant developments had occurred as the result of attempts made to overcome the many structural problems that had impeded it in its recent past – Prodi's long-awaited return from the Presidency of the European Commission in 2004 having been the catalyst for change following three years during which the coalition had spent much of the time flummoxing aimlessly as the parliamentary opposition, unable to agree on a leader or even on single shadow cabinet spokespersons (see Pasquino, 2005).

These fundamental problems and their attempted resolution form the focus of this chapter. Following a brief historical contextualisation of the centre left in the Second Republic, with particular emphasis being given to its electoral strategy, the chapter considers changes in the composition of the coalition and the extension of its boundaries. It then considers the centre left's leadership and the primaries held in October 2005. Finally, it considers the efforts made to address the negative consequences of the fragmentation of the coalition. It is only once these three issues have been considered that conclusions can be drawn as to why the centre left managed to achieve its narrow victory.

The electoral strategy of the centre left between 1994 and 2001

The Italian party-political landscape was almost completely changed by the transformation of the party system and the end of the First Republic, together with the imposition of the 1993 electoral law which allocated 75 per cent of the seats in the two chambers of Parliament according to the single-member simple plurality system and 25 per cent proportionally (see Bull and Newell, 2005). Supporters of the referendum that had led to the 1993 electoral law had hoped that it would bring with it the development of a bi-polar party system based around the formation of alliances, one representing the left, the other the right. Thus the centre-left alliance was first and foremost a consequence of electoral necessity, insofar as it found its origins in the requirement, in the institutional circumstances created by the new electoral law, to formulate an appeal that would enable it to overcome the historic limitations on the extent of its support, which in the post-war era had rarely amounted to more than 40 per cent of the vote (Pasquino, 1998).

The three general elections prior to 2006 provide much evidence of lesson learning by the centre left, confirming that its strategy is essentially Downsian in nature (Rose, 2002). First, the transformation from its first incarnation as the Progressisti (Progressive Alliance) in 1994 to the Ulivo (Olive Tree Alliance) in 1996 was based on awareness that the former had been unsuccessful in large part because the centre had presented itself to the electorate as a separate coalition (the Pact for Italy) and that the Progressisti did not therefore represent a single alliance of sufficient ideological breadth. Second, in including RC, the Progressive Alliance had been too leftist for a majority of voters. Therefore, the Ulivo (see Table 4.1) that was created by Prodi in 1995 represented a strategic shift towards the centre, involving the abandonment of RC, and the co-optation of centrist forces whose democratic (and conservative) credentials were beyond reproach. At the same time, by reaching stand-down arrangements with RC in the single-member colleges in 1996, the leaders of the Ulivo ensured that the centre-left vote would not be divided in the plurality arena. Third, the Progressisti had been penalised by failing to present multi-party lists capable of overcoming the 4 per cent threshold in the proportional arena; and fourth, they had been penalised by their failure to identify, prior to the election, a single prime-ministerial candidate. These deficiencies too were rectified with the formation of the Ulivo (Rose, 2002).

One of Prodi's central aims in creating the Ulivo had been to transcend the existing political forces by means of 'a political package that reflected, and thus attracted, an electorate which was highly critical and sceptical of the traditional parties' (Pasquino, 2005: 99). Consequently, after the Ulivo was victorious in 1996, it was hoped by many that its experience of government would help transform it 'into

Table 4.1 Evolution of the centre left 1996–2006 (list names in italics)

Lists and party components, 1996	Lists and party components, 2001	List and party components, 2006
PDS-Sinistra Europea Partito Democratico della Sinistra (D'Alema) Movimento dei Comunisti Unitari (Crucianelli) Cristiano-Sociali (Carniti) Federazione Laburista (Spini) Movimento per L'Unità della Sinistra Riformista (area Ruffolo) Socialdemocratici (Schietroma) Rete-Movimento Democratico (Orlando)	*Partito dei Comunisti Italiani* Partito dei Comunisti Italiani (Diliberto) *Democratici di Sinistra* Democratici di Sinistra (Veltroni)	*Rifondazione Comunista* Rifondazione Comunista (Bertinotti) *Partito dei Comunisti Italiani* Partito dei Comunisti Italiani (Diliberto) *Ulivo* Democratici di Sinistra (Fassino) Margherita (Rutelli) Movimento Repubblicani Europei (Sbarbati)
Verdi Verdi (Ripa Di Meana)	*Girasole* Verdi (Francescato) Socialisti Democratici Italiani (Boselli)	*Verdi* Verdi (Pecoraro Scanio) *la Rosa nel pugno* Socialisti Democratici Italiani (Boselli) Radicali (Capezzone)
Pop-SVP-PRI-UD-Prodi Partito Popolare Italiano (G. Bianco) Comitati per l'Italia che vogliamo (Prodi, Bressa) Unione Democratica (comprising: Maccanico AD-UDS (Bordon) PRI (La Malfa) SI dissidenti (Giugni) Liberali (Zanone))	*Margherita* Partito Popolare Italiano (Castagnetti) Democratici (Parisi) Unione Democratici per l'Europa (UDEUR) (Mastella) Rinnovamento Italiano (Dini)	*Popolari-UDEUR* Popolari-UDEUR (Mastella)
Lista Dini-Rinnovamento Italiano Socialisti Italiani (Boselli) Patto Segni (Segni) Comitato Dini (Dini) Movimento Italiano Democratico (S. Berlinguer)		*Italia dei Valori* Italia dei Valori (Di Pietro)
Partito Sardo d'Azione Lega Autonomia Veneto Unione Ladina Indipendente	Südtirolervolkspartei Unione Valdôtaine Partito Sardo d'Azione	Partito Pensionati Südtirolervolkspartei Partito dei Socialisti (Craxi) Lista Consumatori Alleanza Lombarda Liga Fronte Veneto

Source: Adapted from Rose (2002: 74) and Di Virgilio (1998: 11, Table 2).

a real political actor capable of imposing its political sovereignty on its component parts and thus eventually absorbing them' (Massari and Parker, 2000: 49).

The centre left's experience of government did not have this effect. Although whilst Prodi was prime minister the project of a sovereign Ulivo remained a possibility, even if a remote one, once his government fell in October 1998, the very concept of the Ulivo came to be questioned.[1] When, for example, DS leader Massimo D'Alema took over the reins of the premiership immediately after Prodi's fall, he did so with the support of former President Francesco Cossiga's UDR, most of whose parliamentarians had originally been elected as part of the centre-right coalition and which made it clear that its support was 'effectively conditional on the "death of the Ulivo"' (Newell, 2000: 179). In short, the Ulivo's difficulties were in no small measure due to the fact that the three governments that followed the collapse of Prodi's bore remarkable similarity, in the circumstances that gave rise to them, to those of the First Republic. That is, all were the consequence of agreements reached in the parliamentary arena with none directly reflecting, in terms of their composition, the distribution of votes cast by the electorate in 1996 (see Rose, 2002).

At the 2001 election, the lessons of the two earlier contests were not forgotten. Although the Ulivo did not die as Cossiga had wanted, neither had it became an actor capable of imposing its sovereignty on its components; and the parliamentary machinations of the period since 1998 had brought within it forces – such as the UDEUR and the PdCI – representing positions located beyond the boundaries of the victorious coalition in 1996. By increasing the heterogeneity of the alliance, these helped to perpetuate its relatively greater fragmentation as compared to the centre right. Once again, then, consideration had to be given to the formation, in the proportional arena, of multi-party lists that would prevent votes being wasted through a failure of single-party lists to reach the 4 per cent threshold. Principal expressions of this necessity were the Margherita (the Daisy) and the Girasole (Sunflower) (see Table 4.1). The coalition also once again chose a prime ministerial candidate from the centre of the political spectrum, avoiding one from the largest party, the DS. Especially given the latter's ideological heritage and Berlusconi's use of anti-communism – especially his tendency to use the term 'communist' 'in an all-embracing way, as signifying arbitrary state power, the deprivation of liberties, the suffocating of private initiative' (Ginsborg, 2004: 91) – it was felt that a candidate drawn from one of the centrist forces had a better chance of winning votes from the widest constituency possible.

However, with the centre right leading by some 15 points from the outset of the 2001 campaign (Newell and Bull, 2002), the fragmented and politically exhausted coalition apparently believed from the start that it would be defeated. Crucially, it proved unable to renew its 1996 agreement with Fausto Bertinotti's RC or to include Antonio Di Pietro's Italia dei Valori (Italy of Values; IdV); and, in choosing Francesco Rutelli as its prime-ministerial candidate, it was unable to exploit the advantages of incumbency (Pasquino, 2002). As Campus shows in chapter 7, in 2006, the centre left did not make the same mistake: learning the lesson of the previous election and standing on the opposite side, it sought to exploit to the full the outgoing government's lacklustre economic performance.

Evolution of the centre-left coalition 2001–2006

Notwithstanding the gradual consolidation of bi-polarity since 1994, then, the contours of the Italian party system continue to demonstrate significant fluidity; and given the latter's degree of fragmentation, electoral outcomes have continued to be highly dependent upon the alliance strategies pursued by the two coalitions. With this in mind, the Italian party system can, to adapt Giorgio Galli's (1966) celebrated phrase, be described as an example of 'imperfect bi-polarism'.[2] This draws attention to two crucial areas: first, the inability of parties outside of the two main alliances to challenge the 'dyadic format' (Diamanti and Lazar, 2002: 50); but second, the imbalance in the distribution of partisan allegiances in favour of the centre right.

Both of these areas have been well documented as reasons for the failure of the centre left in 2001 – while the second was used, in the election's aftermath, to underpin arguments to the effect that the centre left would only be able to beat the centre right to the extent that it was able to expand its boundaries to encompass all significant forces from the left to the centre of the political spectrum. The coalition was unable to do this in 2001, insofar as it failed to include RC and IdV. Had it been able to do so, then it might have succeeded in preventing the centre right from winning a majority in the Senate contest. It won 39.6 per cent of the vote compared with 42.5 per cent for the centre right. Since RC won 5 per cent and IdV 3.4 per cent, joint candidacies involving these two forces might, it may be supposed, have given the centre left a total of 48 per cent. Clearly, however, the argument is one that depends on the assumption that the forces' votes are perfectly 'sumable' and there is evidence to think that this is unlikely to be the case. For example, in both 1994 and 1996, in the single member constituencies (SMCs) where its candidate was supplied by a member of RC, the centre left's plurality vote was substantially less than the sum of the proportional votes cast for its constituent parties in the same SMCs (D'Alimonte and Bartolini, 1997: 126–7). So, for all the efforts made by the centre left to broaden its boundaries for electoral gain, it could not be certain, in the run-up to 2006, that the net impact on its support of the inclusion of forces perceived as 'extreme' would be positive rather than negative. As will be discussed when the issue of fragmentation is considered, this is a problem that appears to affect the centre right to a lesser extent than the centre left insofar as the former appears capable of continuing to attract the support of moderate voters *despite* its inclusion of relatively extreme parties such as the xenophobic Northern League.

Despite concerns about the shift to the left that it was thought might arise from the inclusion of RC within the coalition, the goal of vote maximisation made it seem essential that both RC and IdV be brought into the alliance prior to the 2006 general election. Both had become directly connected with the grass-roots associations and movements that had come to prominence from 2002 onwards, especially the *girotondi* (in the case of IdV) and the anti-globalisation movement (in the case of RC). These had to a certain extent come to dominate the extra-parliamentary opposition to the Berlusconi government and in some respects were even opposed to the leadership of the centre left. If, for example, the *girotondi* helped to mobilise ordinary citizens opposed to the Berlusconi government, then they had emerged in response to the perceived ineptitude and remoteness of the centre-left leadership that had been expressed by the film director Nanni Moretti when, at a centre-left organised rally in Rome in February 2002, he had famously turned to the centre-left leaders present telling them, in front of the crowd: 'We have been waiting for some self-criticism for the errors you have committed, but the bureaucrats have learnt nothing. I am very sorry to say this, but with these kinds of leaders we will never win' (see Andrews, 2005). Subsequently, thousands of *girotondisti*, many from the 'reflexive middle class' (Ginsborg, 2001: 42–44), began filling the piazzas to demonstrate their opposition to the Government's use of political power for Berlusconi's personal benefit. Their name derived from their style of protest: holding hands and encircling buildings, such as the Palace of Justice in Rome, symbolising democratic institutions perceived as under threat. Meanwhile, the anti-globalisation movement had been a significant source of support for the political ambitions of Sergio Cofferati, former general secretary of the CGIL and leader of 'the non-parliamentary opposition against the parliamentary opposition'. For a while he had seemed the only person capable of uniting 'the fragmented centre-left and lead[ing] it to victory' or at the very least providing 'stiffer resistance to the Berlusconi government' (Pasquino, 2005: 103). He eventually left the national political stage to run successfully as the centre left's candidate for the mayoralty of Bologna.

Both IdV and RC were supportive of Prodi's return to Italian politics, and accepted him as leader of the coalition from the European elections of 2004 onwards. They also agreed to his request for their participation in an alliance of all opposition parties which began as the Grande Alleanza Democratica (Great Democratic Alliance; GAD) before becoming the Unione in February 2005. A number of smaller parties also entered the fray on the centre left of which the two most notable examples are the Movimento Repubblicani Europei (European Republican Movement; MRE) and the Radicals. Both had been non-aligned in the 2001 election. The former had seceded from the Partito Repubblicano Italiano (Italian Republican Party; PRI) when it decided to ally with the centre right in 2001. The MRE provided the only female party leader in the coalition, in the form of Luciana Sbarbati. The Radicals, on the other hand, joined in 2005 due in large part to the close relationship they had developed with another coalition member, the SDI, during their campaign for a 'yes' vote in the referendum, held in June 2005, aimed at overturning Italy's restrictive fertility laws. The two parties formed a joint list, la Rosa nel Pugno (literally, 'the Rose in the fist'), to fight the 2006 election.

Finally, following the Margherita's encouraging performance in the 2001 election, its leader, Francesco Rutelli, had sought to exploit the political momentum thus generated by overseeing a transformation of the entity into a single political party.[3] If this increased the level of cohesion, at least to a certain extent, within the centre of the centre left, then some, at least, of the new party's sponsors hoped that its formation would represent a significant step towards the realisation of the Ulivo project as Prodi had originally conceived it. It contributed to ensuring that throughout the period in opposition, several proposals for a reorganisation of the centre left would be discussed, where these often concerned the development of a 'reformist party'. However it was only under Prodi's guidance that these plans saw any signs of coming to fruition, and even then their development was fraught with difficulty. It is to his leadership that we now turn.

Leadership of the centre left

Coalition leaders in the Second Republic have acquired a critical political and institutional role. The creation of two main coalitions and the establishment of bi-polar competition have shifted the spotlight away from parties, and instead focused attention on the coalition leaders, resulting in a growing personalisation of politics, with elections very much reflecting a presidential style of campaigning that has been particularly noticeable in the methods used for the communication of images and messages (Calise, 2000). Visible, authoritative and capable leaders are a must if they are to bring the electoral success that is demanded of them.

According to Campus and Pasquino (2004), coalition leaders in Italy have assumed a plurality of roles – as campaigners, heads of government, mediators between their respective coalition partners, and communicators-in-chief – thus making them the locus of power within their respective coalitions. Power has, however, been much less heavily concentrated in centre-left than in centre-right leaders; for the former have tended to be chosen by the leaders of the parties making up the coalition – although not necessarily in a transparent or accountable manner. Rutelli, for instance, was chosen prior to the 2001 election 'by means of a highly opaque and dubious process (consisting of a meeting of leaders and a few surveys). He was the institutional candidate for the office of prime minister but not the actual political leader of the coalition' (Pasquino, 2005: 97). This is an important distinction: in order to have the authority and capacity truly to lead a coalition, the latter's prime-ministerial candidate needs also to be its political leader. In other words, the two roles need to be assumed by a single individual. If this is not the case then the distribution of power within the coalition is skewed in favour of the parties, who retain a veto (enabling them potentially to paralyse the coalition) and thus the capacity to ensure that their prime-ministerial candidate remains subordinate to them.

Only Romano Prodi has come anywhere near to occupying both of these roles, but even he could not escape being held hostage to the parties, particularly the PPI and the DS, after he formed the Ulivo. Indeed, both expected to profit from his downfall when RC withdrew its support for his government in October 1998.[4] The problem was that Prodi did not himself belong to any of the parties making up the coalition. He deliberately sought to adopt an impartial, 'non-party', stance thinking that it would demonstrate to the electorate that he was above the party conflict that he hoped would be overcome through development of the original Ulivo as a new political subject. This was ultimately viewed by many commentators as a weakness as it left him without a power base in the coalition, exposing him to the constant threat of dismissal (which, in effect, is what happened in 1998) by its constituent parties. It was a situation that drew a strong contrast with the position of Berlusconi, who was able to combine leadership of the largest party on the centre right with leadership of the Cdl coalition. Although Prodi's 'non-party' stance was somewhat blurred by his decision to found the Democratici in 1999 (which later became part of the Margherita), he learnt valuable lessons from the events of 1998, deciding after his return to Italian politics in 2004 once more to position himself visibly above the parties, while demonstrably increasing his legitimacy and authority through primary elections to determine the leader of the centre-left coalition. Not only would an overt victory in such an election place his leadership of the coalition beyond doubt, but by relying on democratic procedures from the bottom up, he would also reconnect the coalition with its rank and file supporters, who 'are necessary to ensure [the coalition's] effectiveness outside Parliament, on the ground' (Bull and Newell, 2005: 56). The road to the primaries can be traced back to the situation the centre left found itself in, in the immediate aftermath of 2001.

Following its defeat in the election of that year, the centre left floundered with no single person able to act as its undisputed leader. By combining leadership of the Ulivo with leadership of the Margherita, Rutelli briefly attempted to do so. However, he soon realised that his party was not powerful enough to enable him to combine the two roles and that he would therefore have to make do with just the latter. The coalition thus became incapable of coordinating its activity and therefore of offering effective opposition to the Government. Thereby, it failed to demonstrate a clear sense of purpose to activists, voters and the public at large (Salvati, 2004). It was in these circumstances that the *girotondi* came (as mentioned above) to vent their frustrations with the Berlusconi government and the centre-left leadership.

The turning point for the coalition came in July 2003 when, in an interview published in *Corriere della Sera*, Prodi suggested that a single unified list, consisting of the component parts of the Ulivo, should be presented for the following year's European elections. The rationale for this was threefold. First, it was easier for the parties to find convergence in the European arena than on the domestic front. Second, the proportional system used for the European elections risked promoting yet further fragmentation and division and therefore increased the urgency of measures that might be expected to counteract them. Finally, Prodi stated that he would return to the leadership only if he were head of an 'organisationally coherent coalition' and would not lead with his hands tied behind his back (that is, at the behest of the parties) (Salvati, 2004: 59–60). Prodi also reiterated the position he had adhered to when previously at the helm of the Ulivo: that of not wishing to lead, nor be a member of any party within the coalition.

By advancing the single unified list, Prodi was reclaiming the leadership role he had lost with the fall of his government in 1998, and presenting a novel approach to the consolidation of the centre left. He was also offering a first step towards the future creation of a 'reformist party' which would absorb the majority of centre-left parties. However, only four parties took up the challenge offered: the two largest parties in the coalition, namely the DS and the Margherita, together with the significantly smaller SDI and MRE. The list, Uniti nell'Ulivo (literally, 'United in the Olive Tree'), did not prove as successful as had been hoped, as with 31.1 per cent of the vote it failed to exceed the combined sum of votes its constituent parties had received in the 2001 election. It also left the Margherita with a strong desire to reassert its separate identity. Thus, although the party became an integral part of the Federazione dell'Ulivo (Federation of the Olive-tree Alliance; Fed) when it was formed in February 2005 by the four parties that had run under the Uniti nell'Ulivo list, it also attempted to slow the process of the eventual creation of a 'reformist party' by opposing the proposal, advanced by Prodi later in 2004, for a single list for future elections.

Therefore, despite the initial warm reception given to Prodi on his return to domestic Italian politics, he was soon on the defensive and having to re-launch the idea of holding primaries to establish his leadership of the coalition.[5] In the immediate aftermath of the April 2005 regional elections, the prospect of a primary receded somewhat; for the centre left's victory in twelve of the fourteen regions contested induced Prodi to declare that the outcome – revealing, among other things, that the centre left had taken 53 per cent of the vote, the Fed 34.2 per cent in the nine regions where its symbol had been present on the ballot paper – had itself legitimated his leadership. As a consequence, he made no secret of his insistence that the Federation parties should agree, without further discussion, to the presentation of a joint list for the elections of 2006. The Margherita's National Assembly swiftly blocked this proposal with 80 per cent of its delegates voting against it and preferring, instead, the proposal that they compete under their own symbol. The rationale for this stance was threefold:

first, the belief that in pursuing the long-term goal of a 'reformist party', Prodi had left unclear the nature of its ideological identity and the 'instruments' by which it would operate; second the results obtained by the party in the regional election (which had given it 13.1 per cent of the vote in the five regions in which it had fought as a separate entity); third, the conviction that, if the Margherita ran as a separate entity, thus maintaining a separate, 'centrist' identity within the coalition, it would be easier for the centre left as a whole to win over the votes of moderates on the centre right. In light of this decision, which he deemed to be political 'suicide', an embittered Prodi was left with no alternative than once again to call for primaries. These were consequently scheduled for 16 October 2005.

Although the centre left had held a primary in Puglia to decide their candidate for the presidency of that region in January 2005,[6] the use of such a mechanism to determine the coalition's national leadership was a novel event, not just in Italy but in Western Europe as a whole. Seven candidates put themselves forward (see Table 4.2), with the favourite, Prodi, being officially backed by the DS and the Margherita. Prior to the primary, the three questions that were uppermost in the minds of observers were: what the turnout would be (Prodi had estimated that somewhere in the region of 750,000 people would participate); the margin of Prodi's, seemingly inevitable, victory; the weight of support that would be received by Bertinotti. This latter issue seemed important for two reasons: first, the belief (roundly dismissed by Pasquino in chapter 1) that centre-right supporters might seek to sabotage the event by turning out to vote en masse for Bertinotti (participation in the primary was not conditional upon any kind of formal affiliation with the centre left or any of its constituent parties) given the general assumption that he would be a much easier opponent than Prodi for Berlusconi to defeat. Second, within the centre left itself, the strength and bargaining position of its radical left would be tempered somewhat by a resounding Prodi victory.

Table 4.2 shows the results of the primary, the most notable features of which were the turnout – 4,311,149 – and the proportion of the vote received by Prodi: 74.1 per cent. Such an unexpectedly highly level of turnout (the more surprising for the fact that the combined membership of the DS and the Margherita stands at around 850,000) together with the overwhelming support for Prodi told several stories; first, that the parties and associations of the centre left were able to act as effective agents of mobilisation. Second, ordinary people utilised the primaries as an opportunity to communicate their dissatisfaction with the remote, oligarchic, nature of the parties, and to impress upon

Table 4.2 **The results of the primary election for the leadership of the centre left**

Candidates	Party	Total number of votes	Valid votes as a percentage
Fausto Bertinotti	RC	631,592	14.7
Antonio Di Pietro	IdV	142,143	3.3
Ivan Scalfarotto	Independent	26,912	0.6
Simona Panzino	No Global	19,752	0.5
Alfonso Pecoraro Scanio	Greens	95,388	2.2
Romano Prodi	Unione	3,182,686	74.1
Clemente Mastella	Popolari-UDEUR	196,014	4.6
Spoiled/blank ballots		16,662	
Total		4,311,149	100.00

Source: www.articolo21.info/documenti/risultati.pdf

them the need to reconnect with their grassroots and with society.[7] Third, the primary offered an opportunity to express a desire for unity amongst the constituent elements of the centre left. Fourth, it was also an opportunity for many to express their dissatisfaction with the Berlusconi government, their unhappiness with the dire state of the economy, and their opposition to the rewriting of the electoral law, the object of which was clearly to prevent, or at least limit the size of, a centre-left victory. Most importantly, however, the primary offered a visible and impressive opportunity to contribute to the legitimation of Romano Prodi's claim to be not only the centre left's prime-ministerial candidate but also its political leader – an opportunity to move him from the position of mere manager/administrator of the coalition to the position of being its unquestionable head. It is to his attempts to bring unity to the coalition that we now turn.

The road towards a more consolidated future?

The fragmented nature of the centre left – and the problems deriving therefrom – stand out in particularly sharp relief if we compare its situation with that of the centre right. As leader and founder of the Cdl, and of its largest, most powerful, party, Forza Italia, Berlusconi is in a position of strength that is currently unmatched on the centre left. Berlusconi leads a coalition having four core elements, among which his party is by far and away the most powerful. There are several reasons for this. First, FI is located close to the centre of the political spectrum in a bi-polar party system characterised by centripetal competition, thus enabling it to attract moderate voters, while the smaller Alleanza Nazionale and the Northern League are positioned to its right. Second, the strength of FI is reinforced by the strategic difficulties faced by both AN and the Northern League: the former continues to have to strive to achieve full acceptance as 'a party like all the rest' (Tarchi and Poli, 2000: 70); the latter continues to face a 'constant struggle to maintain visibility and a distinct identity in the shadow of its larger ally' (Bull and Newell, 2005: 57). If it has sought to meet this challenge by emphasising anti-immigration and xenophobic themes, then this has not proved damaging to the coalition as a whole; for moderate voters 'do not fear voting together with the followers of Fini [AN's leader] and Bossi [LN's leader] because they feel that power is solidly in Berlusconi's hands' (Salvati, 2003: 67). This consideration is particularly significant for the competitive position of the centre right in relation to the centre left for it suggests that alliance with 'extreme' parties poses less of a problem for the former than for the latter.

But the competitive advantage of the centre right does not end there. Although the primaries gave Prodi an unequivocal mandate to lead the centre left, the fact that he lacks the backing of any party (never mind the largest party in the coalition) puts him in a position of considerable weakness as compared with his counterpart on the centre right. Moreover, he leads a coalition whose centrifugal tendencies have been encouraged by its size and heterogeneity and by the paradoxical relationship between the DS and the Margherita – a relationship that is at once competitive, since the two fish in the same pool of voters (Bellucci and Bull, 2002), and mutually dependent, since, as members of the same coalition, each is reliant on the other for its own success. Although it is the largest party on the centre left, the DS is not the bastion of power that FI is on the centre right: it is not substantially larger than its partners, particularly the Margherita; unlike FI, it has significantly sized coalition partners (and therefore competitors) to both its left and right; and its communist heritage leaves it vulnerable to the attempts of the centre right to undermine it by appealing to anti-communist sentiments.

Therefore, in order to become fully competitive with the centre right, the centre left has sought to reorganise itself in such a way that it mirrors the former, seeking in particular to acquire a party similar in weight and positioning to FI. Key to this enterprise has been the attempt to locate its largest, pivot, party at the centre, with the smaller parties located on its left: this is the logic behind the 'reformist party' (or Democratic Party as it has come to be known). As discussed above, Prodi initiated the efforts to build such a party when he launched the Uniti nell'Ulivo list for the 2004 European elections, which was followed by the development of the Fed. The question of a single list for 2006 was resolved by Prodi's success in the primaries, with the Margherita backing away from its earlier rejection of the idea and accepting that in the Chamber of Deputies it should run with the DS and MRE in the Ulivo list (even though it was resolute that it would maintain its autonomy in the Senate election).[8]

Further consolidation of the coalition as an electorally competitive entity came with creation of the GAD and its change of name to the Unione; with the emergence of the la Rosa nel pugno, and with the emergence of the single list, called Insieme con l'Unione (literally, 'Together with the Unione'), fielded by the PdCI and the Greens for the Senate contest. Crucial to the centre left's modest victory in 2006 was, as Chiaramonte explains in chapter 10, the fact that it was for the most part able to line up behind single candidates in the constituencies consisting of Italians resident abroad.

Several additional means were devoted to the effort to maximise cohesion on the centre-left. First, the coalition's 281-page programme *Per il bene dell'Italia* ('For the Good of Italy'), was negotiated and signed by all the parties. Despite the fact that the breadth of its remit inevitably meant that it remained vague in places, it did provide a mandate for the governance of Italy, something that was particularly pertinent in light of RC's involvement and the role it had played in the downfall of the Ulivo government in 1998. Second, an accord was signed between the coalition partners binding them to agree to fresh elections in the event of a government collapse. Third, as a precursor to the Democratic Party, it was decided by Prodi, Fassino and Rutelli that after the election the representatives that had lined up behind the Ulvio would come together to form single groups in both chambers of Parliament.

Conclusion

Lesson learning was key to the centre left's strategic considerations prior to the 2006 general election. Attempts to resolve the fundamental issues of coalition breadth, leadership and consolidation/integration all contributed to the presentation to the electorate of a political subject whose components were more unified than they had been at the previous election. Nevertheless, historically fractious party politics were never far from the surface. Although Prodi was able to exert fairly strong leadership, the democratic occasion of the primaries was, as Pasquino (this volume) notes, never fully exploited by the centre left. Disputes ensued between the coalition partners regarding the future creation of the Democratic Party, construction of the programme (and its interpretation after it had been launched), candidate selection, and the distribution of the spoils of office. Moreover, opinion polls lulled the leadership into believing that victory was assured. Consequently complacency became rife and the election was nearly lost. Valuable lessons still remain to be learned by the parties of the centre left. The future success of the coalition is linked to its ability to become more homogeneous, and fundamental to that endeavour will be the creation of the Democratic Party.

Notes

1 Prodi's government lasted from April 1996 until October 1998 when RC (which, though not part of the Ulivo coalition, had lent the Government external support) declared that it would not support the Government in a confidence vote on the forthcoming Finance Bill (Pasquino, 2002). Following his departure from Government, Prodi formed a new party, the Democratici per l'Ulivo (Democrats for the Olive Tree Alliance), with the goal of re-launching the Ulivo project as well as defending bi-polar competition, which seemed to be threatened by Francesco Cossiga's Unione Democratica per la Repubblica (Democratic Union for the Republic; UDR) and its aim of creating a third force at the centre of the political spectrum (see for example Bufacchi and Burgess, 2000; Newell, 2000).

2 Galli's original conception of an 'imperfect two-party system' was designed to recall the conditions of the First Republic whereby the left was unable to provide a viable governing alternative because the international context of the Cold War led the other parties to deny it legitimacy as a potentially governing actor.

3 In the general election of 2001, the Margherita was a list of four parties, three of which (the Partito Popolare Italiano (Italian People's Party; PPI), Prodi's Democrats and Dini's Rinnovamento Italiano (Italian Renewal)), went on to form the single party led by Rutelli whilst the fourth, UDEUR, decided to remain autonomous.

4 The DS felt that, as the largest party in the coalition, they were entitled to the premiership. Thus, once Prodi's government fell, DS leader Massimo D'Alema was only too happy to replace the professor. The PPI did not object as its leader hoped that he would receive the nomination for the office of President of the Republic in 1999 (see Campus and Pasquino, 2004).

5 The centre left's party leaders had stated explicitly that Prodi was the official leader of the coalition and that the holding of primaries would thus be a redundant exercise.

6 The candidates were Francesco Boccia and RC's Nichi Vendola, who won the primary and the subsequent election for the presidency of the Puglia region.

7 Under the guidance of Prodi, the centre left launched the Fabbrica del programma ('Factory for development of the programme') in February 2005. This was an attempt to encourage deliberative democracy in the construction of the coalition's electoral programme, as it gave ordinary people the opportunity to visit the 'factory' (mainly based in an industrial unit in Bologna, although it did travel) or its website to express views on issues of concern to them and to offer proposals for their resolution (see www.lafabbricadelprogramma.it).

8 Debate surrounding the creation of the Democratic Party rumbled on throughout late 2005 and 2006, with Prodi using his success in the primaries to re-launch the idea, hoping that it would come into fruition more or less immediately. Both the DS and the Margherita had other ideas and eventually all concerned accepted that such an enterprise could not be undertaken until after the April election.

References

Andrews, G. (2005), *Not a Normal Country: Italy after Berlusconi*, London, Pluto.

Bellucci, P. and Bull, M. (2002), 'After the "honourable defeat": the DS, *Margherita* and *Ulivo*', in P. Bellucci and M. Bull (eds), *Italian Politics: The Return of Berlusconi*, Oxford, Berghahn.

Bufacchi, V. and Burgess, S. (2000), *Italy since 1989*, Basingstoke, Palgrave.

Bull, M. J. and Newell, J. L. (2005), *Italian Politics: Adjustment under Duress*, Cambridge, Polity.

Calise, M. (2000), *Il partito personale*, Rome and Bari, Laterza.

Campus, D. and Pasquino, G. (2004), 'Leadership in Italy: the changing role of leaders in elections and in government', paper presented to the Association for the Study of Modern Italy Conference, London, 26–27 November.

D'Alimonte, R. and Bartolini, S. (1997), '"Electoral transition" and party system change in Italy', in M. Bull and M. Rhodes (eds), *Crisis and Transition in Italian Politics*, London, Frank Cass.

Diamanti, I. and Lazar, M. (2002), 'The national elections of 13 May 2001: chronicle of a victory foretold – albeit a little too soon', in P. Bellucci and M. Bull (eds), *Italian Politics: The Return of Berlusconi*, Oxford, Berghahn.

Di Virgilio, A. (1998), 'Electoral alliances: party identities and coalition games', *European Journal of Political Research*, 34, 5–33.

Galli, G. (1966), *Il bipartitismo imperfetto. Comunisti e democristiani in Italia*, Bologna, Il Mulino.

Ginsborg, P. (2001), *Italy and its Discontents*, London, Allen Lane.

Ginsborg, P. (2004), *Silvio Berlusconi: Television, Power and Patrimony*, London, Verso.

Massari, O. and Parker, S. (2000), 'The two lefts: between rupture and recomposition', in D. Hine and S. Vassallo (eds), *Italian Politics: The Return of Politics*, Oxford, Berghahn.

Newell, J. L. (2000), *Parties and Democracy in Italy*, Aldershot, Ashgate.

Newell, J. L. and Bull, M. J. (2002), 'Italian politics after the 2001 general election: *plus ça change, plus c'est la même chose?*', *Parliamentary Affairs*, 55, 626–642.

Pasquino, G. (1998), 'La cosa infinita', *Il Mulino*, 47 (375), 71–85.

Pasquino, G. (2002), 'The political context 1996–2001', in J. L. Newell (ed.), *The Italian General Election of 2001: Berlusconi's Victory*, Manchester, Manchester University Press.

Pasquino, G. (2005), 'Too many chiefs and not enough Indians: the leadership of the centre-left', *Modern Italy*, 10:1, 95–108.

Rose, S. (2002), 'The parties of the centre left', in J. L. Newell (ed.), *The Italian General Election of 2001: Berlusconi's Victory*, Manchester and New York, Manchester University Press.

Salvati, M. (2003), *Il Partito Democratico*, Bologna, Il Mulino.

Salvati, M. (2004), 'The Ulivo: death or transfiguration', in S. Fabbrini and V. Della Sala (eds), *Italian Politics: Italy between Europeanization and Domestic Politics*, Oxford, Berghahn.

Tarchi, M. and E. Poli (2000), 'The parties of the *Polo*: united to what end?', in D. Hine and S. Vassallo (eds), *Italian Politics: The Return of Politics*, Oxford, Berghahn.

5

The parties of the centre right

Roberto Biorcio

The coalition of parties of the centre right, the Cdl, that had governed Italy for five years under the leadership of Silvio Berlusconi, lost the general election of 2006. The result was expected: after the European Parliament elections of 2004 and the regional elections of 2005, opinion pollsters, like public opinion and the majority of media commentators, thought that a victory of the centre left was very probable. However, the results obtained by the centre right were better than expected, and the centre left won by just a few thousand votes. The Cdl managed to recover some of the ground it had lost to the centre left by changing the electoral law in a proportional direction. But in the months leading up to polling day, the attempt to counterbalance the effects on individual electoral behaviour of the unfavourable climate of opinion and of the many expressions of social protest against his policies was above all entrusted to the type of election campaign conducted by Berlusconi.

However, in order to explain the results of the 2006 elections, attention must be focused on the influence of events and processes that unfolded during the years leading up to the poll. At the elections of 2001, the parties of the centre right led those of the centre left by almost 9 percentage points in the proportional arena. In 2006, the percentages of the vote obtained by the two line-ups were almost the same. This was partly due to the broadening of the alliances, something that was more substantial in the case of the Unione. However, the considerable reduction in the gap between the two coalitions also came about because of the changes in political orientations that took place, during the years prior to the elections, in certain geographical areas and social strata.

Disappointment with the Berlusconi government

It may be useful to reflect on the entire sequence of events that led to the outcome of the elections of 9 and 10 April 2006. At the elections of 2001, the victory of the centre right had been clear cut and had been marked by the particular success of Berlusconi and his party (Biorcio, 2002: 88). Forza Italia had obtained almost two-thirds of the votes won by the Cdl (Table 5.1). In contrast, all the other parties of the centre right had suffered a loss of electoral support. For this reason, the balance of power within the coalition had changed substantially. Berlusconi's leadership had been much reinforced and his government was able to count on a broad base of support within the electorate. During its first year in office, the centre-right government enjoyed levels of public confidence which, according to opinion polls, exceeded 60 per cent.

Until the spring of 2004, the government seemed very strong, able to exercise power without particular difficulties owing to its overwhelming parliamentary majority. Effective forms of opposition could come only from street protests, social movements and demonstrations. These were sponsored by a large number of groups, trade unions and associations – often with the support of the parties of the left – as well as by many rank-and-file organisations, around a wide range of themes, in particular the defence of acquired rights. Thus it was that 2002 and 2003 witnessed large-scale trade-union struggles for the defence of article 18 of the Workers' Statute, movements for peace against the war in Iraq, and campaigns surrounding defence of the environment and the judicial system. Opinion polls registered impor-

Table 5.1 Chamber Elections 1994–2006: percentages of the vote obtained by the parties of the centre right

	1994	1996	2001	2006
Proportional arena				
Forza Italia	21.0	20.6	29.4	23.7
National Alliance	13.5	15.7	12.0	12.3
UDC (CCD-CDU)	–	5.8	3.2	6.8
Northern League	8.4	10.1	3.9	4.6
Other centre-right parties	–	–	1.0	2.3
Total centre right	42.9	52.2	49.5	49.7
Total valid votes	38,594,477	37,494,965	37,086,347	38,151,407

tant changes in public expectations as compared to 2001. Among large sectors of the public, hostility towards the Berlusconi government grew considerably. But growing dissatisfaction with the actual results of the government's actions and its failure to keep many of its election promises was also apparent among those who had voted for the Cdl parties. Opinion polls registered a sharp decline in confidence in the government in the spring of 2004 (Figure 5.1).

The effects of the changes in the climate of opinion on both electoral behaviour and the government of public institutions were revealed by the European Parliament elections of 2004, and by a number of local-council and provincial elections. Many of those who in the past had voted for the centre right now abstained. The decline in support was especially steep for Forza Italia, which went from 29.5 per cent in 2001 to 21.0 per cent in 2004. Electors disappointed with the performance of Berlusconi often chose not to vote, only a small number of them opting for the parties of the centre left. These tendencies were accentuated at the regional elections of 2005. The Cdl retained its majority in only two regions of northern Italy (Lombardy and Veneto) and even here it suffered a distinct loss of votes as compared to the previous regional elections. The decline in support was not evenly distributed, geographically, politically or socially. It was greater in the large cities than it was in small towns and villages. Within the centre right coalition, the weight of Forza Italia (with 18.8 per cent) declined still further. The relative disappointment with the performance of Berlusconi's government had without doubt disoriented and demobilised the supporters of his party. The position of the Northern League, by contrast, was somewhat reinforced as it had helped to contain the overall losses suffered by the Cdl, especially in its traditional areas of strength and in the small towns and villages.

There were further changes in the climate of opinion following the centre left's victory in the regional elections of 2005. For the first time, confidence in the opposition exceeded confidence in the Government, which reached its lowest level (27 per cent) in September 2005. Other indicators showed similar trends. Respondents' predictions of the probable winner of the up-coming general election more frequently pointed in the direction of the centre left. And voting intentions surveyed by opinion polls showed a clear majority for the parties belonging to the Unione. Only in the final months of the election campaign did these indicators signal a significant recovery in the chances of victory of the centre right.

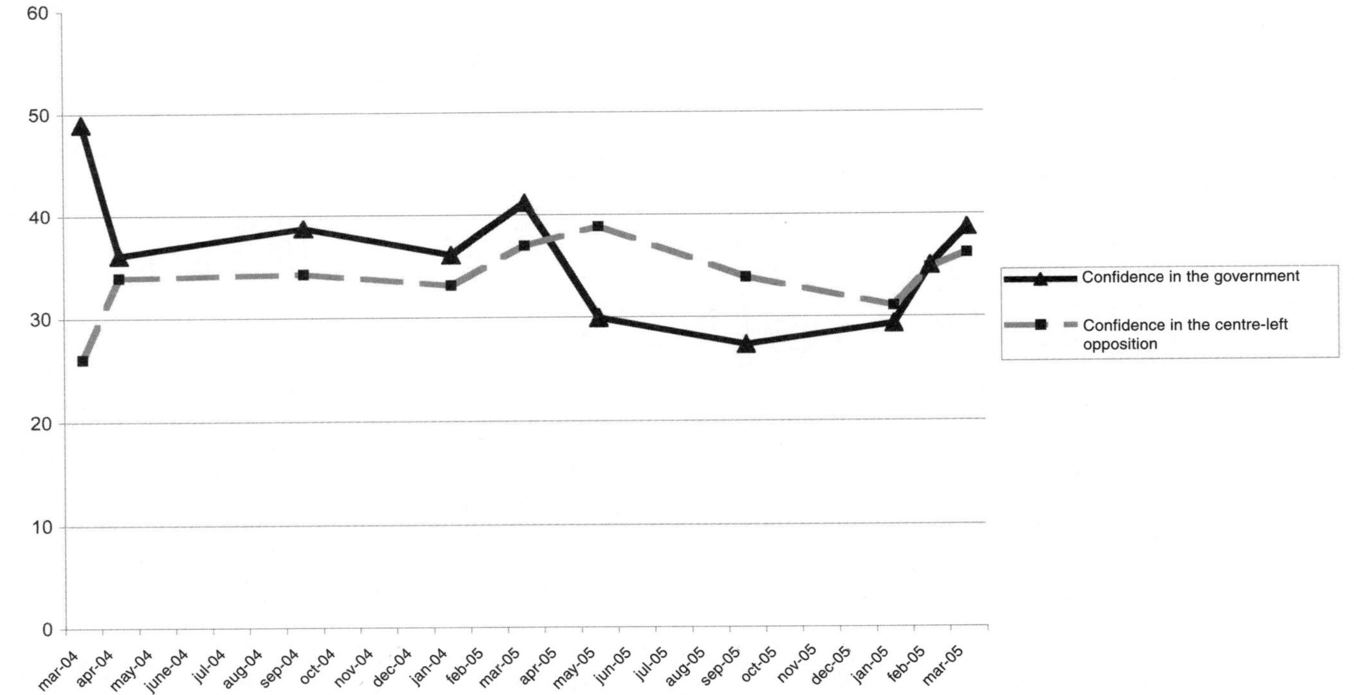

Source: GfK-Eurisko Polls 2006.

Figure 5.1 Confidence in the government and in the centre-left opposion

The counteroffensive of the centre right, and the election campaign

In 2005, beginning with a change in the electoral law from a predominantly majoritarian to a proportional system with a majority premium for the coalition winning the most votes (D'Alimonte and Chiaramonte, 2006), the centre right initiated a counteroffensive in order to overturn the negative predictions of its chances of being re-elected.[1] At the previous elections in 1996 and 2001, in fact, many of the supporters (about 1.5 million) of the parties of the Cdl had not voted for the coalition's candidates fielded in the single-member colleges making up the majority arena. Abolition of the majority arena, and the limitation of electoral options to the simple choice between parties, was expected to favour recovery of a large proportion of the votes that in 2001 had not gone to centre-right candidates (Mannheimer, 2006: 21).

The new electoral law induced the two coalitions to extend their boundaries as much as possible in the attempt to win the majority premium. The centre right thus incorporated – besides a series of minor forces – two far-right formations (the Tricoloured Flame and the Social Alternative), which had in the past fielded candidates independently. Moreover, European Democracy, which in 2001 had presented candidates independently of the Cdl, took part in the formation of the UDC, together with the CCD-CDU. The combination of lists that joined forces in the coalition of the centre right had in 2001 taken 52.4 per cent of the valid votes cast in the proportional arena.[2] But at the end of 2005 the polls continued to suggest considerable difficulties in the way of recapturing the support of earlier Forza Italia voters who in many cases were undecided between voting or abstaining.

In order to change these tendencies, Berlusconi sought to accomplish a kind of new 'taking to the field' (*discesa in campo*[3]) comparable with the one successfully realised in 1994 and 2001. The aggressive election campaign of the leader of the Cdl had two basic objectives: to bring at least 80 per cent of the electorate to the polls, and to recapture 24 per cent of the vote for Forza Italia.

Berlusconi put in an increasing number of appearances on a wide range of television programmes. The public networks of Radiotelevisione Italiana (Italian Radio and Television; RAI) – almost all directed by journalists chosen by the centre right – and the television networks of Mediaset, owned by the Prime Minister's family, certainly facilitated this strategy. But what was decisive was the capacity of the Cdl leader to remain constantly at the centre of the political show through unscheduled appearances and initiatives, often at the limits of what was acceptable in terms of provocation.

During the initial months of the year, Berlusconi's incessant media campaign sought above all to counter the most widespread opinions about his government and the condition of the country. This strategy brought some results: between January and March there was a modest growth in confidence in the Government (Figure 5.1) and in many polls the proportions intending to vote for Forza Italia went up by 2 percentage points. The campaign did not, however, seem capable of reversing the predicted outcome of the elections. Berlusconi thus changed tack during the last two weeks of the campaign, seeking a heightened dramatisation of the contest. The re-awakening of old fears widespread among ordinary people was managed by having recourse to the entire range of arguments in the populist repertoire. The new strategy was initiated by the spectacular clash with the Confindustria leadership at the Italian industrialists' conference in Vicenza. Rather than focusing on future promises or on the performance of his government, Berlusconi shifted attention to the need to defend the interests of his listeners' own sectors, threatened by the possibility of a victory of the Unione. All the populist platitudes were revived with attacks on the powers-that-be, the large newspapers and the large financial conglomerates, accused of betraying the interests of ordinary people and small businesses. The underhand agreements made with the left by these groups, for their own advantage, were denounced. Not even breaches of acceptable public parlance were wanting: the use of vulgar, if widely used, slang expressions revived the linguistic style earlier used by Umberto Bossi in order to establish direct contact with ordinary people. And the indignant or ironical reactions of newspapers and his political opponents were useful for attracting the attention of even the dullest and most absent-minded of electors.

More generally, Berlusconi's campaign sought to arouse the latent fears most widespread among the least politically informed electors: these amounted less to fear of the 'communists' than to anxieties about the more concrete threats of possible taxes on savings, family inheritances, and houses. They were fears that were also rendered credible by the uncertainties and the communications errors of the leaders of the centre left, who put forward conflicting and unclear proposals concerning new measures of taxation.

Berlusconi could not repeat the wide-ranging promises that he had made in 2001. The disappointing performance of his government would have deprived them of credibility. But he used all the same the classic techniques of television sales persons (successfully imitated by many a populist leader) in order to win the votes of marginal sectors of the electorate, the ones least interested in politics. Berlusconi promised that in the event of victory he would take immediate measures concerning certain concrete aspects of citizens' lives. These included the abolition of the ICI and the waste management tax. These promises – though judged difficult to keep by many because of the financial circumstances of Italian municipalities – certainly helped to attract the attention of sections of the electorate undecided about how to vote.[4]

Berlusconi's efforts to mobilise voters was undoubtedly successful among some sectors of the electorate and in particular among those who had voted for Forza Italia at earlier elections and seemed undecided about the choices they would make. These are voters many of whom have little education, no interest in politics and who can be mobilised only by the perception of threats or by the hope of concrete and immediate benefits.

In the Chamber of Deputies election the Cdl thus managed to obtain almost the same percentage support as in 2001, and it lost the election to the centre left by fewer than 25,000 votes. In the Senate election, the votes cast in the home constituencies for the centre right marginally exceeded (by 50.2 to 49.0 per cent) those cast for the centre left. The Unione was able to win a majority of seats in the Senate too only thanks to the senators elected by the Italian citizens resident abroad.

Berlusconi's campaign did not produce victory because the fears he evoked seemed lacking in credibility to young voters and to the overseas residents. And above all it was unable to change the voting choices of the most attentive and informed part of the electorate or of those who had decided their voting preferences some time during the years prior to the campaign.

Territorial differences and the northern question

The parties belonging to the Cdl fractionally increased (from 49.6 to 49.7 per cent) the proportion of votes they had obtained in 2001. But if one takes account of the fact that the coalition was joined by two parties (European Democracy and the far-right formation the Tricoloured Flame) which at the previous elections had stood independently, then the overall share of votes obtained by the parties of the centre right declined by 2.6 per cent. The losses were minor in the northern regions but particularly significant in the south (Table 5.2).

Analysis of the flow of the vote has shown that there were also important shifts and switches of vote between the Cdl and the Unione. Overall, the flows favoured the centre left (Natale, 2006: 63). But this

Table 5.2 Votes for the centre right by geographical area (Chamber)

	% Vote 2006	Difference compared to 2001	
		A*	B**
Piemonte	50.0	0.0	−1.7
Lombardia	56.9	1.5	0.0
Trentino	35.3	3.5	1.9
Veneto	56.8	2.1	−0.1
Friuli	54.5	3.2	1.0
Liguria	46.4	0.9	−0.9
NORTH	*53.8*	*1.5*	*−0.3*
Emilia	40.1	0.6	−0.5
Toscana	38.3	−0.3	−1.3
Umbria	42.5	−0.1	−1.7
Marche	44.8	0.1	−1.4
'RED BELT'	*40.3*	*0.2*	*−1.0*
Lazio	49.9	−0.7	−3.2
Abruzzo	47.0	−3.3	−5.3
Molise	49.1	3.7	−0.6
Campania	48.8	−2.6	−7.8
Puglia	51.5	1.0	−3.2
Basilicata	39.5	2.5	−5.3
Calabria	42.8	−6.9	−12.4
Sicilia	57.9	1.7	−5.4
Sardegna	45.4	−4.1	−6.0
LAZIO AND THE SOUTH	*50.1*	*−1.1*	*−5.6*
Total	49.7	0.1	−2.6

Notes: * A The figures in this column show the difference in the percentage of the vote obtained by the Cdl in 2006, and the combined percentage obtained by the parties belonging to the same coalition in 2001; ** B The figures in this column show the difference in the percentage of the vote obtained by the Cdl in 2006, and the combined percentage obtained by: (a) the parties belonging to the coalition in 2001 and (b) the parties that joined the coalition subsequently (European Democracy and the Tricoloured Flame).

tendency showed itself clearly above all in the central and southern regions, as had already happened at the regional elections of 2005. Less clear cut were the tendencies in the northern regions where there were different movements, sometimes in opposite directions, between large metropolitan centres and the peripheral areas of provinces.

Analysis of the flow of the vote has also shown that there were important shifts and switches of vote between the parties belonging to the Cdl (Natale, 2006: 64). There thus emerged important changes in the distribution of power between the parties of the coalition and in the territorial distribution of support (Table 5.3).

Forza Italia lost almost 2 million votes (and 5.7 per cent) compared with 2001, despite the success of Berlusconi's campaign in re-mobilising some of the electors who had abstained at the European and regional elections. The losses were greater in the northern regions, but took place everywhere. This was the most significant change registered at the last elections as compared with the elections five years previously. The strength of Berlusconi's party within the coalition has been considerably reduced, even if it remains above that of 1994 and 1996.

In the northern regions, the decline in support for Forza Italia was largely compensated by the increases in support for its allied parties, AN and the UDC. In these regions, voters disappointed with Berlusconi did not vote for the Northern League. Only in small numbers did they switch over to the centre left. The fears evoked during the course of the campaign and the dramatisation of the conflict between the two coalitions, prompted on the part of these voters – who in the past had chosen the centre right with greater conviction – choices that were at one and the same time driven by cynicism and prudence.

The centre-right formation that grew the most in 2006 was the UDC, the party born from the joining of forces of the CCD, the CDU and European Democracy. These formations had together obtained 5.6 per cent of the vote in 2001. After their merger, the new formation found itself on an upward trend, obtaining 5.9 per cent of the vote in the 2004 European Parliament elections and 6.8 per cent in 2006. But the territorial distribution of its support has changed in recent years. The most significant increases have, indeed, taken place in the northern regions, while in a number of southern regions support has gone down as compared to the European Parliament elections of 2004. Even though the UDC remains relatively stronger in the south, the distribution of its electoral following is tending to become more even, expanding in the areas that in the past had given more votes to the Christian Democrats.

Table 5.3 Votes for individual parties of the centre right by geographical area

	% Vote in 2006 (Chamber)				Difference compared to 2001			
	FI	AN	UDC	League	FI	AN	UDC	League
Piemonte	23.5	11.8	6.2	6.3	−8.5	2.6	4.0	0.4
Lombardia	27.1	10.2	5.9	11.7	−5.2	1.5	3.8	−0.4
Trentino	16.6	8.1	4.9	4.5	0.1	−1.4	2.8	0.8
Veneto	24.5	11.3	7.8	11.1	−7.6	2.8	4.6	1.0
Friuli	23.4	15.5	7.1	7.2	−4.7	2.9	4.7	−1.1
Liguria	23.5	11.4	6.0	3.7	−5.8	2.0	3.9	−0.2
North	*24.9*	*11.0*	*6.4*	*9.4*	*−6.2*	*2.0*	*4.0*	*0.1*
Emilia	18.6	10.2	5.8	3.9	−5.2	0.6	3.5	1.3
Toscana	16.9	12.6	5.9	1.1	−4.8	−0.5	3.6	0.5
Umbria	17.8	15.2	6.5	0.8	−3.7	−1.8	4.1	0.8
Marche	19.1	14.3	8.0	1.0	−5.9	−0.3	3.8	1.0
'Red belt'	*18.0*	*12.1*	*6.2*	*2.2*	*−5.0*	*−0.1*	*3.6*	*0.9*
Lazio	21.4	18.6	6.9	0.3	−5.1	−1.9	4.2	0.2
Abruzzo	22.8	14.3	6.8	0.5	−6.3	−0.5	1.4	0.5
Molise	26.7	11.1	7.7	0.2	−0.5	1.5	1.4	0.2
Campania	27.1	12.6	5.3	0.2	−6.6	−0.5	2.0	0.2
Puglia	27.3	13.2	7.8	0.7	−2.8	−2.1	3.9	0.7
Basilicata	19.8	10.8	5.9	0.9	−5.8	1.5	5.9	0.9
Calabria	20.7	11.0	7.7	0.8	−5.0	−4.1	2.2	0.8
Sicilia	29.1	10.9	10.0	4.4	−7.5	0.2	2.7	4.4
Sardegna	22.6	12.9	7.7	0.4	−7.7	−0.7	3.1	0.4
Lazio and the South	*25.1*	*13.7*	*7.4*	*1.1*	*−5.7*	*−1.1*	*3.0*	*1.1*
Total	23.7	12.3	6.8	4.6	−5.7	0.3	3.5	0.7

National Alliance's electorate has registered similar tendencies. The modest growth in support for the party (up 0.3 per cent on 2001) is, in fact, the product of a distinct expansion of support in the northern regions balanced by losses in the regions of the south. The party led by Gianfranco Fini too is thus seeing a reduction in the imbalance in the distribution of its support between north and south, and is tending to assume a political position within the centre-right coalition that finds support in all geographical areas.

The Northern League, in contrast, experienced considerable difficulties after it joined the Berlusconi government in 2001. The party has tried, in recent years, to retain contact with popular demands and attitudes in the areas where it is most deeply rooted. Without weakening the alliance and, on the contrary, maintaining a privileged relationship with Berlusconi, the League sought to continue to pose as a party of struggle able to act as a mouthpiece for the discontent and protest of the regions of the north. The old posters against 'Thieving Rome' were taken out and dusted down and the arguments with the allied centre-right parties most deeply rooted in the south were stepped up. In the period of greatest difficulty for the Berlusconi government, the League recovered some of the votes it had previously lost to Forza Italia, reaching 5.0 per cent in the European Parliament elections of 2004, and 5.5 per cent in the regional elections of 2005.

A few weeks before the 2006 vote, Bossi's party tried to expand the reservoir of its support by forming an alliance with Raffaele Lombardo's Movement for Autonomy whose roots lay above all in Sicily. This alliance – which contradicted the traditional anti-southern polemic on which the identity of the Northern League had been based – resulted in an increase in votes as compared with 2001. But the growth was concentrated above all in Sicily (4.4 per cent), being more marginal in the other regions of the centre and the south. In the regions of the north there was no increase in the level of support obtained in 2001. And the trends towards a recovery of support that had manifested themselves at the regional elections of 2005 were halted.

The substantial stability in the level of support for the Cdl in the northern regions was due, as we have seen, above all to the growth of two parties (the UDC and AN) that are more strongly rooted in southern Italy. The tendencies brought to light by the elections of 9 and 10 April cannot therefore be interpreted as a re-explosion of the northern question in the forms that it had assumed in the first half of the 1990s (Ricolfi, Ferragutti and Dallago, 2006).

Social differences

If the share of the vote obtained by the Cdl and the Unione were nearly the same among the electorate as a whole, then within the various occupational categories and/or social classes there were very large differences in favour of one or the other coalition. This therefore suggests that voters' social positions had a strong influence on their choices at the recent elections.

The analysis of electoral behaviour on the basis of the occupational categories or social classes of voters – which is known in the literature as the 'class model' of voting – was for several years after World War II almost entirely useless in Italy. The territorially based sub-cultural traditions, passed from one generation to the next through processes of socialisation within the family, exercised an influence on voting choices that was often far greater than that exercised by membership of a specific social class. And at the same time, membership of the Catholic community cross-cut social divisions, orienting the votes of believers independently of the occupational categories to which they belonged.

The nature of the relations between voters, social classes and parties has, however, changed considerably since the crisis of the 'First Republic'. First the Northern League, then Forza Italia, sought to provide representation, in the political arena, for a series of interests which, in the past, had simply been mediated within the framework of the general programmes of the large, mass-membership parties. The two new parties – which created the basis for the formation of the new coalition of the centre right – sought thus to offer direct expression to interests emerging from civil society that had in the past struggled to gain a hearing within the traditional political establishment. The League from the beginning sought to act as a mouthpiece for the interests and values expressed by the small-business districts of the regions of the North. Forza Italia was founded by a successful entrepreneur who had 'lent his services to politics', continually reaffirming his identification with the values, the mentality and the genuine interests of the category from whence he came. Fiscal protest, the criticism of state bureaucracy and inefficiency, the promotion of private enterprise – all themes to which particular socio-economic categories are sensitive – thus acquired a growing profile on the political agenda.

If at the elections of 1994 the electorate of the centre right as a whole had had a cross-class profile (Mannheimer, 1994), then starting from the elections of 1996, and to an even greater extent in 2001, the class distribution of the vote acquired a very distinct profile. The centre right – and above all Forza Italia – showed a great capacity to attract support among entrepreneurs and the self-employed (shop-keepers and artisans). The votes of housewives were most likely to go to the centre right. But even among workers employed in the private sector, voting choices predominantly favoured the parties of the centre right. Support for the Cdl thus tended to go beyond the traditional confrontation between bourgeoisie and working class (ITANES, 2001: 65). The centre left won significantly above-average support only among public-sector workers, in particular among middle-ranking white-collar employees.

In the elections of 2006, the Cdl succeeded in maintaining its very strong capacity to attract votes across the entire range of categories of the self-employed. Entrepreneurs, independent professionals, shop-keepers and artisans gave more than twice as much support to the parties of the centre right as they gave to the centre left (Table 5.4). Greater difficulties for the Cdl emerged, however, among the various categories of employee.

The centre right no longer enjoys majority support among private-sector workers. If among directors, middle managers and routine white-collar employees there is substantial parity between the two coalitions, then a majority of manual workers voted for the Unione.

Table 5.4 Votes for the centre right by occupational category and geographical area (Chamber, %)

	Italy	North	'Red belt'	Lazio and the South
Entrepreneurs/independent professionals	57.6	68.5	51.4	49.9
Artisans/shop-keepers/self-employed workers	64.5	73.3	45.5	61.7
Directors/middle managers/executives	49.5	51.4	53.9	39.7
Routine white-collar workers/teachers	48.5	49.3	37.7	50.9
Manual workers	45.3	49.5	29.1	46.4
Housewives	54.0	58.8	48.2	50.5
Students	46.9	47.5	49.1	47.1
Pensioners	45.4	52.8	28.8	46.9
Unemployed	46.2	29.5	62.7	49.8
All	49.7	53.8	40.3	50.1

Source: GfK-Eurisko Polls 2006.

This is an important change as compared with 2001. In those elections, the centre right had won above-average support among manual workers (Biorcio, 2002: 92). Analogous changes of electoral support also took place among the unemployed. In 2001, this part of the electorate, which is of significant dimensions especially in southern Italy, had to a large extent been attracted by the promises contained in Berlusconi's programme to broaden the range of available employment opportunities. At the most recent elections the unemployed and those in search of a first job voted predominantly for the Unione.

Important changes as compared to 2001 can also be observed in other categories of elector outside the labour market. Among pensioners, support for the Cdl has declined considerably. The percentage of votes going to the Unione has also grown among housewives, in the past much more willing to vote for the coalition led by Berlusconi.

In the regions of northern Italy, the predominance of the centre right among entrepreneurs, shop-keepers and artisans is very marked. In these regions the Cdl remains the coalition of choice among employees too, but its advantage over the Unione appears much reduced, especially among manual workers.

Less decisive was the outcome of the competition between the two coalitions for the votes of employees in the various geographical areas. In 2006, the Unione emerged in the lead.

The differences between the parties of the centre right

Did the transformations that took place in the social profile of the vote for the two coalitions also change to any significant degree the characteristics of the vote for the principal parties making up the Cdl?

Forza Italia retained its considerable over-representation among the self-employed (entrepreneurs, shop-keepers and artisans) and among housewives (Table 5.5). The effective campaign run by Berlusconi from the initial months of 2006 on undoubtedly limited his losses, remobilising a good part of his electorate among almost all social strata. The Forza Italia electorate of 2006 appears, in social terms, almost a photocopy, just slightly smaller, of its 2001 electorate – with one major exception. The most significant losses (both in percentage terms and in terms of the absolute number of votes cast) in fact took place among the various lower strata (manual workers, the unemployed, pensioners). In 2001, Berlusconi had been able to make promises to these social groups that had led them to hope for the possibility of an improvement in their standards of living. Disappointment with the performance of the centre right government

Table 5.5 Votes for individual parties of the centre right by occupational category (%)

	Centre right	Forza Italia	National Alliance	UDC	Northern League
Entrepreneurs/independent professionals	57.6	28.9	21.3	3.7	3.4
Artisans/shop-keepers/self-employed workers	64.5	30.9	14.9	6.0	8.5
Directors/middle managers/executives	49.5	18.2	14.3	9.7	3.8
Routine white-collar workers/teachers	48.5	21.1	14.6	8.1	2.3
Manual workers	45.3	20.5	11.2	3.3	6.8
Housewives	54.0	33.2	6.6	8.4	3.6
Students	46.9	19.4	16.9	6.2	2.8
Pensioners	45.4	20.6	10.1	8.2	4.8
Unemployed	46.2	19.9	12.0	6.6	4.3
All	49.7	23.6	12.1	6.8	4.7

Source: GfK-Eurisko Polls 2006.

was not outweighed by the effects of the campaign based on the possible dangers of a government of the Unione.

The votes lost by Forza Italia in 2006 were for the most part compensated, as we have seen, by the growth in support for the other parties of the coalition, above all in the regions of the north. These changes partly modified the social profile of the parties. National Alliance obtained much-above-average levels of support among entrepreneurs and professionals in particular. The UDC obtained especially high percentages among senior managers, executives and among middle-ranking employees. The League continued to find its highest levels of support among the self-employed *petit bourgeoisie* (shop-keepers and artisans) and among workers in the regions of the north.

Supporters of the parties of the centre right are also significantly different in terms of their levels of education and their degrees of political engagement (Tables 5.6 and 5.7). These differences reflect the social differences we have highlighted.

Forza Italia is under-represented among university and secondary-school graduates, while it obtains much more support among electors with middle- and lower-level educational qualifications. In general, Berlusconi's party does better among electors with little or no interest in politics. Northern League supporters have very similar characteristics, with a clear preponderance of voters with middle and low levels of education and who say they have no interest in politics. Those who

Table 5.6 Votes for parties of the centre right by educational qualification (%)

	Centre right	Forza Italia	National Alliance	UDC	Northern League
Degree	39.3	16.4	13.0	6.6	2.2
Secondary-school diploma	52.0	23.3	15.1	6.7	3.8
Middle-school diploma	52.7	25.6	12.6	6.9	5.4
Elementary-school certificate/ no qualification	45.3	23.4	8.0	6.9	5.4
All	49.7	23.6	12.1	6.8	4.7

Source: GfK-Eurisko Polls 2006.

Table 5.7 Votes for parties of the centre right by levels of interest in politics (%)

	Centre right	Forza Italia	National Alliance	UDC	Northern League
A great deal/some	45.6	21.6	12.1	5.5	4.2
A little	50.2	23.6	12.8	7.7	3.7
No interest	54.9	27.2	11.0	7.6	7.1
All	49.7	23.6	12.1	6.8	4.7

Source: GfK-Eurisko Polls 2006.

voted for AN have very different characteristics insofar as they have higher levels of education and appear to be more interested in politics. The profile of UDC supporters is different again insofar as their proportions do not vary with the level of education of voters.

In general we can observe that the four principal parties of the Cdl have very different chances of winning support in the various social environments that make up Italian society. The difficulties encountered by Forza Italia in maintaining the support it had won in 2001 were translated into a significant loss of support for the centre-right coalition as a whole, especially among the lower social strata.

Conclusion

In the elections of 2006, Silvio Berlusconi once more played a central role: he set the agenda for the entire campaign and enabled the centre right to make an unexpected come-back. The recovery staged by the leader of Forza Italia during the course of the campaign allowed him to recapture a large proportion of those electors who had remained undecided about how to vote (or whether to abstain) until the final weeks: a sector of the electorate with little interest in politics, tending to be moderate and without a clear preference in favour or against either of the two main coalitions (Sani, 2006: 60). The recovery of the Cdl was not, however, sufficient to outweigh the effects of the attitudes of mistrust (or hostility) against the centre-right government that had become widespread during the preceding years and that had given rise to a kind of general mobilisation against Berlusconi. This was a mobilisation that changed the political orientations prevalent among the lower strata of the electorate. This vast social swathe – consisting of manual workers, their families, and pensioners with a manual-worker background – had in 2001 given most of their votes to the Cdl. In 2006, driven by a range of different factors, the support of these voters went mostly to the Unione, especially in the central and southern regions of Italy. The factors that drove them included, first, the perception that they had grown poorer, together with the difficulties they faced in making ends meet on a daily basis. The realignment of the preferences of manual workers and their families was also certainly influenced by the trade union protests against the centre-right government that unfolded during the course of 2002 and 2003.

Using a military metaphor, one can say that in the elections of 2006 Berlusconi once again succeeded in winning an important battle while losing the war (perhaps definitively). The referendum that was held a few months after the election rejected by a large majority the constitutional reform that had been passed by the centre right in Parliament. The reform provided, among other things, for the introduction of devolution (an increase in the powers given to the regions) a measure that the Northern League considered a non-negotiable condition for its participation in the coalition of the centre right.

The election and the referendum defeats, together with the exit from government and the decline in support for Forza Italia, throw a question mark over the leadership and the most fundamental characteristics of the Cdl. The coalition is faced with a difficult dilemma. On the one hand, the leadership of Berlusconi appears indispensable to coalition unity and thus to the possibility of a future election victory. On the other hand, the 2006 defeat has created the need for a redefinition of the characteristics of the Cdl, with a reduction in the role of Berlusconi himself and a new candidate. These problems have been raised especially by the UDC, which has already taken independent positions on a range of issues debated in Parliament. But AN too has questioned the management of a Cdl that has hitherto often been conditioned by the close alliance between Berlusconi and Bossi.

The electoral strength of the two coalitions turned out to be almost equal in the elections of 2006, and in the end, victory was decided by just a few thousand votes. Can Italy now be considered a country split into two opposing halves? Voting choices that were the expressions of very different processes of reasoning, often driven by attitudes of cynicism and arrived at only in the final days of the campaign, cannot legitimately be projected onto the entire society, freezing them in the process. The principal contradictions and latent conflicts with the potential to explode and divide Italian society (on social, economic, cultural and religious issues) are also ones that divide the two political coalitions. At the same time, only a limited proportion of the electorate (not more than about 40 or 50 per cent) has more than a slight interest in politics or strong and stable partisan convictions. Even though among this proportion there is a slight preponderance of supporters of the centre left, competition among the electorate as a whole continues to be wide open.

Translated by James L. Newell

Notes

1 The majority premium in the case of elections to the Chamber of Deputies is awarded to the coalition that wins most votes nationally. In the case of Senate elections, the majority premium is assigned at the regional level.
2 In 2001 the parties belonging to the Cdl obtained 46.6 per cent of the votes, while European Democracy and the Tricoloured Flame obtained 2.4 and 0.4 per cent of the vote respectively.
3 This is a footballing analogy that has become famous since it was used by Berlusconi in January 1994 when announcing his intention of forming a coalition capable of resisting 'the communist threat' (*pericolo comunista*), and to be led by him personally. A populist expression, its implication was that only the direct intervention in politics of a person with his own extraordinary qualities could 'save the day'.
4 These promises raised the proportions of those intending to vote for the Cdl by between 0.5 and 1.0 per cent according to a number of polls (Mannheimer, 2006: 23).

References

Biorcio, R. (2002), '*Forza Italia* and the parties of centre right', in J. L. Newell (ed.), *The Italian General Election of 2001: Berlusconi's Victory*, Manchester and New York, Manchester University Press.

D'Alimonte, R. and Chiaramonte, A. (2006), 'Proporzionale ma non solo. La riforma elettorale della Casa delle libertà', *Il Mulino*, 56:1, 34–45.

ITANES [Italian National Election Study] (2001), *Perché ha vinto il centrodestra*, Bologna, Il Mulino.

Mannheimer, R. (1994), 'Forza Italia', in I. Diamanti and R. Mannheimer (eds), *Milano a Roma*, Rome, Donzelli.

Mannheimer, R. (2006), 'La campagna elettorale del 2006 e la mobilitazione delle "terza Italia" politica', in R. Mannheimer and P. Natale (eds), *L'Italia a metà. Dentro il voto del paese diviso*, Milan, Cairo Editore.

Natale P. (2006), 'La fedeltà leggera alla prova: i flussi elettorali', in R. Mannheimer and P. Natale (eds), *L'Italia a metà. Dentro il voto del paese diviso*, Milan, Cairo Editore.

Ricolfi, L., Ferragutti, P. and Dallago, F. (2006), 'Le elezioni di aprile e la "questione settentrionale"', in *Polena*, 3:1, 170–176.

Sani, G. (2006), 'Vincere la campagna e perdere le elezioni', in ITANES [Italian National Election Study], *Dov'è la Vittoria? Le elezioni del 2006*, Bologna, Il Mulino.

6

The processes of alliance formation

Mark Donovan

Alliances and party-system structure

By 2001, most observers agreed that after four elections the Italian party system had come to be organised around competition between two alliances (D'Alimonte and Bartolini, 2002; Caciagli and Corbetta, 2002; Pasquino, 2002). At the same time, however, there was also agreement that both alliances were fragmented and heterogeneous. Indeed, there has been a strong implication that both alliances are internally multi-polar, or at least bi-polar, in which case the party system must be multi-polar, rather than bi-polar, even if its format is clearly 'binary', that is rooted in competition for government between two blocs of forces. For these reasons, in the chapter on alliance formation in the volume devoted to the 2001 election, I argued that Italy had an 'imperfect two-bloc party system' (Donovan, 2002). This suggestion recognised the centrality of alliances to government formation and electoral behaviour whilst also acknowledging the complexity of inter-party relations, and particularly the attempts to reconstruct a centre pole, as well as the dissatisfaction of many voters, elites and observers with what the political elites were offering. No one suggests that Italy has a two-party system. Indeed, precisely the lack of cohesion within the alliances led Romano Prodi and Silvio Berlusconi, the two leaders, to seek some form of organisational integration. Both faced strong resistance from the party leaders: the barons against the would-be kings. Whilst little happened on the right – which, though fragmented, was more strongly led – a significant step towards aggregation took place within the left at the beginning of the 2001–2006 legislature. Subsequently, a series of faltering moves were taken not only towards aggregation, but also towards integration. Yet internal opposition was strong, and it was reinforced by the electoral reform, or 'counter-reform', as its opponents dubbed it, introduced by the government in December 2005 (see chapter 10).

The new electoral systems (for the two chambers) were intended by the Government to lessen the magnitude of its expected defeat, although they also responded to the repeated demands of the UDC that proportional representation be re-established. The restoration of this principle, abolishing the single-member constituencies introduced by the mould-breaking 1993 reform, promoted continuing fragmentation. And in fact this was another reason why the right enacted the reform: it threw a spanner in the works of party-building that, with immense difficulty and in very limited form, was under way on the left. Thus, despite the reform, the latter's two leading parties, the DS and the Margherita, presented themselves for the Chamber of Deputies election under the tried-and-tested banner of 'the Olive Tree', first used in 1996. At the same time, nonetheless, each presented itself separately for the Senate election, thus maintaining its distinct identity. The new electoral regulation did not do away with the need to form alliances, however. Rather, it shifted the emphasis from the constituency to nationwide support for a common prime-ministerial candidate. Nor was majoritarianism entirely done away with, since the prime-ministerial candidate who gained most votes in the Chamber of Deputies was guaranteed a minimum of 55 per cent of the seats there. In the Senate, the new electoral system also restored proportional representation whilst retaining an element of majoritarianism via the allocation of bonus seats, but the bonus operated at the regional level. At the aggregate, national, level the new electoral system did not guarantee a 'working' majority in the Senate and, in the event, the outcome was a very near tie: the left gained 158 seats, to the right's 156, whilst one overseas independent was also elected.[1] In any event, in order to secure the vitally important majority of votes in the Chamber, Prodi and Berlusconi sought the support of as many parties and lists as they could. Eventually, each prime-ministerial candidate came to be supported by between twelve and eighteen electoral lists (see Tables 6.1 and 6.2). The outcome in the Chamber was also extremely close. The lists supporting Berlusconi received 18,977,843 votes compared to 19,002,598 for those supporting Prodi – 24,755 votes less, or 0.0649 per cent of the total. Nevertheless, as intended by the new electoral law, this miniscule plurality (49.8 per cent of the total) triggered a seat bonus sufficient to allow the formation of a strong majority in the Chamber.

Perhaps the most striking outcome of the competitive aggregation of lists was the creation of a 'pan-left' and a 'pan-right', with virtually no 'third' forces. In fact, these latter took under 1 per cent of the vote (Table 6.3). This was a radical decline from the nearly 20 per cent

Table 6.1 Lists supporting the candidacy of Romano Prodi as Prime Minister

Chamber of Deputies			Senate		
List	No.	Vote	List	No.	Vote
Olive Tree	26	11,930,983	Olive Tree	1	59,498
Left Democrats	–	–	Left Democrats	17	5,977,347
Margherita	–	–	Margherita	17	3,664,903
MRE	–	–	MRE	8	51,219
RC	26	2,229,464	RC	18	2,518,361
la Rosa nel Pugno	26	990,694	la Rosa nel Pugno	18	851,604
Greens	26	784,803			
PdCI	26	884,127	'Together with the Unione'	18	1,423,003
United Consumers	–	–			
IdV	26	877,052	IdV	18	986,191
UDEUR	26	534,088	UDEUR	17/16	477,226
Pensioners' Party	26	333,278	Pensioners' Party	18	340,565
Partito dei Socialisti (Craxi)	16/11	115,066	Partito dei Socialisti (Craxi)	10/8	126,431
Consumers' List – DC	11/4	73,751	Consumers' List – DC	8/4	72,199
LFV	2	21,999	LFV	1	23,214
Alleanza Lombarda	1	44,589	Alleanza Lombarda	1	90,855
SVP	1	182,704	–		
			PSDI (Social Democracy)	11/10	57,343
			United Christian Democrats	2	5,442
Total	13	19,002,598	Total	16	16,725,401

Notes: No. = Number of constituencies in which lists were approved/finally presented (if different); Vote = Actual numbers.

Sources: Chamber: Court of Cassation; otherwise adapted from Ministry of Interior data.

Table 6.2 Lists supporting the candidacy of Silvio Berlusconi as Prime Minister

Chamber of Deputies			Senate		
List	No.	Vote	List	No.	Vote
Forza Italia	26	9,048,976	Forza Italia	18	8,202,290
National Alliance	26	4,707,126	National Alliance	18	4,235,808
UDC	26	2,580,190	UDC	17	2,309,442
Lega Nord – MPA	26	1,747,730	Northern League – MPA	17	1,530,667
DC – New PSI	26/25	285,474	DC – New PSI	14/12	190,717
AS con Mussolini	26	255,354	AS with Mussolini	18	214,526
MS – FT	26	230,506	MS – FT	18	204,498
No Euro	17/14	58,746	No Euro	5/4	30,527
FIPU	9/5	28,317	Pensioners	8/6	61,681
Ambienta-lista	7/6	17,145	Ambienta-lista	7/5	36,458
Italian Liberal Party	5/4	12,265	Italian Liberal Party	6/3	15,657
SOS Italia	7/4	6,781	SOS Italia	5/2	4,993
Italia di Nuovo	1/0	–	Italia di Nuovo	2/0	–
			Italian Republican Party	11/9	45,098
			New Sicily	1	33,485
			Pact for Sicily	1	20,825
			Extended Christian Pact	1	9,735
			Liberal Reformists	5/4	7,571
Total	13/12	18,977,843	Total	18/17	17,153,978

Notes: No. = Number of constituencies in which lists were approved/finally presented (if different); Vote = Actual numbers.

Sources: Chamber: Court of Cassation; otherwise adapted from Ministry of Interior data.

obtained by such parties in 1994, when the new party system first came into being. Even in 1996, they obtained nearly 15 per cent (not including RC)), largely thanks to the Northern League's abandonment of Berlusconi, whilst in 2001, difficulties in combining the different lists, particularly on the left, and the reassertion of a centrist Catholic force kept third-party support at 10 per cent (again, not including RC, which made its independence of the rest of the left quite clear). With third-party support approaching zero, the binary nature of Italian politics seemed to have been convincingly confirmed.

This chapter examines how Italy got to this point, focusing on the processes of alliance formation (and non-formation) from 2001, and their significance for the 2006 election.

The left: fragmentation, transformism and attempted unification

Romano Prodi was backed by 13 lists in the Chamber and 16 in the Senate (see Table 6.1 and Figures 6.1–6.4). Since the alliances differed slightly in the two chambers, and since some lists were composite, 21 different parties, quasi-parties and organisations can be identified as backing Prodi.[2] The new electoral system 1) promoted aggregation of lists in support of prime-ministerial candidates; 2) encouraged at least a minimal degree of aggregation of intra-alliance lists to overcome the low thresholds for such lists (2 per cent in the Chamber, 3 per cent in the Senate); but 3) enabled the smallest lists to run separately, given that they had the potential to prove that they mattered by contributing to the total vote of the prime-ministerial candidate in the Chamber. Since Prodi won in the Chamber by under 25,000 votes, the 115,066 votes of Vittorio Craxi's Socialists were arguably decisive to the outcome – and several lists could argue this (Table 6.1). Prodi's government thus included not only representatives of the nine parties which founded the Unione (see below), but also personalities such as Vittorio Craxi and Elidio De Paoli (whose Lombard League – Pensioners' List, called Alleanza Lombarda (Figure 6.2), obtained 44,589 votes).

Three major features of this fragmented unity were: the overcoming of mutual vetoes; several cases of transformism; and a series of attempts to rationalise and even integrate some or all of the alliance. This election was the first in which a single, 'pan-left' alliance existed – the Unione. It included RC, which ran separately in 1996 and 2001, and Antonio Di Pietro's IdV. This was created in 1997, and it too ran separately in 2001 when its vote, together with that of RC, amounted to 8.9 per cent. The new pan-left, then, ranged from the communist

Table 6.3 'Third' forces, Chamber of Deputies (PR vote), millions

'Third' forces votes:	1994		1996		2001		2006	
	No.	%	No.	%	No.	%	No.	%
MS – FT	–[a]	–	0.34	0.9	0.14	0.4	–[a]	–
Northern League	–[a]	–	3.78	10.1	–[a]	–	–1	–
Pannella (& other)	–[a]	–	0.70	1.9	0.83	2.2	–2	–
PPI	4.29	11.1	–	–	–	–	–	–
Segni Pact	1.81	4.7	–	–	–	–	–	–
European Democracy	–	–	–	–	0.89	2.4	–[a]	–
IdV	–	–	–	–	1.44	3.9	–[b]	–
RC	–	–	3.21	8.6	1.87	5.0	–[b]	–
Other	1.36	3.3	0.63	1.6	0.38	1.0	0.17	0.5
Total excluding RC	7.46	19.1	5.45	14.5	3.68	9.9	0.17	0.5
Total including RC	7.46	19.1	8.66	23.1	5.55	14.9	0.17	0.5

Notes: [a] Formed part of the coalition of the right; [b] Formed part of the coalition of the left.

Source: Ministero dell'Interno, Archivio storico delle Elezioni.

left to the centre, represented by the UDEUR, a decidedly moderate force.

The overcoming of mutual vetoes

The vetoes overcome in this process of aggregation reflect three lines of division within the left:

- The 'left left' – that is, RC, the PdCI and the Greens – opposes 'neo-liberal' economics and proposes a pacifist foreign policy, in contrast to the rest of the alliance and especially, on both counts, the Radicals. Nevertheless, the construction of the Unione was precisely about integrating these forces, and above all its largest component, RC, into a governing alliance, overcoming its 'opposition of principle', which had led to the fall of the first Prodi government in 1998.[3]
- Second, Di Pietro had not been part of the left in 2001 as a result of friction with the SDI and the PPI which had seen their predecessor parties destroyed in the corruption scandal, Tangentopoli. Di Pietro, a public prosecutor in Milan, had been the lead protagonist in this immense political drama.
- Third, the Margherita majority and the UDEUR excluded the Radicals until January 2006, preoccupied by the impact their inclu-

Figure 6.1 Consumers' List – DC

Figure 6.2 Lombard Alliance

Figure 6.3 'Together with the Unione'

Figure 6.4 'the Rose in the fist'

sion would have on Catholic voters who had been mobilised by the referendum on artificial insemination, in June 2005, when the Church played an unusually interventionist (and arguably unconstitutional) role.

Cases of transformism

Transformism was a significant aspect of alliance-building on the left.[4] In particular, two interest groups, hitherto aligned with the right, were transformed, or 'captured' by the left. First, Carlo Fatuzzo, leader of the Pensioners' Party, which gained a third of a million votes, had previously been associated with the National Alliance, the centre-right European People's Party (EPP) and Forza Italia. In the 2005 regional elections, the party backed candidates of left and right, according to local circumstances, and in February 2006, following a meeting with Prodi, Fatuzzo formally broke with Berlusconi, arguing that the government had failed to stand by its promises on pensions. Second, the Consumers' List – DC, comprising both an interest group and a minor party fragment, was also won over to the left. This list's successful senatorial candidate, Pietro Fuda, had been elected provincial president of Reggio Calabria by the right in 2002.[5]

Transformism might also be argued to characterise Vittorio Craxi's Socialists. Vittorio, known as Bobo, was a prominent member of the New PSI formed in January 2001 from the fragmented remnants of the

Italian Socialist Party (PSI) destroyed by Tangentopoli. More specifically, the New PSI was formed by those who would not ally with the Left Democrats, the successor to the Italian Communist Party (PCI), believing that the PSI's destruction, and the humiliation of Bettino Craxi, its leader (from 1976 to 1993), had resulted from the political bias of public prosecutors inspired by and/or sympathetic to the PCI. Bobo was Bettino's son. The New PSI fought the 2001 election allied with Berlusconi, but whilst Bettino Craxi and Berlusconi had themselves been allies from the 1980s, by 2001 Berlusconi was the leader of the right. From 2005, Bobo tried to lead the party back to the left. However, the party split (again), and Bobo formed the Partito dei Socialisti – in effect, a 'personal party', that is, a (quasi-)party consisting of the supporters of a prominent politician. Arguably, this party returned part of the socialist elite and its associated electorate to their ideological homeland. Nevertheless, the more bitter anti-communist socialists saw Bobo as betraying his father's memory and as opportunistically jumping on the band-wagon of the opposition's expected victory.

A further reason for the failure of the New PSI to rejoin the left was the alliance strategy of Enrico Boselli the leader of the SDI – the party that brought together those socialists who had joined the left, albeit remaining apart from the DS. Rather than promote the reunification of the SDI and the New PSI, Boselli allied with the Radicals, forming la Rosa nel Pugno (literally, 'the Rose in the fist': see Figure 6.4) and inviting the New PSI to do the same. This was all too much, and Craxi formed his own list, backing Prodi.

The SDI/Radical alliance also involved a degree of transformism. The Radicals are a politically ambiguous, libertarian force which was part of the anti-communist left in the so-called First Republic. In 1994, the party's leader, Marco Pannella, allied with Berlusconi, hoping for a 'liberal revolution'. Rapidly disillusioned, Pannella re-established his independence, although a handful of so-called Reformists (Riformatori) remained loyal to Berlusconi. After 2001, Pannella sought alliance on left or right to enable his party to survive. In the June 2005 referendum campaign to abrogate the government's conservative legislation, the SDI and Radicals worked closely together, and in the regional elections of the same year Radicals in the Abruzzo region, Pannella's birthplace, allied with the left's candidate for the regional presidency, Ottaviano Del Turco, a prominent SDI leader. Del Turco won the election and, later that year, after much further prevarication, the Radicals and the SDI formed la Rosa nel Pugno.

Throughout 2005, individual cases of transformism – especially ones involving shifts from the moderate, Catholic right to the moderate, Catholic left, that is, to the UDEUR and the Margherita – were much reported by the press. A particularly significant example of what might be termed molecular transformism, or alliance-switching, is that of Sergio D'Antoni, the secretary general of the Catholic trade union, the CISL, from 1991 to 2000. In 2001, D'Antoni was the principal founder of Democrazia Europea (European Democracy; DE), a substantially Catholic, explicitly centrist, 'third force' which obtained almost 1 million votes (see Table 6.3). In December 2002, DE fused with the UDC. However, in late 2004, D'Antoni switched to the left taking many of his supporters with him, allegedly in response to the Government's 'anti-southern' stance.[6] And, in fact, territory is an aspect of the processes of alliance formation that also deserves attention, although it is not specific to the left. A particularly significant example has its origins, at least, in DE.

A leading ally of D'Antoni's in the DE was his fellow Sicilian, Raffaele Lombardo. When D'Antoni left the UDC in 2004, Lombardo remained, but in early 2005 he too departed, forming the Movement for Autonomy to fight the local and regional elections. The right did badly in these elections, but in Catania Lombardo's lists, which remained as part of the right, gained 20 per cent of the vote, giving a symbolically important victory to Berlusconi. In the run-up to the 2006 election, Lombardo emphasised his movement's centrist identity, seeking alliance with either of the blocs. Massimo D'Alema, the president of the DS, sought to persuade the UDEUR to ally with Lombardo, but in the event Lombardo allied with the League (Figure 6.5). Whilst both parties claimed that the alliance was programmatically based, supporting regional self-assertion in a state undergoing a process of federalisation, most onlookers regarded it as an electoral ploy to overcome the electoral thresholds.[7] In fact, after the election, the alliance fell apart.

Another aspect of alliance-building that included a territorial

Figure 6.5 Northern League – Movement for Autonomy

dimension was the proposal advanced by an array of forces to present civic lists backing Prodi. For many, this was not only a way of mobilising support for Prodi, it was also a way of pressuring party secretaries to act loyally towards Prodi, and to take serious steps towards unification of the left. A number of regional presidents contributed to this initiative, seeking to back Prodi with their own lists. These grassroots initiatives, had they gone ahead, might have tipped the balance in one or more of the regions eventually won by the right (Ricolfi, 2006; Weber, 2006), most notably Friuli-Venezia Giulia, Piedmont and Lazio (see Chapter 10, Table 10.3), but they were blocked by the DS and the Margherita. These two parties' representatives argued that such lists would further fragment the left, compounding its coordination problems and increasing the risk that the smaller parties would fail to reach the 2 per cent threshold.[8]

Attempts to rationalise and integrate the alliance

Whilst further fragmentation via these civic lists did not take place, steps towards unification were slow to make progress. Importantly, three of the four forces that had formed the Margherita electoral alliance in 2001 (Donovan, 2002) did go on to unify, in 2002, as a party of the same name.[9] The UDEUR maintained its independence. Francesco Rutelli, the prime-ministerial candidate in 2001, became the Margherita's leader. Whilst this reduction in fragmentation was welcome, the four-party alliance had only gained 15 per cent of the vote. Moreover, its ambition to grow resulted in a damaging rivalry with the DS, especially as the DS found itself to be the 'sandwich filling', at risk of being squeezed out of existence between this reformist left and the 'left left'. The danger of polarisation within the left, between the moderates and the radicals, was exacerbated by the 'primary' election held to select a prime-ministerial candidate in October 2005. The steps that led to this were tortuous.

The 2001 defeat was followed by a failure of leadership on the left. In July 2003, Prodi, now President of the European Commission, entered this vacuum to urge the left to present a unified list at the 2004 European Parliament election. The proposal generated intense dispute, primarily in terms of whether such a list really could include all the parties of the left, forming a pan-left, or whether just the more centrist parties should unite, forming a reformist core, excluding the 'left left' and perhaps Di Pietro's IdV – on which the SDI insisted. Ironically, then, Prodi's proposal for unification deepened divisions, especially because the proposal to unify just the centrist components encouraged others to promote unification of the left left. However, to many, for

example those on the left of the DS, the prospect of an organisationally divided left was disastrous, playing into Berlusconi's hands by
strengthening his claim that the opposition remained dominated by
communists. In the event, the DS and Margherita, as well as the SDI
and the tiny Movimento Repubblicani Europei (European Republican
Movement; MRE) fought the 2004 European Parliament election
presenting a single electoral list – Uniti nell'Ulivo (literally, 'United in
the Olive Tree'). The result was disappointing, although perhaps not
as bad as initial reactions suggested (Vassallo, 2004).

Despite the setback, the sub-alliance staggered on, becoming the
Olive Tree Federation (known as the 'Fed') in September 2004. Some
form of at least limited organisational integration was supposed to
follow, with supporters of the Fed seeking ultimately to create a
'people's party', that is, a politically moderate and electorally large
force (over 30 per cent) capable of dominating coalition formation
within its half of the political spectrum (Smith, 1990). Advocates of
this strategy believed that creating a centripetally orientated centre of
gravity within the left would enable it to compete in the centre ground
and thus win the forthcoming election. Opponents challenged this,
arguing that it was doubtful that the election could be won in the
centre if, as the consequence of such a strategy, left-wing voters
abstained. Others argued that the implied abandonment of even social
democracy in favour of 'third way' social liberalism would so split the
left that it would be unable to maintain a government even if it won
the election. Consequently, in order to prevent the threatened division,
Prodi and Fausto Bertinotti, the leader of RC, worked on building a
coalition uniting all the left – the Great Democratic Alliance (GAD), as
it became known – which was launched in October 2004. In February
2005, it took the name 'Unione' and comprised nine parties:

- The four of the Fed: DS, Margherita, SDI and MRE
- The UDEUR
- Di Pietro's IdV
- The 'left left': the Greens, the PdCI and RC.

At the end of February 2005, the Fed formally established a supra-
party organisation with Prodi, as president, nominally having power
over such key issues as foreign and European policy, and structural
reform. The presidential executive, however, was dominated by the
party elites, primarily those of the DS and the Margherita. This made
it impossible to reach agreement on the presentation of a common,
Federation, list in all fifteen of the regions where elections took place

in the spring. Thus it was that the Fed presented itself in only nine of the fifteen, mostly in the north. In the south it was argued, particularly by the Margherita, voters were mobilised by individual parties and would be put off by the absence of their party symbols on the ballot slips.

Despite the success of the spring elections, the failure of the Fed to make a decisive breakthrough plus the near disintegration of the government alliance led the highly tentative integration process to come to a halt. Particularly significant was the fact that the government crisis, at the end of April, was forced by the UDC; for this helped to feed speculation that the so-called Catholic parties would seek to recreate a centre pole, given the conflictual heterogeneity of left and right. If this strengthened those forces, within the Margherita, opposed to further development of the Federation project, then they were strengthened still further when, at the end of June, the New Christian Democratic party was launched. Though electorally insignificant, the New DC's legal possession of the original DC party symbol made it a potential focus for aggregation of the UDC, UDEUR and the majority of the Margherita.

Speculation about such an eventuality was matched by suggestions that Prodi and the DS should forge ahead with the minority of the Margherita wanting to develop the Federation project further, and by the SDI's declaration that it would leave such a diminished body to seek unity with the New PSI. Amidst this confusion an opinion poll confirmed that whilst a narrow majority (51 per cent) of the public still favoured bi-polarism, 34 per cent preferred a return to tri-polar politics with a centrist Catholic party (Mannheimer, 2005).

To overcome this turmoil, the parties of the Unione agreed to hold the primary which Prodi had long pushed for – to select who should lead the Unione. This provoked yet further division, not least given the uncertainty surrounding the outcome. It was intended as a plebiscite for Prodi, but in the end seven candidates stood. Crucially, the two main parties, the DS and the Margherita, refrained from competing, so the key question was what proportion of the vote Prodi would get compared to Bertinotti, the radical. In the event, the primary was a stunning success, generating a turnout of 4.3 million, far higher than expected, of which 74.1 per cent backed Prodi, and 14.7 per cent Bertinotti.

As the general election approached, parties and lists had to make final decisions as to whom they would run with. For the left's small parties, the marginally higher Senate threshold (3 instead of 2 per cent) was an issue. The PdCI pushed for an alliance of the left left, but

Bertinotti was resolutely opposed to this, so the Greens and the PdCI (together with a consumers' association) formed a joint list on their own (Figure 6.3). The SDI confirmed its break with the Fed and its alliance, instead, with the Radicals, who were allowed to join the Unione at the last minute. In the Chamber, several of the smaller parties gained representation via the Olive Tree list, mostly on a quota grudgingly conceded to Prodi during extremely hard bargaining by the DS and the Margherita.

The centre right

Although less fragmented than the left, the right too underwent an early process of intra-alliance consolidation when, in December 2002, the CCD and the CDU, together with the newly formed DE, formed the UDC. On this basis, the second Berlusconi government (2001–2005) comprised just four parties: FI, AN, the Northern League and the UDC. The Government also received the external support of the tiny New PSI and even smaller Italian Republican Party, both of which entered the Berlusconi III government in April 2005. The alliance was dominated by Berlusconi, but he was far from unconstrained by his allies. In particular, in privileging the link with Umberto Bossi's League, creating a so-called 'northern axis', he provoked considerable opposition from AN and the UDC (Donovan, 2004, 2005). Their electoral strength lay from Rome southwards, and the most important policies promoted by the Government either damaged, as in the case of the pension reform, or jeopardised, as in the case of constitutional reform, their interests. Given these deep internal conflicts, the issue of integration, or unification, was also an issue on the right.

A further source of tension within the right was Berlusconi himself and particularly preparation for the 'post-Berlusconi' scenario – which through most of 2005 seemed to draw ever closer. This issue fuelled tensions within FI itself, particularly between the Christian democratic and liberal tendencies within the party. These intra-coalition and intra-party tensions peaked during elections: beforehand over candidate selection, and after, in the form of mutual recrimination for the poor results. This was particularly the case from 2004 by when it became clear that the right consistently underperformed in sub-national votes. A key reason for this was electoral demobilisation resulting from the Government's failure to cut taxes. The other reason was that FI, electorally the right's largest party, remained an organisational pygmy. Whilst Berlusconi surmounted these difficulties fairly easily in 2002–03, tensions following the 2004 European elections led to the forced resignation of Giulio Tremonti, the Economics Minister and key link figure between Berlusconi and Bossi. More dramatically, the 2005 regional election debacle led to a formal parliamentary crisis. Reluctantly backed by the AN, the UDC forced Berlusconi's resignation as Prime Minister by threatening to withdraw its ministers. Infuriated by the UDC's assertiveness, Berlusconi relaunched the idea of a single party of the right, this time with some vigour, immediately after winning the parliamentary vote of confidence in his new government. Unification was necessary, he said, to overcome the alliance's self-destructive tendencies, and to respond to the left's continuing drive towards integration. Berlusconi threatened his allies that if they refused his challenge, he would refuse to continue to lead the alliance. In fact, for much of 2005, the UDC sought precisely this, and, despite the unequal size of the protagonists, the battle between Berlusconi and his coalition partner dominated much of the year, fuelling speculation about a return to neo-centrist government.

The most supportive of Berlusconi's allies in the project to build a single party – or federation, the precise nature of the project was an issue itself – was Gianfranco Fini, at least from July 2005. Until then, Fini rejected it, like the other leaders. But Fini never overcame a sense of dependence upon Berlusconi and the possibility of a return to government formation from the centre deepened his determination to maintain the alliance with Berlusconi at all costs – enabling him to overcome the fear of cannibalisation. This fear was strong in the UDC too, and not without good cause. In the immediate aftermath of the regional election disaster, when Berlusconi was fighting off pressure from Fini and UDC leader, Marco Follini, to hold an early parliamentary election, Berlusconi allegedly told Fini (but it applied equally to Follini) that he already controlled half his party (Galluzzo, 2005a).

Berlusconi's desire to dominate his allies was, paradoxically, linked to his drive – launched in view of the regional elections but nevertheless anticipating his strategy for the 2006 election – to enlarge the alliance. Potential allies included the Radicals, the New DC and the far-right parties grouped together in the Alternativa Sociale (Social Alternative) led by Alessandra Mussolini (Figure 6.6).[10] All provoked controversy both for their policy implications (for example the UDC opposed alliance with the Radicals on the same ethical grounds that the Margherita and UDEUR did), and for the way in which Berlusconi sought to use these parties to undermine and discipline his allies. Thus, Fini opposed the inclusion of Mussolini's new allies in the alliance since their neo-fascist identity outflanked his party electorally and challenged his attempt to 'normalise' the right. The alliance went

Figure 6.6 Social Alternative with Alessandra Mussolini

Source: Ministry of the Interior: http://politiche.interno.it/liste2006/simboli.htm

ahead, but the leaders of Mussolini's allied parties did not stand as candidates. Similarly, the New DC, though tiny, was used by Berlusconi in his battle against the UDC.

The issue of the nature of the integration of the right was never resolved. Rocco Buttiglione of the UDC proposed building a party from members of the EPP – that is, excluding the League and the AN – although Fini was known, notwithstanding official denials, to want membership for his party. Buttiglione's proposal also implied the possibility of reuniting with the UDEUR and the Margherita, also members of the EPP. Fini instead proposed a 'Gaullist' alliance of FI, AN and the UDC, plus a looser alliance with the League and other minor parties. Third, there was the 'Republican', in other words 'pan-right', model, named after the US conservative party, including all six of the government parties. At the end of July 2005, three days after the Unione's leaders agreed a 'Manifesto of Values' to which voters in the October primary would sign up, the right held a 'constituent assembly'. The UDC had been won over by the promise of primaries and a return to proportional representation, while the League was willing to consider, at least, the idea of a federation with the other parties, supposedly akin to the German CDU/CSU model.[11] The assembly saw the right split. Berlusconi and Fini agreed to postpone further action until after the election whilst the UDC continued its battle, calling for immediate action and 'discontinuity' – in other words a change of leader, perhaps to the UDC's Pierferdinando Casini. Buttiglione, a leader of the pro-Berlusconi tendency in the UDC, instead came out in support of Roberto Formigoni, the FI (but ex-DC) president of Lombardy. Formigoni was not only one of just two successful right-wing candidates in the 2005 regional elections, he also presided over Italy's richest and most populous region and made the most of his support from the world of Catholic associationism. In his youth, Formigoni had been a leading figure in Communion and Liberation, founding, in 1976, an explicitly political movement to flank it – the Popular Movement. Moreover, sharing the UDC's dislike for Bossi's Northern League, Formigoni had fought a long war of attrition against the League in Lombardy. And Casini now backed Fini's model, but still in terms of EPP membership, implicitly supporting a future application for membership from the AN. As the leader of the New DC colourfully put it, the tiny UDC, acting like a small, but aggressive business firm, was bidding to take over a larger, but presumed ailing rival – FI (Rotondi, 2005).

The conflict between FI and the UDC came to a head in the autumn on the back of calls from the business world, including the international community, for a return to technocratic and or centrist government in Italy (Radice, 2005; Scalfari, 2005). In September, the UDC threatened to withdraw from the alliance unless an alternative to Berlusconi was found to lead it into the next election. Berlusconi conceded the idea of holding primaries, as on the left, but then used the electoral reform, launched the same month, to argue that the elections themselves would constitute a form of primary, given the return of the proportional principle, with the three main leaders – Berlusconi, Fini and Casini – competing for precedence. At the end of October, the UDC admitted defeat, electing a new party secretary, Lorenzo Cesa, having allegedly been threatened with electoral annihilation by Berlusconi's media if it stood independently (Galluzzo, 2005b). Tentative offers by the left to stand down in some constituencies in favour of the UDC were no counter to this. Berlusconi was back in the saddle, and went on to campaign mightily for re-election – only narrowly failing, perhaps because of the left's greater success at alliance-building.

The right lost the election, and the significance for the Chamber vote of the left's winning over of Craxi's Socialists, the Pensioners and the Consumers has already been discussed. Also significant, arguably, was the right's failure to embrace Project Northeast, given its 92,000 votes. Another personal party, created in June 2004 when the wealthy industrialist Giorgio Panton split from the League in protest at the moderation of the government's constitutional reform project, the left could not ally with it, but Berlusconi sought to. Given the acrimonious relations between Panton and the League, however, this proved impossible. Panton's party, accounting for about a half of the total of 'third force' votes, was the only movement of any size not to be included in one or other of the alliances.

Conclusions

Did the greater success of the left in alliance-building win it the election? Many believe so (chapter 10; Feltrin and Fabrizio, 2006). There has been a strong tendency in analyses of Italian electoral politics in the last decade to emphasise the 'supply side' of the electoral equation – that is, what the political elites offer to voters – rather than the demand side, the stability of which is emphasised. But the approach is hotly contested (Pappalardo, 2006). Let us consider the case, for the Chamber, of the Socialists (115,066 votes), the Pensioners (one-third of a million votes) and the Radicals (perhaps half a million votes).

Even those who argue for the stability of electoral behaviour concede that some 5 per cent of voters typically switch between the two main coalitions at elections (Natale, 2006). Craxi's Socialists may have had a role to play in this in 2006 – perhaps winning the election for Prodi. Certainly, it is simplistic to assume that the shift of parties or lists from right to left will mean that past voters for those lists will remain loyal, thus transferring their votes to the left, but in this case the hypothesis is not difficult to believe. What of the Pensioners' list? The greatest area of uncertainty regarding electoral behaviour concerns so-called 'third Italy' voters: that is, those who do not identify with either of the blocs, and who tend to be uninterested in politics, even hostile to it, drifting in and out of abstention. It is these, some argue, who have determined election outcomes since 1994 (Mannheimer, 2006). Perhaps these apolitical voters are precisely the ones likely to be mobilised by interest-group lists, such as the pensioners'. Moreover, if the left was as weak among older voters as appears to be the case (Orbach 2006), the pensioners' list may have 'plugged' an electoral weak spot for the left. So, again, it is not implausible that the left benefited from this particularist mobilisation of support on its behalf.

The case for the Radicals is less clear. A poll carried out by the party in February 2005 (Roncone, 2005) suggested that two-thirds of their supporters preferred an alliance with the left, and many of its voters may have voted left in 2001 anyway. Furthermore, there is evidence that the preference of regular practising Catholics for the centre right over the centre left increased slightly in 2006 (Segatti, 2006), perhaps partly as a reaction to the intense polemics over a series of 'lifestyle' or ethical issues which were highlighted by the 2005 referendums. The Church not only took a forceful position in this debate, but equally strongly opposed the Radicals joining either electoral alliance. So inclusion of the Radicals might have cost the left many votes. In sum, then, the overall balance of gains and losses from the additional lists supporting the left may be less clear than is often argued by those emphasising the importance of party 'supply' over electoral 'demand'.

What this chapter shows more clearly is that at the elite level, at least, the idea of the creation of a centre alliance, a third pole, still motivates key actors. Their efforts may prove wasted if it is true that in practice no centre pole can be recreated in a democracy no longer threatened by anti-democratic movements (Sartori, 2005). But it remains true, first, that Fini took the threat seriously enough in the summer of 2005 to break the informal alliance with the UDC against the 'northern axis', throwing in his lot more clearly with Berlusconi. Second, the party created by Prodi in 1998–99 precisely to combat the neo-centrist threat (which he clearly took seriously), and which is now a component of the Margherita, continued to be a significant actor in 2005 in the shape of those who rebelled against the Margherita's abandonment of the project to build the Fed. Third, Formigoni, the powerful centre-right President of Lombardy, backed also by a number of former left-wing politicians, seems to have generated, and perhaps himself is interested in, the possibility of creating a centrist pole that would build a new *conventio ad excludendum*, this time against the League on the one hand and and RC on the other (Meli, 2005).

Finally, there can be little doubt that the creation of a pan-left in 2005–06 is a tremendous achievement. Whilst not guaranteed to survive, its creation was a necessary, if not sufficient, condition for the left's victory. The two crucial figures in that process were Prodi and Bertinotti. In June 2004, Sartori concluded one of his regular *Corriere della Sera* editorials by writing that 'The idea of a serious left saved by Bertinotti is truly frivolous' (Sartori, 2004). Perhaps it is not so frivolous: if in the coming months and years the left demonstrates not only that it can win elections but also govern successfully, then the achievement of Prodi and Bertinotti will show itself to have been the most significant act of alliance-building in the last five years – at least.

Notes

1 The left's advantage of two seats was augmented by the overseas candidate who supported the majority as he had said he would before the election – whoever formed it. The seven life senators also backed the majority, at least in making the key initial appointments, partly to promote governability.

2 Composite lists: 1) la Rosa nel Pugno, comprising the SDI and Radicals; 2) the Consumers – DC; 3) Lega Lombarda – Pensioners; 3) 'Together with the Unione', comprising the Greens, the PdCI and another consumers'

movement; 4) the Olive Tree comprising, in the Chamber, the DS, and the Margherita and MRE. See also Figures 6.1–6.4.

3 Rifonazione Comunista was not part of the government between 1996 and 1998 but until October of the latter year its external support provided the minority government with a parliamentary majority.

4 'Transformism' is a controversial term, often used polemically, that has many nuances of meaning. Broadly speaking, it refers to opposition politicians switching allegiances (being transformed) to become supporters of the Government. The switch may actually precede an expected government alternation, such that Government supporters join the current opposition, as part of a 'band-wagonning' process.

5 Fuda's election resulted, in fact, from the backing given to the list in Calabria by that region's President, Agazio Loiero, who split from his party, the Margherita, following a dispute over candidate selection in the 2005 regional election. Subsequently, this dispute had major repercussions when one of the candidates elected in 2005 was accused of association with organised crime and, indeed, linked to the murder of a party rival. This led one Margherita politician to distinguish between acceptable and unacceptable forms of transformism.

6 In 2006, D'Antoni was elected to Parliament and became a deputy minister.

7 Individual lists forming part of an alliance – such as the League – required 3 per cent to achieve representation in the Senate. Lists not part of an alliance – such as the Movement for Autonomy up to that point – required 8 per cent. In the Chamber, they required 2 and 4 per cent respectively.

8 Four parties on the left got between 2 and 3 per cent of the vote in the Chamber. They were: la Rosa nel Pugno (2.59), the PdCI (2.31), IdV (2.29) and the Greens (2.05). In addition, the UDEUR obtained 1.40 per cent of the votes and was included in the distribution of seats as the first list below the threshold.

9 The PPI, the formal heir of the Christian Democratic Party that dominated Italian government from 1947 to 1993; the Democrats, founded by Prodi in 1999 to defend the DS–left Catholic alliance, and hence bi-polarism; and Italian Renewal, a personal party created by Lamberto Dini, Prime Minister during the transition year of 1995–1996.

10 The dictator's granddaughter split from AN in November 2003 when its leader declared, during a visit to Israel, that Fascism had been 'absolutely evil'. Her new allies included: the Movimento Sociale – Fiamma Tricolore (Social Movement – Tricoloured Flame; MS–FT – formed in 1995 to maintain the identity of the Movimento Sociale Italiano [Italian Social Movement] against the revisionism of Fini's AN), the National Social Front, which split from the latter in 1997 to pursue a more hard-line position, and Forza Nuova, a neo-fascist party.

11 In that model, the CSU organises the right in Bavaria, the CDU in the rest of the country. However, the League does not monopolise the right in any of Italy's regions.

References

Caciagli, M. and Corbetta, P. (eds) (2002), *Le ragioni dell'elettore*, Bologna, Il Mulino.

D'Alimonte, R. and Bartolini, S. (eds) (2002), *Maggioritario finalmente? La transizione elettorale 1994–2001*, Bologna, Il Mulino.

Donovan, M. (2002), 'The processes of alliance formation', in J. L. Newell (ed.), *The Italian General Election of 2001: Berlusconi's Victory*, Manchester and New York, Manchester University Press.

Donovan, M. (2004), 'The governance of the center-right coalition', in S. Fabbrini and V. Della Sala (eds), *Italy Between Europeanisation and Domestic Politics*, Oxford, Berghahn.

Donovan, M. (2005), 'Intra- and inter-alliance relations after the 2004 European and provincial elections', in C. Guarnieri and J. L. Newell (eds), *Italian Politics: Quo Vadis?*, Oxford, Berghahn.

Feltrin, P. and Fabrizio, D. (2006), 'Politiche 2006: risultati e principali tendenze', in R. Mannheimer and P. Natale (eds), *L'Italia a metà*, Milan, Cairo editore.

Galluzzo, M. (2005a), 'Il Cavaliere litiga con i due vicepremier', *Corriere della Sera*, 8 April.

Galluzzo, M. (2005b), 'E il premier avvertì Casini: Marco ti sta portando alla rovina', *Corriere della Sera*, 3 October.

Mannheimer, R. (2005), 'Elettori attratti dal terzo polo moderato, lo vuole il 34%', *Corriere della Sera*, 21 June.

Mannheimer, R. (2006), 'La mobilitazione della "terza Italia" politica', in R. Mannheimer and P. Natale (eds), *L'Italia a metà*, Milan, Cairo editore.

Meli, M. T. (2005), '"Addio Ulivo": i riformisti e il fascino dei governatori', *Corriere della Sera*, 16 January.

Natale, P. (2006), 'Un milione e mezzo dalla Cdl all'Unione', *Polena*, www.polena.net/it/index.htm (accessed on 10 September 2007).

Orbach, Massimo (2006), 'Il voto degli over 64', http://brunik.altervista.org /20060604183704.html (accessed on 6 June 2006).

Pappalardo, A. (2006), 'Il bipolarismo italiano e le elezioni del 2006. Capolinea o fermata intermedia?', paper presented to the workshop 'Il voto del 9 e 10 aprile 2006: Analisi dei risultati e delle loro conseguenze sistemiche', University of Pisa, 15–16 June.

Pasquino, G. (ed.) (2002), *Dall'Ulivo al governo Berlusconi*, Bologna, Il Mulino.

Radice, G. (2005), 'Un analisi condividibile. L'Unione ispira poca fiducia', *Corriere della Sera*, 10 August.

Ricolfi, L. (2006), 'Così la dea bendata ha fermato la grande rimonta', *La Stampa*, 12 April.

Roncone, F. (2005), 'Polo o Gad, per scegliere i radicali si affidano ai sondaggi', *Corriere della Sera*, 5 February.

Rotondi, G. (2005), 'Rotondi: l'UDC ha lanciato un'Opa sugli azzurri', *Corriere della Sera*, 18 August.

Sartori, G. (2004), 'La sinistra frammentata', *Corriere della Sera*, 23 June.

Sartori, G. (2005), 'Il polverone del centro. Il bipolarismo resterà (ma va fatto funzionare)', *Corriere della Sera*, 26 August.

Scalfari, E. (2005), 'Quel circo equestro chiamato centro', *La Repubblica*, 21 August.

Segatti, P. (2006), 'Cattolici e voto', in R. Mannheimer and P. Natale (eds), *L'Italia a metà*, Milan, Cairo editore.

Smith, G. (1990), 'Core persistence: system change and the "Peoples' Party"', in P. Mair and G. Smith (eds), *Understanding Party System Change in Western Europe*, London, Frank Cass.

Vassallo, S. (2004), 'Analisi dell'istituto cattaneo sui risultati delle elezioni amministrative ed europee', www.cattaneo.org/pubblicazioni/analisi/pdf/AnalisiCattaneo17–06–04.pdf (accessed on 28 September 2007).

Weber, R. (2006), 'L'Italia uscita dalle urne: un paese a fluidità variabile', http://brunik.altervista.org/20060525221730.html (accessed 25 May 2006).

III

The campaign

7

Campaign issues and themes

Donatella Campus

Introduction

Each of the general elections held since the end of the First Republic in the early 1990s has differed from each of the others in terms of its characteristic style of competition. The 1994 election, the first to be held on the basis of the plurality electoral law introduced in 1993,[1] was exceptional owing to the sudden appearance of Forza Italia and the formation of a centre-right coalition just a few weeks before election day.[2] The 1996 election seemed to represent a step toward a 'normalisation' insofar as it was marked by the clash of two coalitions that were internally divided (Campus, 2001), but at least able to compete quite fairly on the basis of substantive themes and issues (Sani and Segatti, 1997). The 2001 campaign was marked by a greater degree of cohesion of the two coalitions, and more solid programmatic alliances – but the election was not contested on traditional policy issues (Campus, 2002). Rather, the election turned out to be a referendum on Berlusconi's fitness to lead the country and it was characterised by a high degree of partisanship (Roncarolo, 2002).

The 2006 election was also quite distinct as compared to earlier contests. Two new elements exerted a notable impact on the style of competition: the introduction of a new proportional electoral law, and the appeal to electors to cast their votes on the basis of retrospective assessments of the performance of the incumbent government. In this chapter, I will analyse the most distinctive features of the electoral competition. First, I will try to highlight the differences between the two main coalitions in terms of their internal dynamics: their degree of cohesion, the strength of their leaderships, the characteristics of the platform-writing process. Second, I will examine the campaign strategies that each coalition employed to try to defeat its opponent and the issues that dominated the campaign. Finally, I will try to make sense of why some themes, in particular ethical issues, had a much lower profile, although they may reveal themselves to be the issues that dominate political debate in the coming months, now that the election has taken place.

Two coalitions, two different approaches

As stressed elsewhere in this volume, the 2006 election began with an early favourite, the centre-left coalition, which in opinion polls consistently led by several percentage points. The centre left's main advantage was that, for the first time, all the parties of the wide constellation of the Italian left, from the Catholic and centrist Margherita ('Daisy') to the party furthest to the left, Rifondazione Comunista (Communist Refoundation), managed to agree on the creation of a common electoral cartel, the Unione. Moreover, the return of Romano Prodi to the leadership of the centre left was a clear asset. Prodi was an experienced candidate, who had already led his coalition to victory in 1996 and had served as Prime Minister between 1996 and 1998. Above all, Prodi had been selected through primary elections from which he had emerged as the overwhelming choice of centre-left voters.

The primaries had been the culmination of a long and complex process of negotiation among the several parties of the centre left. As Pasquino (in this volume) has explained, Prodi insisted on the elections in order to gain recognition as the exclusive leader of the entire centre-left coalition. His run-away victory on 16 October 2005 had the clear effect of strengthening his leadership. As a consequence, the mechanisms he had put in place to develop the election programme by creating the Fabbrica del programma ('Factory for development of the programme')[3] also obtained a sort of legitimation. If Prodi was the undisputable leader of the coalition, then the elaboration and the writing of the centre left's election platform had to take place under his direction. The Fabbrica del programma, based in Bologna, Prodi's home city, became a sort of advanced laboratory where the professor's collaborators and volunteers organised regular seminars and hearings (some of which saw the participation of Prodi in person). Their purpose was to consider evidence and information concerning the priorities of the centre left's electorate and to gather suggestions from civil-society representatives and ordinary people through a process of platform-development that worked from the bottom up. From the point of view of communication, such an initiative was a success in building a positive image of Prodi as a leader who was willing to listen to the variety of voices of the left but, at the same time, also capable of developing a synthesis of different viewpoints.

The process of drafting and reaching agreement on the final version of the centre left's manifesto was, however, a less-than-tranquil process. According to press leaks, several of the meetings of the coalition's leaders that were devoted to discussions of the programme were the scenes of sharp controversy and bitter argument. In particular, issues like Pacs (Patti civili di solidarietà or 'Civil solidarity agreements', which sought to extend to gay and unmarried heterosexual couples some of the rights currently enjoyed by people who are married) and the curtailing of public funding for private and Catholic schools divided the Catholic parties from la Rosa nel Pugno (literally, 'the Rose in the Fist'), composed of former Radicals and Italian Socialists. Eventually, a common agreement was reached on a very detailed text, 281 pages long, entitled, *Per il bene dell'Italia* ('For the Good of Italy'). Its conspicuous length may be viewed either as an attempt to give space to as wide a range of issues and viewpoints as possible, or as a way of reconciling the differences between the allies. The manifesto was presented to a huge convention, held in Rome, on 11 February 2006.[4] With the single exception of the leaders of la Rosa nel Pugno, who did not participate, the leaders of the centre left's constituent parties publicly reaffirmed their commitment to the Unione in an atmosphere of apparent harmony and confidence in the likelihood of victory. If the heterogeneity of the Unione was a matter of fact that nobody could hide, everybody could at least see that the centre left had made a serious effort not only to create an electoral cartel, but, more importantly, also to build a political coalition able to form a solid and stable government.

If, at the beginning of the election campaign, the centre left thus emerged from the process of mediation and integration of its several components in a state of heightened strength, then the centre right found itself in the opposite situation. The coalition which had triumphantly won the 2001 election was clearly worn out and weakened after five years of uninterrupted but turbulent government. The first evident breakdown had occurred at the 2004 European election from which the Cdl and, in particular, Forza Italia had emerged clearly dented.[5] As a consequence of the decline of the largest party and its leader, the other centre-right parties, which had been willing to take a back seat in exchange for a satisfactory distribution of the rich spoils of the 2001 victory, started to make new claims and to challenge Berlusconi's leadership. In the summer of 2004, the AN and the UDC forced the Prime Minister to replace one of his closest and most trusted collaborators, Minister for the Economy and Finance, Giulio Tremonti. Following a further heavy defeat in the 2005 administrative elections, the level of conflict between Berlusconi and his allies, and in particular the UDC, reached such a height that, in order to secure the Government's survival, it was necessary for Berlusconi to resign and to form a new government. This was, in terms of composition, almost a carbon copy of the previous one, but it was based on a fresh programmatic agreement. In staying in office from 11 June 2001 to 23 April 2005, Berlusconi's government had, as Pasquino notes in chapter 1, lasted long enough to break the record for the longest surviving cabinet in republican Italy, but such troubles tarnished irremediably the reputation of the Prime Minister, whose leadership emerged from the trauma much weakened.

While the centre left went through a process of growing integration that saw all of its components making serious efforts to smooth out their differences and to project a convincing image of cohesion, Berlusconi's allies tried deliberately to differentiate themselves from each other and, especially, to distance themselves from Berlusconi, who was left to account for the performance of the centre-right government on his own. By taking advantage of the new electoral law, both Gianfranco Fini and Pierferdinando Casini, respectively leaders of the AN and of the UDC, declared that they were running for the post of Prime Minister and that, in the event that the coalition was victorious, the identity of the future head of government would depend on the electoral performance of his party (though it was never made clear whether this referred to the distribution of votes, or to the *change* in the distribution of the votes, between the parties). They called it a *gioco a tre punte* (roughly, a 'three-pronged attack') drawing a clear soccer analogy in order to emphasise that such a strategy would maximise the electoral prospects of the coalition as a whole. However, the common feeling was that they were trying to challenge Berlusconi's leadership with a view to getting rid of him once the election had taken place.

On these premises, it was unlikely that the members of the centre right would engage in the kind of elaborate process of platform-writing that the centre left had undertaken. In 2001, the Cdl had presented, first, a sort of preliminary pact, subscribed to by all four of its components and outlining the general themes that were later developed in a proper and more detailed manifesto, the *Plan for Government*. Both documents could be regarded as expressions of the viewpoints of all of the coalition's partners (Campus, 2002: 193). Also, the much emphasised 'Contract with the Italian People', which

Berlusconi signed on TV, promised to achieve policy goals consistent with the common manifesto and shared by the whole of the centre-right coalition. In 2006, by contrast, the Cdl apparently had greater difficulty in formulating an agreed programme. Having rejected Berlusconi's proposal of a new contract with the Italian people, the other parties of the coalition agreed only to subscribe to a brief text, one that in the end turned out to be very concise, at 22 pages. In a campaign that was highly theatrical and that featured a thick schedule of media events, the occasion of the programme's official public presentation – a press conference given by Silvio Berlusconi – was unusual for its low profile. The absence of the other leaders marked a significant contrast with the centre left's convention.[6] Throughout the campaign, leaders of the centre-right parties made few references to the common election platform. For instance, while all of the parties included the text of the manifesto among the material they made available via their websites, they were clearly trying to draw the attention of Internet users to aspects and materials more closely related to themselves, such as the performances and achievements of their own leaders and ministers. More generally, the lack of emphasis on the common programme can be regarded as an interesting indicator of the centre right's degree of disharmony. If they did not go as far as to present and distribute their own alternative manifestos, then it nevertheless appeared clear that the centre-right parties no longer considered the Cdl to be a political project, but merely an electoral cartel necessary to obtain the majority premium assigned by the new electoral law to the coalition that won the most votes.

In the light of all this, one may argue that in the 2006 campaign the contrasting features of the electoral programmes were paradigmatic of the nature and orientations of the two coalitions, and that they pointed in opposite directions. On the one hand, the centre left followed a bi-polar logic and, notwithstanding its heterogeneity, used the process of platform-writing as a useful opportunity to bring together and to reconcile different opinions. From the point of view of political communication, the launch of the common manifesto was a symbolic means of emphasising unity and agreement. On the other hand, the lack of commitment of the centre-right parties to the task of producing a common manifesto, and the consequent lack of emphasis on it, can be viewed as the effect of the adoption of a proportional style of competition. Parties like AN and the UDC made it clear that they were running for themselves. Although more loyal to the leadership of Berlusconi, the Lega Nord (Northern League; LN) could not refrain from marking its profound differences with all of the other parties. As for Berlusconi, his highly personalised conception of politics suggested to him how to deal with the challenge posed by Fini and Casini. No longer obliged to mediate between his allies and to accept compromises, as he had been forced to do as head of government, Berlusconi felt completely free to conduct his own campaign. This led, as I will show later, to almost total monopolisation of the campaign by Berlusconi himself, with very little space being left to the other centre-right parties.

The strategy of the centre left: transforming personalisation into accountability

In countries where alternation in government is a regular feature of politics, voters, it is assumed, engage in a retrospective reasoning (Key, 1966; Fiorina, 1981): rewarding the government if the economy is in good shape and punishing it for bad times. For this reason, evaluations of economic performance are regarded as powerful predictors of voting choice. For a long time, retrospective voting has been quite unfamiliar to the average Italian voter. The political system of the First Republic prevented alternation, thus depriving of significance voting based on punishments and rewards. According to Parisi and Pasquino's (1977) well-known typology of the vote of belonging, of opinion and of exchange, in Italy the two prevailing models of voting – the first and the third – were grounded on solid relationships between voters and parties and on the search for individual advantage rather than on the evaluation of past performances.

The 2006 election, however, posed a challenge to the well-established habits of Italian voters. This occurred for at least two fundamental reasons. First, the bi-polar competition that had emerged in the early 1990s had reframed the political context. In 1996, the centre left took over from a government of 'technocrats', and, in marking a return to full party government, brought to office parties that had spent the previous fifty years in opposition. In 2001, the victory of Berlusconi and the Cdl, and the defeat of the incumbent centre left, marked the first true alternation in government. In short, both alternation and retrospective voting had become possible and available options. Second, the 2001 campaign established an apparently irreversible trend by attributing responsibility for coalitions' electoral programmes to prime-ministerial candidates (Campus, 2002: 193). Berlusconi made the point very clearly when signing the 'Contract with the Italian People': he personally was in charge of implementation of the electoral platform of the Cdl. 'The most striking feature of recent campaign strategies', according to Calise

(2005: 101), 'has been the personalization of issues and platforms' with the most prominent issues being linked to the leader himself. In other words, leadership-centred electoral contests have become a precondition for the application of a mechanism of accountability. A leader who claims a personal mandate encourages voters to develop high expectations about his/her capacities to solve the country's problems. If the performance turns out to be disappointing, citizens tend to hold the leader accountable and to punish him/her accordingly. Evidence of this phenomenon can be found in the 2004 European election, when the decline of Berlusconi's popularity damaged his own party, FI, more than the other parties of the centre-right coalition (Campus and Pasquino, 2006: 34).

If in 2001 the centre left forfeited the advantages of incumbency and did not claim credit for what it had done in government (Pasquino, 2002), then in 2006 the Unione did not make the same mistake and, standing on the opposite side, was quick to take advantage of the critical condition of the economy. During Berlusconi's tenure, Italy had suffered from the unfavourable international economic conjuncture more than any other European country and had ended up with a declining growth rate and a rising level of public debt. As most polls confirmed, pessimism was widespread. The poll shown in Table 7.1, carried out some weeks before the elections, is an instance of the state of public opinion concerning the main problems facing Italy. One may observe that economic issues rank highest in the list of priorities, surpassing even crime, which had been regarded as the key problem in 2001 (Campus, 2002: 190).

Table 7.1 The importance of various issues in voting choices, 2006 (% of respondents)

How important to you is the following issue when it comes to deciding how to vote?	*Very important*	*Quite important*	*Not very important*	*Not at all important*	*Don't Know*
Unemployment	84	8	4	3	1
Social services (education / health / welfare)	81	11	5	2	1
Economic development	78	13	5	3	1
Inflation / price control	77	12	4	5	2
Crime	77	15	5	2	1
Immigration	66	18	9	5	2
Foreign policy and Italy's international role	53	26	11	6	4

Source: ISPOS Public Affairs, telephone interviews, 23 February 2006, available at www.sondaggipoliticoelettorali.it

On these premises, the most elementary rule of electoral positioning – that is, that it should be based on a careful assessment of one's own and one's opponent's strengths and weaknesses (Newman, 1999: 45) – suggested to the centre left that it should focus its campaign on Berlusconi's poor performance. According to the most detailed assessments (Ricolfi, 2005; Ricolfi, 2006), the 'Contract with the Italian People' had been only partly fulfilled: this provided the centre left with a wide array of powerful arguments. Further support came from the fact that, alarmed by the economic crisis, big business interests represented by Confindustria had made several declarations criticising the way the Government had handled the economy.

The strategy of transforming Berlusconi's personalisation of politics into accountability with the aim of eliciting a vote based on retrospective judgments was extremely well suited to the characteristics and the peculiarities of the Unione. First, Prodi had the right credentials for dealing with economic problems. He is Professor of Economics; as a prime minister, he had led Italy into the single currency; he had been president of the European Commission. He could successfully position himself as the leader who would fix the problems created by the centre-right government. Second, by making Berlusconi's economic record the main issue of the campaign, the Unione aimed at focusing voters' attention on what was supposed to be safe ground. If the campaign had concerned ideas about how to change the country and had focused on the details of the centre left's programme, then it would have risked revealing several areas of potential disagreement among the centre-left parties. Ethical and social issues – such as stem-cell research, gay marriages and private education funding – seemed to be particularly controversial. By contrast, the economic problems facing the country and the level of collective anxiety on this matter suggested that appeals focused on the economy would offer a message capable of meeting the hopes of a wide range of constituencies.

In principle, the strategy of the centre left was the one most appropriate to the goal of setting the campaign agenda in the most advantageous way. However, Berlusconi too had agenda-setting plans and he was not keen to be cornered. As a result of this struggle, economic policies became the main battleground – but not in the way the centre left had anticipated and desired.

The centre right: transforming taxes into an emotional matter

While the centre left decided to make the Berlusconi government's performance the main campaign issue, on the other side, Berlusconi's coalition partners gave every indication that they were determined to leave the Prime Minister on his own to account for the performance of his government. It is hard to say whether Berlusconi was actually damaged by his allies' withdrawal. However this may be, he tried to transform his political isolation into an asset: as a matter of fact, he conducted a campaign that was entirely focused on his leadership and orchestrated to fit the man. Once more, he thrust himself into the centre of the electoral stage, hoping to win by the force of his personality and by relying on his consummate communicative skills.

In a first phase of the campaign, Berlusconi seemed determined to play the role of the incumbent. In other words, he spent the first weeks of the campaign promoting the achievements of his government and defending it from the attacks of the centre left.[7] However, as election day drew closer, he realised that such a strategy was not as effective as he had previously believed. The gap in the polls had been reduced, but the centre right was still trailing. Voters continued to be sceptical about the performance of the government.[8] Berlusconi became aware of what political marketing experts know too well: 'if the economy is not strong and people are hurting financially, then the incumbent is seen in a much more negative light than the challenger' (Newman, 1999: 73). Not even his almost daily appearances on the most popular television and radio talk-shows had the power to reverse the situation.

It was clear that Berlusconi needed to reposition himself. His goal thus became one of shifting from the image of a lame duck incumbent to that of the political outsider who fights on behalf of ordinary people and opposes the return to power of the ruling élite. As is well known, the language of anti-political sentiments has always been one of the most powerful weapons in Berlusconi's armoury. In some ways, it may be argued that anti-political sentiments are the essence of Berlusconi's leadership (Campus, 2006b). In 1994, he took to the political field as an outsider who claimed to be able to bring about political renewal and to return government to the people (Taguieff, 2003; Tarchi, 2003). Later on, he used anti-political rhetoric whenever it seemed it might be useful, being versatile enough to adapt it to a wide variety of different circumstances (Surel, 2003; Tarchi, 2003). Towards the end of the 2006 campaign, Berlusconi understood that he had to revert to his old style of campaigning, one much closer to that of a challenger than to that of an incumbent prime minister.

In order to do so, a winning theme had to be found to shake up the final weeks of the campaign. For some time, Berlusconi tried to play his favourite card of the communist threat, but it was clearly too old and too artificial an argument. Remarkable help came from his adversaries. At a certain point in the campaign, leaders of the Unione made controversial declarations about the centre left's fiscal plans. In particular, Fausto Bertinotti, leader of Rifondazione Comunista, drew attention to the centre left's intention to reintroduce the inheritance tax that had been abolished by Berlusconi in 2001. The tax had had quite a low exemption ceiling, and reintroduction on the same basis would affect a large part of the electorate, including most middle-class families, most of which own their own homes.[9] For this reason, Bertinotti's statement created a lively controversy – to which the Unione did not immediately react with the necessary clarity and decisiveness. Only at the end of the campaign, with the centre right refusing to let go of the matter, did Prodi make clear the terms on which the tax would be reintroduced, insisting that it would be relevant only for estates valued at several million euro.[10] The formal commitment of the coalition leader on this policy certainly reassured middle-class voters, but the general feeling was that the centre left was not as united as it wanted people to believe. There was speculation that the most leftist members of the coalition, namely Rifondazione Comunista and the Comunisti Italiani, might be more influential than had been assumed in the drafting of economic and fiscal policies. This was clearly disturbing for those centrist voters to whom the Unione had tried to present a moderate message and who were inclined to vote for the centre left. The inheritance tax issue had created a hole in the solid alliance of the Unione.

The centre right had finally discovered a weak point in the defences of their adversaries and was determined to transform it into a weakness that was decisive. Due to the centre left's strategy of focusing on the serious economic problems facing the country, pocketbook issues had become the principal yardstick by which voters were assessing candidates and their proposals. The issues were unlikely to have an impact on voters with strong party and ideological affiliations, but they were likely to be relevant in the case of swing or uncertain voters. As the incumbent prime minister, Berlusconi was damaged by public dissatisfaction with the economy; however, if he could convince voters that the centre left would hurt the middle class financially with an avalanche of new taxes, then he might have a chance of refocusing voters' fears on his adversaries.

In this sense, Berlusconi's speech at the convention of Confindustria (the association representing Italian entrepreneurs), held in Vicenza on 17 and 18 March, marked the turning point of the campaign. Instead of playing the role of the incumbent and defending his government's performance from the criticisms of Confindustria's ruling circles – in particular those of its president, Luca Cordero di Montezemolo – Berlusconi offered a typically populist appeal. He launched a coarse attack on the leadership of Confindustria, accusing it of representing only the interests of big business and declaring that his message was directed at the medium- and small-sized firms representing the true body of Italian entrepreneurship. As a matter of fact, his intention was to reach an audience much larger than Confindustria. The Vicenza speech was carefully planned as a 'media event':[11] Berlusconi appeared unexpectedly after it had been announced that he was ill and could not participate; there was a conspicuous and vocal group of his supporters in the audience; his talk was straight and aggressive. As a consequence, Berlusconi obtained an extraordinary amount of coverage, which lasted for several days. While the press debated whether it was all the result of improvisation by a desperate man, or a calculated risk by an overconfident leader, Berlusconi succeeded in achieving his objective, namely, sounding the alarm for the middle class – especially the part consisting of small entrepreneurs, tradespeople and shopkeepers – concerning the risks to their businesses and savings that were posed by the prospects of a centre-left victory.

In the meantime, Giulio Tremonti, the FI champion of tax cuts and restrictive fiscal policies, helped to frighten the centrist electorate by insinuating that, in order to sustain its economic programme the Unione would be obliged to raise social security contributions. Prodi was quick to reject the charge and accused Tremonti of *delinquenza politica* (literally, 'political delinquency'). However, the bitter tone of Prodi's rebuttal betrayed a growing uneasiness in the centre-left camp. This suggested that taxes might really be an issue capable of putting in jeopardy the almost certain victory of the Unione. Berlusconi decided to take full advantage of it. In the final days of campaign, he stressed the point on every possible occasion, using the most colourful expressions. These included the famous sentence uttered before the assembly of Confcommercio, the association for salespersons and shopkeepers, when he said that he was confident of winning the election because he could not believe that Italian voters were such *coglioni* (dickheads) as to vote against their interests. Of course, such a declaration had devastating effects on the general tone of an already bitter and aggressive campaign. Berlusconi was heavily criticised for having insulted centre-left supporters and was accused of political cynicism for having invited the electorate to vote according to self-interest without considering collective values or the wellbeing of the community.[12]

If the first criticism is undisputable – clearly Berlusconi had pushed his predisposition for political entertainment and showbiz too far – the second deserves a closer look. As a matter of fact, Berlusconi has never considered taxes to be simply a matter of individual economic interest. From the perspective of free-market liberalism, tax cuts represent a sort of symbolic policy, a means to free citizens from State control and to encourage free enterprise.

Berlusconi's real attitude towards the tax issue emerged clearly in the appeal he made at the end of his second debate with Romano Prodi. In the dying seconds, when Prodi had no further right of reply, Berlusconi played his best card: the promise to abolish ICI, a measure not in the centre right's manifesto and one that had never been mentioned before. Beyond this, the whole of his final appeal was centred on the theme of taxes as a necessary evil, and on the need to limit the extent of state intrusion into the lives (and businesses) of ordinary citizens. As Pierluigi Battista, deputy editor of the important daily newspaper, *Corriere della Sera*, pointed out, Berlusconi 'introduced the emotional aspect of taxes into Italian politics'.[13] There is a golden rule that politicians know quite well: 'emotion is what sells products and politicians' (Newman, 1999: 89). In talking about taxes, Berlusconi was able to appeal not only to voters' pocketbooks, but also to the ideals and values of a large part of the electorate.

Forthcoming electoral analysis will no doubt show whether the tax issue had a significant impact on voters' choices. Until the relevant survey data becomes available, a plausible indicator is offered by the evidence suggesting a last-minute recovery by Berlusconi, who seems to have closed the gap in the polls in the last two weeks of the campaign.[14] In any case, what is clear is that Berlusconi marked the substantial difference between two opposing visions of life and politics: on the one hand, a leader who would work hard to prevent new taxes; on the other hand, a coalition with totally different economic priorities and for which some kinds of taxes, such as the inheritance tax or the tax on public bonds, should be regarded as fair measures to obtain a certain degree of redistributive justice. If Berlusconi's strategy was insufficient to win him re-election, then it should, however, be acknowledged that he was able to campaign successfully on a theme that many Italian voters evidently consider of the utmost importance and that will also influence their assessments of the performance of future governments.

Final remarks: issues in the background

In analysing the issues and themes of the 2001 election, I stressed that it could be regarded as one of the elections least focused on programmatic platforms (Campus, 2002: 183). This was not true of the 2006 campaign, which, as argued above, was in contrast explicitly focused on economic issues. According to most observers, other issues remained largely in the background, even though they were by no means without great potential significance. In particular, I am refer-ring to the ethical issues that repeatedly surfaced in political discussion as a result of the initiatives of third parties (above all, the Catholic Church), but which never really became central to the debate.

There are a number of possible explanations as to why controversial issues such as gay rights, stem-cell research, artificial insemination and the liberalisation of policy towards drugs have not become the battle-field that they are in other Western democracies, especially the United States. The first lies in the profile of the Italian centre left. Clearly, it is reasonable to suppose that those on the left will be the natural supporters of progressive views on these points. However, at least two components of the Unione, the Margherita and the UDEUR, are Catholic parties that seek votes among those who are not opposed to State intervention on economic matters, but are much more conserva-tive on ethical issues. Since the Catholic Church made clear at the beginning of the campaign – through the declaration of Cardinal Camillo Ruini[15] – that the duty of Catholic voters was to support politicians willing to defend the traditional family and 'pro-life' stances' it would have been counterproductive for the centre left to stress certain themes. At the beginning of March, polls suggested that a part of the Catholic electorate was still undecided;[16] therefore, both coalitions had an interest in attracting or, at least, not discouraging Catholic voters. Moreover, during the period of platform-writing, it had emerged quite clearly that issues such as Pacs and stem-cell research had strong divisive potential within the coalition itself. On these premises, ethical issues clearly represented ground that was very slippery for the centre left. If some parties, like la Rosa nel Pugno, campaigned on these issues, then it is not surprising that the official approach of Prodi and of the remainder of the centre left was to keep them as far as possible off the campaign agenda.

Less evident are the reasons why the centre right did not take advan-tage of the centre left's lack of unity on the ethical issues. Although the 'official' Catholic component of the centre right, the UDC, is smaller and less influential than the Margherita is on the centre left, the parties of the Casa delle Libertà are all pretty conservative on matters like the family, gay rights and so forth. If some leaders of the centre right, namely Berlusconi and Casini,[17] had expressed the intention of visiting the Pope during the election campaign with the clear aim of raising their profile as defenders of Catholic values, then it is, however, true that the Cdl has never campaigned intensely on these issues. When, the year before, the referendum on artificial insemination was held,[18] the centre right, instead of seeking to defend legislation they themselves had passed, followed instead the line of abstentionism, an easier way of defeating their adversaries, but not the best way of championing the issue. Even more blatantly, Gianfranco Fini had declared himself to be in favour of a 'yes' vote in the referendum. As for Berlusconi, moral issues have never really been his forte: although an observant Catholic, he holds quite liberal views on religious matters (for instance, he is divorced). Moreover, within Forza Italia there is a strong minority with different viewpoints, notably those surrounding the former Minister for Equal Opportunities, Stefania Prestigiacomo, who was among the most vocal promoters of the artificial insemination referendum. For all these reasons, Berlusconi preferred to focus on a theme, tax cuts, that suited him much better and to which the larger part of Italians were probably more sensitive.

Moral and social issues will, however, certainly come back to the centre of the political debate in the post-election period. There is little doubt that some members of the centre left, namely the radical left, la Rosa del Pugno and also a part of the DS, will attempt to reform the legislation on several issues. In order to be seen to be keeping their election promises, they will probably be required to put pressure on the Unione to take the initiative. However, without the support of the Catholic parties, the government is without a majority of votes in Parliament. A way of dealing with ethical issues may well therefore lie in the formation of 'cross-cutting' alliances (lining up Catholics and conservatives on one side; liberals and progressives on the other). This may well help to avoid a legislative *impasse*, but it is also likely to have the unwelcome side effect of weakening the solidity of both the Government and the opposition. To conclude, the themes so studiously avoided in the election campaign cannot be ignored for ever and it is easy to predict that they will, in the coming months, present a significant challenge for all parties and, in particular, for the Prodi government.

Notes

1 Technically this was a mixed system, but it was one with strong plurality components (75 per cent of the seats being distributed according to a plurality system, 25 per cent proportionally).
2 Much has been written on the 1994 campaign. Interested readers will find

a complete set of references in the special issue of *Compol-Comunicazione Politica*, no. 1, 2004, where a number of scholars and communications experts deal with a wide range of aspects of the campaign.

3 The Fabbrica del programma, housed in a former industrial plant in the suburbs of Bologna, was inaugurated on 16 February 2005. Its main purpose was to organise meetings and hearings, details of which can be found on the website www.fabbricadelprogramma.it. The latter also provided a useful forum for citizens to express their views on a variety of topics: from economic policy to immigration, from education to women's rights, and so on.

4 The convention was held at the Eliseo Theatre.

5 The sum of the votes cast for the centre-right parties at the 2004 European election was slightly higher than the sum of the votes cast for these parties at the previous European election in 1999. With respect to the 2001 election, however, there was a clear loss especially for Forza Italia (whose support declined from 29.5 to 21.0 per cent). All data have been drawn from the Ministry for Internal Affairs' website, www.interno.it.

6 See the report in *Corriere della Sera*, 23 February 2006, p. 5.

7 Campus (2006a) offers a more detailed analysis of Berlusconi's campaign strategies.

8 According to a poll carried out by IPSOS Public Affairs on 20 February 2006, 60 per cent of respondents still said that the Berlusconi government had achieved little or nothing of the aims set out in its election programme. Data available at: www.sondaggipoliticoelettorali.it. According to Mannheimer (2006: 24), the percentage of those who approved of the government's performance rose from 31 to 41 percent between January and the end of March 2006. This was not enough, however, to guarantee the victory of the centre right.

9 The official programme of the Unione was undetermined on this point (p. 204) as it referred only to the plan to introduce inheritance tax for 'large estates'.

10 As he declared to Lucia Annunziata during the course of the television programme, *In mezz'ora*, broadcast on RAI Tre on 2 April 2006.

11 Dayan and Katz (1992) define media events as political events that are theatrical and adjusted to the demands of the media system.

12 On this last point, see Claudio Magris, 'Il vero insulto', *Corriere della Sera*, 6 April 2006, p. 1.

13 Declaration published in *Il Foglio*, 5 April 2006, p. 1.

14 Publication of polls is banned by law in the final two weeks of the campaign. Since the campaign, it has been revealed that certain polls conducted during the final week were showing a very close election (Mannheimer, 2006: 24).

15 Inaugural speech to the winter session of the Consiglio Permanente della Conferenza Episcopale Italiana (Standing Committee of the Italian Episcopal Conference) held on 23 January 2006.

16 See the polls published in *Corriere della Sera*, 7 March 2006 and, for a

more detailed analysis of Catholic voters' orientations, see Segatti (2006).
17 Following negative reactions by the centre left, both Berlusconi and Casini renounced their intentions of meeting Pope Benedict during the campaign.
18 The referendum, held on 12 and 13 June 2005, aimed at striking from the statute book certain limitations on the practice of artificial insemination, and on the treatment of embryos.

References

Calise, M. (2005), 'Presidentialization, Italian Style', in T. Poguntke and P. Webb (eds), *The Presidentialization of Politics*, Oxford, Oxford University Press.

Campus, D. (2001), 'Party change, electoral platforms, and issue ownership: a study of the 1996 Italian election', *Modern Italy*, 6:1, 5–20.

Campus, D. (2002), 'Two coalitions in search of an issue: the role of policy stands in the campaign', in J. L. Newell (ed.), *The Italian General Election of 2001: Berlusconi's Victory*, Manchester and New York, Manchester University Press.

Campus, D. (2006a), 'The 2006 election: more than ever a Berlusconi-centred campaign', *Journal of Modern Italian Studies*, 11:4, 516–531.

Campus, D. (2006b), *L'antipolitica al governo: De Gaulle, Reagan, Berlusconi*, Bologna, Il Mulino.

Campus, D. and Pasquino, G. (2006), 'Leadership in Italy: the changing role of leaders in elections and in government', *Journal of Contemporary European Studies*, 14:1, 25–40.

Dayan, D. and Katz, E. (1992), *Media Events: The Live Broadcasting of History*, Cambridge, MA, Cambridge University Press.

Fiorina, M. (1981), *Retrospective Voting in American National Elections*, New Haven, CT, Yale University Press.

Key, V. (1966), *The Responsible Electorate*, Cambridge, MA, Harvard University Press.

Mannheimer, R. (2006), 'La campagna elettorale del 2006 e la mobilitazione della terza Italia politica', in R. Mannheimer and P. Natale (eds), *L'Italia a metà*, Milano, Cairo Publishing.

Newman, B. (1999), *The Mass Marketing of Politics*, Thousand Oaks, CA, Sage.

Parisi, A. and Pasquino, G. (eds) (1977), *Continuità e mutamento elettorale in Italia*, Bologna, Il Mulino.

Pasquino, G. (2002), 'The political context 1996–2001', in J. L. Newell (ed.), *The Italian General Election of 2001: Berlusconi's Victory*, Manchester and New York, Manchester University Press.

Ricolfi, L. (2005), *Dossier Italia: A che punto è il 'Contratto con gli italiani'*, Bologna, Il Mulino.

Ricolfi, L. (2006), *Tempo scaduto: Il 'Contratto con gli italiani' alla prova dei fatti*, Bologna, Il Mulino.

Roncarolo, F. (2002), 'Virtual clashes and political games: the campaign in the print and broadcast media', in J. L. Newell (ed.), *The Italian General Election of 2001: Berlusconi's Victory*, Manchester and New York, Manchester University Press.

Sani, G. and Segatti, P. (1997), 'Programmi, media e opinione politica', in R. D'Alimonte and S. Bartolini (eds), *Maggioritario per caso*, Bologna, Il Mulino.

Segatti, P. (2006), 'Cattolici e voto', in R. Mannheimer and P. Natale (eds), *L'Italia a metà*, Milano, Cairo Publishing.

Surel, Y. (2003), 'Berlusconi, leader populiste?', in O. Ihl, J. Chene, E. Vial and G. Waterlot (eds), *La Tentation populiste au coeur de l'Europe*, Paris, Editions la Découverte.

Taguieff, P. (2003), *L'illusione populista*, Milano, Mondadori.

Tarchi, M. (2003), *L'Italia populista*, Bologna, Il Mulino.

8

'And the winner is …': competing for votes in the print and broadcast media

Franca Roncarolo

Introduction

The striking result obtained by the centre right (which was expected to lose many more votes than it did) and the narrow victory of the centre left (which was expected to win easily) calls for close investigation. In all mediated democracies, including Italy, communication has become a crucial factor and it certainly was in 2006.

Exactly as in 2001, there was an early favourite coalition which, during the two years prior to the election had 1) received growing support at each local and European election; 2) retained a lead in the polls; and 3) been crowned winner by journalists who played a strategic role by representing each leader as front-runner or likely loser. However, things started to change during the final weeks before the vote so that, helped by what was once again a highly dramatic campaign of mobilisation (Mannheimer, 2001), the coalition that was supposed to have no chance of success came much closer to victory than had been expected.[1]

Of course, there are many differences between the two campaigns, not least the difference in electoral laws (which meant that the gap between the two coalitions in 2001 was made greater by the proportional arena where, as is well known, the parties of the centre right performed much better than in the majoritarian arena). But repetition of the earlier scenario is interesting. And even if at present it is impossible to tell whether this is mere coincidence or whether it indicates the emergence of a more deeply seated pattern, the dynamic that it reveals is puzzling and worth exploring.

With this as the point of departure, I will investigate three issues. First, I will consider the problem of predicted victories and the relationship between the rationale of the permanent campaign and the hyper-dramatic communication strategies that mobilise voters during the final days before voting. Second, I will discuss the very different styles of campaigning of Prodi and Berlusconi and try to highlight the more general lessons that can be learned from their experience. Finally, I will explore the role of political journalists, highlighting the elements of continuity and discontinuity that emerge from comparison of the 2006 and the 2001 election campaigns.

Victories announced in the media and final rushes among voters: more on the Italian style of permanent campaigning

Many scholars have in recent years adopted the theoretical model of the permanent campaign[2] to explain the new pattern of competition introduced by Berlusconi since the early 1990s (Mazzoleni, 2004). Underlying this pattern is a very intensive communication process that unfolds long before the election campaign starts and turns every opportunity – including those offered by 'second-order elections' (Reif and Schmitt, 1980) – into a key moment of a single, coherent strategy (Marletti, 2000). Despite the strategy's effectiveness, the institutional features of the Italian political system reduce its potential. The same election campaign that in 2001 showed Berlusconi's almost paradigmatic ability as a permanent campaigner also revealed how the original model has been adapted to the needs of a political system that had never completely repudiated its proportional soul (D'Alimonte, 2003) and has since gone back to it.[3]

According to the model, the election campaign is closely linked with the following phase of government and the future election; for, not only do leaders use the same propaganda techniques during the electoral and non-electoral phases, but the programmatic agenda plays a strategic role.[4] Even if popularity can be, and often is, courted without reference to a political programme, in Italy this tendency is favoured by systemic factors. This is so above all because the model of permanent campaigning does not work in the same way in a majoritarian system, where just one party is invested with the responsibility of government, and in a multi-party system, with a coalition government that must negotiate most decisions. As Berlusconi discovered during his five turbulent years in power, even a leader who has been elected after publicly signing a formal 'Contract with the Italian people' cannot easily put the agenda at the centre of his permanent campaign (Roncarolo, 2005). And the introduction of a new proportional electoral law only produced more difficulties – as the dynamics documented by Campus in this volume show. Despite the many appeals of social scientists on the front pages of various dailies (Ricolfi, 2005), neither the centre right nor the centre left coalition used its programme as a strategic tool in order to win the election. As a consequence of the negative polls, Berlusconi's allies chose to differentiate themselves in order better to compete for the coalition's leadership, while the centre left's campaign was driven by the opposite logic. Given the high expectations of victory and the shared acceptance of Prodi's leadership, the very heterogeneous centre-left coalition needed to present itself in as harmonious a light as possible. Consequently, the allies laboriously built a general agreement based on a wide-ranging programme that carefully avoided facing the more divisive issues in the attempt to avoid detailed discussion for as long as possible.

That these attitudes depend on systemic factors is easy to see. During the election campaign, the proportional rationale driving each party to 'run for itself' competes with the opposite principle encouraging aggregation by awarding a majority premium to the winner. But in the best case, political actors use caution in their statements about the programme until votes have shown which party is strongest.[5] Moreover, as both the first Prodi government and Berlusconi's coalition discovered, the inclination to differentiate does not stop when in office because, with respect to the next elections, political parties are at least as much competitors as allies. So it is difficult for the premier to engage in a true permanent campaign focused on critical issues and aimed at supporting the political agenda. And the result is that the model of permanent campaigning loses its policy significance to become an almost uninterrupted succession of electoral tests, or a kind of 'horse race', whose most important moments occur during the last two years before the general election. Indeed, as the two election campaigns of 2001 and 2006 show, the electoral cycle begins with the European election (about two years before the national election), continues with the regional elections (the following spring) and ends with the new general election (with possibly one more test if there are primary elections).

Perhaps more so in Italy than in other mediated democracies, each electoral test is interpreted by journalists and politicians as an occasion to check the strength both of the Government and of the opposition parties. While offering the political actors new elements enabling them to decide alliances and negotiate electoral lists, the permanent campaign feeds the media with the data that make forecasts easier, thus strongly contributing to the creation of an 'expected winner'.

What follows from these considerations is that while the 'original' model of the permanent campaign is supposed to strengthen the leader, the Italian version ends up weakening the incumbent coalition – first, because it cuts the links with the political agenda and pushes parties in government to seek their own electoral success on the basis of differentiated strategies; second because, in this context, campaigning is easier for the opposition than for government. Not surprisingly, during the 2006 campaign, Berlusconi finally decided to run more as the challenger than as the incumbent, pushing Prodi into the corner of political responsibilities.

No less important is the high degree of mobilisation that the competitors can obtain by fully exploiting the potential of the media during the final period before the vote. This mobilisation can produce relevant changes in the climate of opinion deriving from the initial phases of the permanent campaign and can overturn the bandwagon effect – that initially prevails by virtue of the existence of an expected winner – for some voters, rendering them vulnerable to the underdog effect caused by the hyper-dramatic communication strategies adopted during the final weeks by the expected loser.

We might therefore wonder whether the permanent campaign helps, in the Italian context, to reduce the reliability of electoral predictions, by increasing the likelihood of the emergence of a dual climate of opinion (Noelle Neumann, 1993). Of course this risk is present in all mediated democracies. In Italy, however, it seems to be particularly relevant – partly because there the permanent campaign is aimed less at involving citizens in the political process than at positioning political actors in the public arena, and partly because of the peculiar elements of the Italian media-political system. In a country where political journalism has little autonomy and is very partisan (Roncarolo, 2002; Hallin and Mancini, 2004), the permanent electoral competition between majority and opposition often continues without the necessary journalistic filters in the media arena, where it encounters the natural tendency of the media to simplify and dramatise. As a consequence, the habit of reading the results of each electoral competition as signals of future victories (or defeats) ends up producing true social constructions of reality that amplify the opinions of the interested and informed public while paying little attention to the (often more silent) moods widely circulating in other sectors of society.

This offers a special opportunity to the communication strategies of the expected loser – strategies that aim at mobilising those voters whose indifference toward politics (Campus, 2000) is usually only overcome when somebody raises the stakes and when they perceive their votes as decisive or especially important. As we have seen in the 2001 and 2006 elections, if these conditions are satisfied the strategies of mobilisation can increase turnout[6] and obtain the (at least partial) recovery of those political actors who, many months before the election, pollsters and journalists had already considered defeated.

From a predicted defeat to a post-modern campaign of re-conquest: Berlusconi's strategic communication on television and elsewhere

Needless to say, the case of Berlusconi in the 2006 election campaign is, from this point of view, almost paradigmatic. During the last three months before the vote, indeed, the Forza Italia (FI) leader changed the climate of opinion amazingly (Mazzoni, 2006), moving the incumbent centre-right coalition from being the almost certain loser to a position that many observers considered very close to victory.

As is well known, until the beginning of December 2005, the centre right looked as though it was in very serious trouble. At that time Berlusconi led a highly divided coalition and faced the declining support of a disappointed public opinion. Not surprisingly, and as the media chorus repeated continuously, the incumbent was, according to the polls, headed for almost certain defeat. The only chance of success for the premier was to re-conquer disappointed citizens by means of a strategy that was successful in countering the effects of *fedeltà leggera* (weak partisanship).[7] In order to do it, he had to pursue a double aim, on the one hand preventing centre-right voters from abstaining, and raising turnout above the threshold of 80 per cent as in 2001 (Feltrin, 2006); on the other hand recapturing the trust of those voters who might have been tempted to choose a different party among those belonging to the centre-right coalition. With these goals in mind, Berlusconi developed a strategy consisting of three complementary phases: the first aimed at capturing public attention by defending the government's performance; the second aimed at delegitimising the opposing coalition while creating a widespread feeling of fear of the consequences of the possible centre-left victory and the third aimed at definitively mobilising every potential voter by promising advantages in the case of centre-right confirmation (Cornia 2006).

The turning point was the traditional end-of-year press conference, on 23 December 2005, which launched the first phase. During the two-hour meeting with journalists, the FI leader stressed that over 25 per cent of Italians were still undecided about whom to vote for; he passionately defended his government's record, and excluded any possibility of losing the elections. Then, in the first week of January, he launched an impressive media offensive (see Table 8.1), fully exploiting both his privileged access to the television networks and the temporary absence of any rules regulating election campaigning.[8] On 9 January, during prime time, the FI leader appeared on *Otto e mezzo* – a kind of bi-partisan political talk show[9] – and shortly after he participated in a very popular – not to say cult – programme about football, *Il processo di Biscardi*. Two days later, on 11 January, Berlusconi appeared on *Porta a porta* denying the existence of any conflict of interest caused by his dual role as Prime Minister and media magnate, stressing the various political achievements of the Government and blaming the opposition for all its problems. On 13 January, the Prime Minister went to the public prosecutor's office in order to give evidence concerning the DS' responsibilities in a banking scandal – which, according to some observers, risked threatening the latter party's reputation as the guardian of morally sound conduct (Scalfari, 2006) – and, the day after, he repeated his allegations during a broadcast press conference. Then he made new remarks on this and other issues during a centre-left-oriented political talk show, *Ballarò*, when – on 17 January – he phoned in live and talked for about twenty minutes, raising the audience from 4.2 to 5.4 million people in the process (Siliato, 2006). Thanks to his indefatigable vitality, a few hours later Berlusconi was on a morning television programme – *Unomattina* – and immediately after on the radio talking to the listeners of *Isoradio*, a specialised programme for car-drivers.

Having obtained a postponement of the dissolution of Parliament after a trial of strength with President Ciampi, day by day the FI leader proceeded to produce a barrage of propaganda in a way that was so unfair as to lead the President openly to disapprove of the premier's

Table 8.1 Some key moments in Berlusconi's media assault

Format	Programme	Time schedule	Network	Date	Average audience
Face-to-face Berlusconi–Bertinotti	*Porta a Porta*	Late evening	Rai Uno	11 January	3,000,191
Telephone call by Berlusconi	*Ballarò*	Prime time	Rai Tre	17 January	4,616,941
Berlusconi star guest	*Uno mattina*	Early morning	Rai Uno	18 January	1,592,935
Berlusconi	*Dopo Tg1*	Access prime time	Rai Uno	19 January	6,947,000
Face-to-face Berlusconi–Rutelli	*Matrix*	Late evening and night	Canale 5	20 January	1,968,000
Face-to-face Berlusconi–Rutelli (repeat)	*Matrix*	Prime time	Italia1	21 January	2,626,000

Source: Punto.com, 'L'offensiva del Cav: 21 milioni di spettatori', 24 January 2006.

campaign. Claiming that the Government had done a lot of important things during the previous five years but had failed properly to inform the Italian people of its achievements, Berlusconi argued that his position as Prime Minister made it appropriate, indeed essential, that he be on television as much as possible, especially in view of the *par condicio* law (or 'Marx condicio law' as he preferred to call it), which would soon unfairly prevent him from going public as much as he wished, and particularly in the way he wished.

Despite the new proportional electoral law, the FI leader adopted both the majoritarian and the proportional model of communication (Marletti and Roncarolo, 2000).[10] With its focus on the strategic role of the premiership, the former allowed him to exploit all the advantages of incumbency such as, for instance, the greater visibility and the exceptional aura that it offers the premier (as the live coverage of Berlusconi's visit to the United States in March 2006 well showed). Then, during the final phases of the 2006 election campaign, strongly engaged in the attempt to save his party (and himself) from the predicted electoral collapse, Berlusconi exploited the advantages of the proportional model, adopting a strategy of differentiation that let him distance himself both from his allies (who were more or less openly accused of being responsible for the unfulfilled election promises) and from the critical economic situation.

In order to reach his potential voters, and communicate with them in the appropriate tone, more effectively, Berlusconi exploited the rationale of narrowcasting, which above all plays on differences between people. On the other hand, in order to change potential votes into actual votes, he used the rationale of broadcasting which, in contrast, appeals to shared elements (such as fears and concerns), trying to unify the fragmented audiences. In so doing he succeeded both in alerting almost all the citizens to the importance of the coming election and in mobilising the latent mental schemes of some of them about the dangers associated with a centre-left victory.

Finally, Berlusconi adopted a highly integrated communications strategy. If television played a central role, it was exploited in conjunction with a variety of different media, from the Internet to newspapers and local television. In this way, the Prime Minister was successful in intensifying citizens' tendency to engage in 'selective exposure' and in weaving the main campaign events inside and outside the media into a coherent strategy. For example, on 13 March, during a live interview with the journalist and former television executive Lucia Annunziata, Berlusconi left the television studio in protest against what he called true 'one-sidedness' with a *coup de théâtre* which, even if not fully original (Ceccarelli, 1999), was obviously destined to capture public attention. In the afternoon of the same day, he appeared at a FI election rally in Pescara where he projected the recorded programme on a large screen at the front of the conference hall and gave a running commentary on it, thereby obtaining two different results: amplifying the effect of a programme that only the most attentive would have seen on television and framing it in the context of a propaganda discourse aimed at highlighting the groundlessness of criticisms of him, while stressing the adversarial attitude of many journalists.

Significantly, the populist traits that featured as part of Berlusconi's communications strategy also shaped the final phase of the campaign, which started about a week later. On 14 March, the premier was unsuccessful in the first television debate with Prodi, because – he complained – the rules imposed by his adversary prevented him from presenting his message effectively. Then, four days later, he went to the Confindustria conference in Vicenza and created an event that – once again – put him at the centre of the stage in a context in which it was easier to by-pass the rules and talk to different publics in the spotlight of television. First of all he brought with him a claque of about 250 people whom (according to some rumours) his loyal supporter, Veneto Region President Giancarlo Galan, had expressly organised in order to amplify the effect of consent. Then, the FI leader passionately addressed both the public present at the conference and the public who would have seen the speech on television (at least partially), and did so without respecting any time limits because, he said, 'Having made 1,700 regulations it is hard to squeeze all the many things done into just three minutes and half'. Striding back and forth across the stage, he criticised entrepreneurs and journalists, whom he accused of conspiring to bring about a centre-left victory. And while he was feeding the anti-élitist feelings of many potential voters he demonstrated to the general public that, despite all the polls, he could still win.

From that moment, the FI leader changed tactic: he definitively ceased respecting the rules and put at the centre of his communications strategy the fiscal issue raised – precisely during the Vicenza meeting – by his Minister for the Economy and Finance, Giulio Tremonti.[11] At meeting after meeting, from Genoa to Naples, Berlusconi linked the idea of a Prodi victory with the prediction of an increase in taxation so establishing the Achilles' heel of the centre left and creating the Trojan Horse with which he would enter the media arena and put strain on journalists' definitions of reality. While the dailies sponsored by the more radical left-wing parties were debating the advantages of more taxes, Lucia Annunziata (2006) signed a leading article that was very

critical of the position of progressive parties on the fiscal issue, and
even the centrist newspaper *Corriere della Sera*, which openly supported the opposition leader, published a cartoon showing Prodi wearing
the uniform of 'Tax Willer'.[12] Needless to say, these arguments found
greater visibility on television where the image of a surely divided, and
maybe dangerous, coalition was at the centre of the stage – at least
until the second broadcast debate, when – in the final seconds, with
Prodi unable to respond – Berlusconi pulled off a tactical coup by
promising an end to ICI, the local property tax, if re-elected.

Let's meet far from the media: the centre left's model of collective campaigning

Starting from very different political needs and a personal style radically different from that of the incumbent, Prodi chose the opposite
model of communication. For many months he wrote letters to the
daily newspapers in order to intervene in the political debate with
calm authoritativeness; gave interviews (sometimes to the radio);
campaigned from posters promising '*la serietà al governo*' (reliability
in power); organised an up-to-date website, and travelled throughout
Italy with a yellow truck to meet people. But, above all, he used television as little as possible, devoting more attention to the effort of
building consensus among his allies than to citizen-centred communication. Two main elements underlay this choice, besides Prodi's
disinclination to exploit mediated communication and the more
general suspicion of television that is widespread on the left.

First, there was the rejection of Berlusconi's style of leadership and
the belief that the failure of his approach had become clear to the great
majority of the electorate. Indeed, after the positive outcome of the
regional elections and the success of the primary election that crowned
Prodi as the opposition's leader, the centre left had taken for granted
the final emergence of the new climate of opinion emphasised by so
many journalists. So it ended up overestimating its chances of electoral
success (Vassallo, 2006) believing that a campaign aimed at maintaining the advantage by generically stressing the need for change was
good enough. Unlike what Berlusconi had done in 2001 – when,
though expected to win, he had nevertheless continued to feed his
advantage with a citizen-oriented, communication-intensive strategy
that never stopped until election-day – Prodi continued to work on
political goals without spending much time on campaigning – at least
until Berlusconi's challenge forced him to join the fray in the media.

The second element that helped to shape the centre-left model was one that arose from the plurality of interests and voices that a coalition with a high degree of internal diversity brings with it. At first, the opposition parties seemed to find in the 'Fabbrica del programma' (see chapter 7; Santagata, 2006) the perfect means for turning its diversity into a resource. Besides being a good device for the promotion of consensual procedures useful for integrating the several components of the coalition, at the beginning the 'Fabbrica del programma' was indeed a well functioning tool, both for direct communications strategies and from the point of view of media logic. While offering people the opportunity to participate, the Fabbrica met the need of the media for a single image able to symbolise the radical differences – both in style and content – between the incumbent and the challenger coalitions. Moreover, the fact that this difference leant, among other things, on the greater ability of the centre-left parties to find a synthesis of their different points of view in a shared – even if general – programme, and the fact that they worked hard to integrate their respective positions instead of spending their time on television, were opening strengths for the centre left.

For some time, the less personal and spectacular style of campaigning adopted by the coalition helped to raise the profile of Prodi's image as a serious leader, demonstrating that an effective alternative to the unsuccessful centre-right majority was on the table. But with the competition becoming tougher, the political limits of this representation and the problems in terms of communications strategy started to become evident. Almost immediately after the convention of 11 February 2006 where the leaders of the Unione parties had signed the 281-page programme, evocatively entitled *Per il bene dell'Italia* (For the Good of Italy), arguments about controversial issues that had not been thoroughly tackled started. And as time went by, things worsened – first, because, as we said above, Berlusconi's provocations and the dynamics of electoral competition made more and more visible the differences between the centre-left parties, darkening the coalition's image of unity and eroding its credibility; second, because, as many observers noted, the centre left's electoral communication was overly self-referential. Thus, from 1 January to 24 February, the coalition spent about 360 minutes (or 38 per cent) of its time on TV talking about itself and little more than 90 minutes debating economic issues (Davi, 2006). Moreover, having adequately given expression to the disappointment of many citizens until the end of 2005, when Berlusconi tried to change the climate of opinion, the Unione failed to drive the agenda-setting process. Instead of developing the coalition's themes and proposals, the opposition's leaders reserved more space for criticism of the incumbent, so that – not surprisingly – remarks against him ranked fourth among the centre left's top ten issues, while the problems of work, for instance, were only sixth (Davi, 2006). And Prodi's several statements aimed at reacting, more than at clearly making proposals,[13] were another indicator of this difficulty.

It thus emerged that, in comparison with the premier's huge personal engagement, the centre left's investment in the campaign was too weak. Limiting the appearances of the coalition's leader on television, refusing – as Prodi did – to participate in any election broadcast on Mediaset's channels, and stressing the importance of meeting people directly instead of through television screens, might have been an effective strategy. But it would have needed many more meetings, for a longer period, with a better and more integrated organisation. For example, the electoral project *Incontriamoci* (Let's meet), which was aimed at increasing the intensity of networking with ordinary people, started too late,[14] had too little visibility and, on the whole, failed to achieve its aims. It was neither able really to replace electronic links with true contacts nor to influence the battle for issues and images in the media. The same was true of the campaigns conducted by Bertinotti, Rutelli and Fassino, who – as in 1996 and 2001 – used symbolic vehicles in order to make the campaign visible outside the media. Theoretically, the fact that each leader travelled throughout the country and met his/her own constituencies with a specific message was a good idea in order to exploit a real weakness of the centre-right coalition, namely its lack of rootedness at the local level. But again, the travelling started too late, suffered from tensions among the parties and failed to mobilise activists. In short, locally rooted direct propaganda had limited effects and this was not surprising, given the fact that the proportional electoral law, which did not allow voters to express preferences for candidates, had removed any incentive for the latter to campaign.

The point is that campaigning outside the media without the large and stable organisational networks that the traditional political parties once offered is very difficult, demanding and expensive. But in the context of mediated politics it is also very hard to keep control of the public agenda and of the image-building process without fully controlling the media logic and exploiting the special visibility that television offers. Thus, a leader who tries to limit his presence on television risks finding himself in the spotlight mainly when the attention of the media is attracted by conflicts and controversies. Of course, one can leave the task of representing the coalition on television to one's allies, as Prodi frequently did before coming to agreed rules for the broadcast debates.[15] But if this offers a means of including the other leaders in a collective model of leadership then it also involves significant risks. These – as the Unione discovered – are that increasing the range of spokespersons when the agreed programme is quite generic increases the possibility of discrepancies and contradictions in what they say. Indeed, in a context where the electoral law pushes parties toward differentiation, the opportunity of presenting your own specific point of view is difficult to resist. And it hardly needs adding that the media, strongly attracted to conflict and controversy, encourage this propensity.

The effects of these problems on the public's perception became clear in the context of Berlusconi's very aggressive campaign. So, while the Prime Minister's fortunes began to rise, the image of the coalition led by Prodi began to lose attractiveness: if in November and December, more than half the people (51 to 54 per cent) interviewed for the Ispo polls said that they expected the centre left to win, around mid-March the percentage had dropped to 39 per cent.[16]

The changing nature of Italian political journalism between covert propaganda and open endorsement

In the second part of the campaign, however, Prodi increased his presence on television, sometimes even obtaining very good results as the two debates with Berlusconi showed. But the overall television information context was not favourable to the opposition.

According to data gathered by the media monitoring institute, Centro d'Ascolto dell'Informazione Radiotelevisiva,[17] even when the *par condicio* law was in force, the centre-right parties received greater coverage on the television news broadcasts of all the public and commercial networks but one (the traditionally left-oriented Tg3). The lack of balance shows clearly in terms of measures of the amount of time different political actors talked on screen (called 'word time'; see Table 8.2.

Not surprisingly, the lack of balance was greater on Berlusconi's networks[18] and was even greater with reference to the visibility of parties and leaders. Indeed, as documented below, the Prime Minister and his party were so much at the centre of the television stage that no other political actor could compete: not only did FI occupy a quarter of the total 'word time' that was devoted to the political parties on RAI news during the campaign, but the percentage grew to over a third on La7 and it exceeded 50 per cent on the Mediaset channels (Table 8.3). The difference became monumental in the case of

Table 8.2 Word time devoted to the two coalitions by each television
network in news broadcasts from 11 February to 7 April 2006

	RAI		Mediaset		La7	
	time	%	time	%	time	%
Centre right	5h 58' 05''	50.99	6h 07' 59''	66.33	0h 28' 44''	55.03
Centre left	5h 35' 38''	47.79	3h 04' 12''	33.20	0h 21' 36''	41.37
Others	0h 08' 35''	1.22	0h 02' 35''	0.47	0h 01' 53''	3.61

Source: Centro d'Ascolto dell'Informazione Radiotelevisiva.

Berlusconi and Prodi: while on Mediaset news broadcasts the opposition leader was given 17 per cent of time, the Prime Minister was given
52 per cent (Table 8.4). Needless to say, the principal reason for the
greater visibility enjoyed by Berlusconi and the centre-right parties
was the fact that the entrepreneur was the incumbent. And Prodi's
difficulties in driving the communication process in the media certainly helped to increase this advantage. However, the systematic
imbalance was evident and, once again, it showed the effects that the
close connection between the media and politics in Italy can produce.

Even if no direct relationship can be found between the amount of
time enjoyed by the political actors on television and the votes that
they obtain – as the 2006 election results demonstrate – the issue of
fairness remains important. This is so because differences in leaders'
visibility create differences in their agenda-setting power, with relevant
effects on their chances of capturing the attention of uninterested
voters, and consequently on their chances of influencing the climate of
opinion.

With regard to the partisan role of television, it is interesting to note
that Mediaset joined the fray as in 1994. In other words, whereas in
2001 Berlusconi's networks basically amplified the promotional activities of the leader, without offering any special space to the campaign
or changing their programme schedule, things went differently in
2006. Old and new programmes made special room for the premier,
reserving him preferential treatment. Two former politicians anchored
talk-shows that offered special hospitality to the leader of FI.[19] And
during an afternoon programme watched by those who usually do not
watch political programmes, a popular television character claimed
that despite her antipathy towards politicians, she really loved
Berlusconi;[20] while three days before the vote a quip in a reality show
amplified the premier's proposal to abolish ICI, the local property tax.

Unlike Mediaset, and again in contrast with what happened in 2001
(Roncarolo, 2002), the public service broadcaster did not join the fray.
Beyond some arguments about the limits of satire and the advantage

Table 8.3 Word time devoted to the first five parties by each television network in news broadcasts from 11 February to 7 April 2006

	RAI		Mediaset		La7	
	time	%	time	%	time	%
Forza Italia	2h 56' 33"	25.14	5h 17' 45"	57.28	0h 17' 56"	34.34
Unione	1h 43' 12"	14.69	1h 37' 23"	17.55	0h 06' 29"	12.42
AN	1h 19' 25"	11.31	0h 24' 37"	4.44	0h 06' 25"	12.29
UDC	1h 00" 55'	8.67	0h 11' 57"	2.15	0h 01' 43"	3.29
DS	1h 00' 01"	8.55	0h 29' 19"	5.28	0h 07' 05"	13.57
Margherita	0h 56' 12"	8.00	0h 17' 01"	3.07	0h 03' 345"	6.83
la Rosa nel						
Pugno	0h 32' 38"	4.65	0h 17' 44"	3.20	0h 00' 34"	13.57

Source: Centro d'Ascolto dell'informazione Radiotelevisiva.

Table 8.4 Word time devoted to Berlusconi and Prodi by each television network in news broadcasts from 11 February to 7 April 2006

	RAI		Mediaset		La7	
	time	%	time	%	time	%
Berlusconi	1h 56' 08"	16.54	4h 49' 25"	52.17	0h 13' 08"	25.15
Prodi	1h 42' 33"	14.6	1h 36' 21"	17.37	0h 06' 16"	12

Source: Centro d'Ascolto dell'Informazione Radiotelevisiva.

traditionally given to the governing parties, on the whole RAI kept out of the electoral competition and was reasonably fair. This change was probably connected with the expected victory of the opposition and the centre left's battle for more adequate campaign rules. In making room for this battle RAI also contributed to the emergence of the new, less partisan and show-oriented, approach represented by the two serious – and sometimes boring – debates between Berlusconi and Prodi watched by sixteen and twelve million people respectively.

The feeling that, paradoxically, something was starting to change in the landscape of Italian political communication was confirmed by two further elements, ones referring respectively to journalism in the press, and on TV. In the 2006 campaign the newspapers went back to playing a strategic role in interaction among politicians. Thrust once more to the centre of the communication process by the new proportional electoral law, the daily newspapers acted as an arena in which parties' leaders exchanged messages and managed their relationships. Two factors rendered this interaction less self-referential, however: first, the changes in the Italian electoral market, a market that – beginning in the 1990s – had moved closer to the traditional model of most other Western democracies thanks to the (final) achievement of alternation in government; second, the majoritarian component of the electoral law that both Berlusconi and the media helped greatly to highlight. They did it by emphasising those aspects (from personalising the competition between the two coalitions to increasing the simplification implied in the rationale of bi-polarism) that were more attuned to their logic and by stressing the crucial importance of each vote in order to win the majority premium. Not surprisingly, therefore, the forms of journalistic endorsement started to change too, as the case of *Corriere della Sera*, the biggest-selling non-specialist daily, suggested. The front-page leader backing the centre left, signed by the newspaper's editor, Paolo Mieli (2006), represented a break both with reference to the traditional political parallelism of the press and with regard to the habit – initiated in the second half of the 1970s by Eugenio Scalfari – of joining the fray by turning a daily into a political actor (Marletti, 1984). As far as we can tell, Mieli's editorial was a temporary stance that implied neither a stable alliance with the centre left nor any conversion of the traditionally centre right daily: as is usual in majoritarian democracies, it was merely an influential newspaper's judgment about the political offer in a specific election.

Some further examples of the slow changes involving Italian political journalism came from the television sphere. The most debated and meaningful case was that of Lucia Annunziata. In her strict and minimalist programme, the former head of RAI tried to interview Berlusconi without the usual compliant attitude, challenging him until he angrily left the studio before the programme had finished, as was mentioned above. But the point is that some days later she interviewed Prodi with the same rigour, highlighting the weakest points in his proposals and the contradictions in the fiscal programme of the centre left. If Annunziata put herself forward as the champion of watchdog journalism, then Enrico Mentana used his political talk show *Matrix*, broadcast by Canale5, to anchor a sequence of face-to-face debates between Berlusconi and various leaders of the centre left with such balance that Oliviero Diliberto offered him honorary membership of the PdCI (Guerzoni, 2006). Finally, the model of a double anchorship – successfully pursued by Giuliano Ferrara on La7[21] since March 2002 in order to ensure the presence of different opinions even in the anchor team – mixed a rejection of lap-dog journalism with the belief that aside from addressing the problem of balance in television broadcasting it could maximise the quantity of information offered to the public.

Final remarks

From the point of view of political communication, there were three lessons to be drawn from the 2006 campaign. First, the centre left won thanks to political factors that were strengthened by the personal and structural limits which caused the premier to fail to really link his communication strategy with the government's agenda and the electoral programme that was supposed to be the basis of that agenda. This lesson should be carefully kept in mind by the current government in order to avoid two very dangerous risks: forgetting the importance of agenda and splitting the communication from the political process.

Second, the permanent campaign does not give any guarantee of victory to the expected winner because it is unable to eliminate the risk of changes in the climate of opinion. Actually, if the theoretical model comes down to a mere sequence of polls and electoral tests, then the permanent campaign increases the risk of last-minute switches. As Prodi discovered, the tendency of the media to create an expected winner can favour the emergence of a dual climate of opinion and makes more effective the campaigns aimed at breaking the spiral of silence, or at generating support for the predicted loser.

Finally, in the mediated democracies, campaigning from one election to the following is a categorical imperative but this does not imply the need continuously to be on television. Even if Berlusconi's style of campaigning easily achieves great attention in the media system, in the 'third age' of political communication (Blumler and Kavanagh, 1999) other models – which are based more on direct, locally rooted messages – are possible. Indeed, as the centre left demonstrated for the second time in 2006, a coalition can win despite the lack of a telegenic leader or a high degree of personalisation – especially if the competition is conducted within the framework of a proportional electoral law. But those who want to be really successful in the strategy of limiting the space for media logic must develop a genuinely intensive communication strategy. That is exactly what the centre-left coalition failed to do, so weakening its victory.

Notes

1 Of course, in 2001 the centre-right coalition won by a large margin. But in that case too, while the polls had registered a very large gap between the two coalitions, the difference in terms of plurality votes for the Chamber of Deputies was small (45.4 to 43.8 per cent).

2 According to the scholars (Blumenthal, 1980; Kernell, 1986) who first

suggested the concept, the permanent campaign represents a structural adaptation of the political system to an environment made more complex by the challenges of media logic and the effects produced by the crisis of parties.

3 Among other things, the notion of the 'permanent campaign' draws attention to the use of governing as an instrument to build and sustain popular support. For this reason, and because of the multi-party character of Italian democracy, the model cannot be applied without qualification to that political system, as we explain in the paragraphs that follow.

4 Using skills offered by political marketing (Newman, 1994), the leader first wins with an electoral agenda focused on widespread concerns and then prepares the bases for the next election by supporting the policies of that agenda with an intensive communication process that includes – if necessary – the strategies of going public (Kernell, 1986).

5 On the basis of the proportional principle, each party is induced to represent the interests and opinions of a specific – although small – segment of voters, without committing itself too closely to the programme of the future government.

6 In 2001 turnout fell slightly – from 82.9 to 81.4 per cent for the Chamber of Deputies election – but was much higher than had been expected (Newell and Bull, 2001: 25). In 2006, depending on the bases used for the calculation, turnout rose – from 81.4 to 83.6 – or (more correctly) remained essentially the same (at 81.4 per cent): for details see Newell (2006) and Istituto Cattaneo (2006). This must be seen against the background of declining turnouts in the advanced democracies generally.

7 According to Natale (2002) weak partisanship is a typical feature of the Italian electoral market; it is a kind of political tie that is strong enough to prevent voters from betraying their chosen coalition, but insufficiently strong to prevent them from voting for a different party belonging to the same coalition or failing to vote at all.

8 According to law no. 28/2000 the restrictions on political advertising, as well as the remaining *par condicio* rules, come into force with the dissolution of Parliament.

9 *Otto e mezzo* is a daily political talk show that is hosted by two journalists of different political orientation: Giuliano Ferrara, the conservative journalist who was a minister in the 1994 Berlusconi government and is now editor of the centre-right daily *il Foglio*, together with a man or a woman with the opposite political opinions (during the election campaign the anchorwoman was Ritanna Armeni, a journalist with the radical-left daily *Liberazione*).

10 From this point of view we could say that while during the previous ten years the almost majoritarian law adopted in 1993 had been 'proportionalised' (D'Alimonte, 2003), following the electoral law reform passed in December 2005 the majoritarian elements still present in the proportional law were stressed and heightened. About Berlusconi's majoritarian style of communication see also Santalmassi (2006).

11 The role played by Tremonti in the communication strategy of Berlusconi is well documented in Feltri (2006).

12 Tex Willer is the main character of an Italian popular comic. He is a Texan ranger who protects people from bandits.

13 According to the research data collected by the Department of Political Studies at the University of Turin, the proportion of defensive events in Prodi's communication was almost double the proportion in Berlusconi's (about 40 per cent to 21 per cent).

14 *Incontriamoci* was created within the framework of the Fabbrica del programma immediately before Christmas while it actually started on 26 February 2006. It was meant to offer an opportunity to participate and was based on voluntary managers who organised meetings of 10 to 20 persons in private arenas (often people's homes) with the participation of representatives of the Unione. More detailed information about the project can be found at www.incontriamoci.fabbricadelprogramma.it.

15 Before the first debate with Prodi, Berlusconi had face-to-face encounters with the leader of the Margherita, Francesco Rutelli (*Matrix*, 20 January) and with the leader of Communist Refoundation, Fausto Bertinotti (*Porta a porta*, 12 January). A couple of months later he again met Bertinotti, along with the Radical Emma Bonino (*Ballarò*, 28 March) and the leader of the PdCI, Oliviero Diliberto (*Matrix*, 10 March).

16 See Mannheimer (2006: 24). As is well known, the question was suggested by Elizabeth Noelle-Neumann as a useful indicator of the climate of opinion and was originally worded: 'Of course, nobody can know for sure, but what do you think: Who is going to win the election?' (Noelle-Neumann and Petersen, 2004: 348).

17 The data are available on the website of the Centro d'Ascolto at www.centrodiascolto.it.

18 Data concerning Mediaset are strongly negatively influenced by the news broadcasts of Rete4, the channel where the most devoted supporter of Berlusconi (Emilio Fede) anchors the news. Here the 'word time' given to the centre right and to the centre left was 74 to 26 per cent respectively. It is worth noting that, though less evidently so, the news broadcasts of the other two Mediaset channels were also less balanced than the public channels (Tg5 shows a distribution of 'word time' between centre right and centre left of 56 and 44 per cent for the former and the latter respectively, while the corresponding percentages for 'Studio aperto' are 58 and 41 per cent). The lack of balance on the part of Tg5 was to be expected as the 'fair' Mentana had been fired at the end of 2004. He had been the editor of Tg5 since its foundation and his removal was directly linked to the opening of the more crucial phase in Berlusconi's permanent campaign.

19 The former League Deputy and President of the Chamber of Deputies Irene Pivetti anchored the talk show *Liberitutti*, which reserved a full episode to Berlusconi, while Claudio Martelli, a well-known Socialist deputy during the Craxi era, anchored *L'incudine*, which gave a very

generous form of hospitality to Berlusconi, letting him use his own personal director and a whole team of media advisers.

20 Continuing the approach inaugurated in 1994 by her husband (another popular actor), Sandra Mondaini joined the fray with an interview on *Verissimo*, a gossip programme broadcast by Canale 5. She said: 'He is a man who must be known in order to love him. And being in a free country, I say it: I love Berlusconi very much'.

21 La7 is a small but well-respected TV company that at present is owned by Telecom Italia Media. Together with Mtv it represents the so-called Third Pole of the Italian television system.

References

Annunziata, L. (2006), 'La sinistra e il paese che non c'è', *La Stampa*, 1 April, p. 12.

Blumenthal S. (1980), *The Permanent Campaign*, New York, Simon and Schuster.

Blumler, J. and Kavanagh, D. (1999), 'The third age of political communication: influences and features', in *Political Communication*, 16:3, 209–230.

Campus, D. (2000), *L'elettore pigro. Informazione politica e scelte di voto*, Bologna, Il Mulino.

Ceccarelli, F. (1999), 'Adesso in tv conta soltanto chi se ne va', *La Stampa*, 7 June, p. 6.

Cornia, A. (2006), 'La rimonta di Berlusconi, tra glaciazione dell'elettorato ed effetti della televisione', paper presented to the annual conference of the Società Italiana di Scienza Politica, University of Bologna, 12–14 September.

D'Alimonte, R. (2003), 'Mixed electoral rules, partisan realignment, and party system change in Italy', in M. S. Shugart and M. P. Wattenberg (eds), *Mixed-Member Electoral Systems. The Best of Both Worlds?*, Oxford, Oxford University Press.

Davi, K. (2006), 'Tv, l'Unione nella trappola del Cavaliere', *La Stampa*, 1 March.

Feltri, M. (2006), 'L'ex antipatico che ha riaperto una partita chiusa', *La Stampa*, 1 April, p. 5.

Feltrin, P. (2006), 'La partecipazione elettorale', in R. Mannheimer and P. Natale (eds), *L'Italia a metà. Dentro il voto del paese diviso*, Milano, Cairo Publishing.

Guerzoni, M. (2006), 'Diliberto: caro Romano, a me Matrix ha portato 1500 nuovi iscritti', *Corriere della Sera*, 28 March, p. 6.

Hallin, D. C. and Mancini, P. (2004), *Comparing Media Systems. Three Models of Media and Politics*, Cambridge, Cambridge University Press.

Istituto Cattaneo (2006), 'Elezioni politiche 2006 – L'affluenza alle urne non è cresciuta', http://www.istcattaneo.org/pubblicazioni/analisi/pdf/Analisi _Cattaneo_ Affluenza_2006_(13_aprile_2006).pdf (accessed on 15 July 2006).

Kernell, S. (1986), *Going Public: New Strategies of Presidential Leadership*, Washington, DC C.Q. Press.

Mannheimer, R. (2001), 'Le elezioni del 2001 e la "mobilitazione drammatizzante"', *Rivista Italiana di Scienza Politica*, 31:3, 543–560 [now also in G. Pasquino (ed.) (2002), *Dall'Ulivo al governo Berlusconi*, Bologna, Il Mulino].

Mannheimer, R. (2006), 'La mobilitazione della "Terza Italia" politica', in R. Mannheimer and P. Natale (eds), *L'Italia a metà. Dentro il voto del paese diviso*, Milano, Cairo Publishing.

Marletti, C. (1984), *Media e politica*, Milano, F. Angeli.

Marletti, C. (2000), 'Elezioni europee e campagna permanente. Una discussione dei primi risultati di ricerca', *Comunicazione politica*, 1:2, 169–180.

Marletti, C. and Roncarolo, F. (2000), 'Media influence in the Italian transition from a consensual to a majoritarian democracy', in R. Gunther and A. Mughan (eds), *Democracy and the Media: A Comparative Perspective*, New York, Cambridge University Press.

Mazzoleni, G. (ed.) (2004), 'Il grande comunicatore. Dieci anni di Berlusconi sulla ribalta politica', special issue of *Comunicazione politica*, 1:5.

Mazzoni, M. (2006), '"Chi vince e chi perde". Un modo per influenzare il clima di opinione', paper presented to the annual conference of the Società Italiana di Scienza Politica, University of Bologna, 12–14 September.

Mieli, P. (2006), 'La scelta del 9 aprile', *Corriere della Sera*, 8 March, p. 1.

Natale, P. (2002), 'Una fedeltà leggera: i movimenti di voto nella "Seconda Repubblica"', in R. D'Alimonte and S. Bartolini (eds), *Maggioritario finalmente? La transizione eletorale 1994–2001*, Bologna, Il Mulino.

Newell, J. L. (2006), 'The Italian election of 2006: myths and realities', *West European Politics*, 29:4, 802–813.

Newell, J. L. and Bull, M. J. (2001), 'The Italian General Election of May 2001', Keele European Parties Research Unit (KEPRU) Working Paper no. 4, Keele University.

Newman, B. (1994), *The Marketing of the President: Political Marketing as Campaign Strategy*, Thousand Oaks, CA, Sage.

Noelle–Neumann, E. (1993), *The spiral of silence. Public Opinion – Our Social Skin*, Chicago, University of Chicago Press.

Noelle-Neumann, E. and Petersen, T. (2004), 'The spiral of silence and the social nature of man', in L. L. Kaid (ed.), *Handbook of Political Communication Research*, Mahwah, NJ, and London, Lawrence, Erlbaum Associates.

Reif, K. and Schmitt, H. (1980), 'Nine second order national elections: a conceptual framework for the analysis of European election results', *European Journal of Political Research*, 1:8, 3–44.

Ricolfi, L. (2005), 'Programmismo, contrattismo', *La Stampa*, 5 December, p. 1.

Roncarolo, F. (2002), 'Virtual clashes and political games' in J. L. Newell (ed.), *The Italian General Election of 2001. Berlusconi's Victory*, Manchester, Manchester University Press.

Roncarolo, F. (2005), 'Campaigning and governing. An analysis of Berlusconi's rhetorical leadership', *Modern Italy*, 1:10, 75–94.

Santagata, G. (2006), *La fabbrica del programma. Dieci anni di Ulivo verso il Partito democratico*, Rome, Donzelli.

Santalmassi, G. (2006), 'Se il Cavaliere buca lo schermo', *Il Sole 24 Ore*, 29 January, p. 6.

Scalfari, E. (2006), 'Perché Berlinguer è di nuovo attuale', *La Repubblica*, 31 December, p. 1.

Siliato, F. (2006), 'Vince la star, anzi il gioco di sguadra', *Il Sole 24 Ore*, 23 January, p. 2.

Vassallo, S. (2006), 'Le elezioni regionali. Quando vincere troppo può essere dannoso', in G. Amyot and L. Verzichelli (eds), *Politica in Italia. I fatti dell'anno e le interpretazioni*, Bologna, Il Mulino.

9

Italian elections online: ten years on

Wainer Lusoli, Rachel Gibson and Stephen Ward

Introduction

This chapter examines the use of the Internet by Italian parties and candidates in the 2006 general election using data drawn from the candidates themselves as well as systematic content analysis of party websites. The key question posed is the extent to which Italian parties managed to exploit the potential of the online campaign more fully, ten years after their web debut in 1996. Accounts of their performance in 2001 did not give cybercampaigners many reasons to be cheerful, the parties being roundly criticised for their failure to utilise the immediacy and interactivity of the new medium (Gibson *et al.*, 2002). More creative uses surfaced in the 2004 European elections, however, with the Left Democrats establishing an online volunteer centre, and again in 2005 when Fausto Bertinotti, a candidate for the leadership of the Unione, set up a fully interactive site to boost his primary election campaign. In addition to these obvious signs of an increasing interest in web campaigning, the changing institutional context in Italy across the past decade has arguably created a fertile environment for parties to adopt more adventurous campaigning techniques. The apparent shift to a more presidentialised and personalised system of elections and wider use of the Internet among the public means that parties and individual politicians may be more alert to the opportunities it presents for targeted and individualised communication.

In order to assess the current maturity of Internet campaigning in Italy this chapter is divided into three main sections. First we review recent changes in the political communication environment as a backdrop to the rise of Internet campaigning. Second, we examine the key claims about the contribution of the Internet to political campaigns, both in general and in relation to recent Italian elections. Finally, we trace the development of online campaigning in Italy and present our findings for the 2006 election. We conclude by placing the findings in the wider context of the shifting campaign context and the rise of the so-called 'third age' or post-modern era of political communication. How far does online campaigning in Italy contribute to broader changes in political message transmission taking place elsewhere in the world?

Changing political communications

There is wide agreement that Italian political communication is in transition, following the 'thawing' of the First Republic's political-media complex after the events of 1994. Inherent tensions between party-based and candidate-based forms of electoral campaigning are acute in Italy. On the one hand, there are evident signs of 'Americanisation' of the Italian political process (Pasquino, 2005). It has been claimed that Italian party organisations are in decline, leading to a more candidate-centred type of electoral politics. This, in turn, opens up the space for business interests to try to shape public policy outside the electoral circuit (Hopkin, 2005). More money, both public and private, is now available to Italian parties to spend more freely, with fewer constraints and controls (Della Porta, 2001). Alternatively, the participation of Italian magistrates in the legislative process, their almost militant activism, and the related tendency to arouse political controversy and their capacity to exercise a power of judicial review further subtracts representative blood from the traditional institutional vessels (Newell, 2001). Institutionally, the results of the reconfiguration of party financing, party structures, the rise of the candidates' star and the perceived 'judicialisation' of the polity place Italy in a hybrid ground between the European and American models of partisan democracy.

Political processes have also changed considerably since 1996. The introduction of mayoral campaigns for large cities such as Rome and Milan (Mazzoleni, 1996) and the first ever primary elections held for selection of the leader of the centre left (16 October 2005), are a clear example of the unfolding of a mixed party/candidate model. The October 2005 primaries in particular had unexpected consequences regarding citizen mobilisation and involvement across traditional party channels (see chapter 1; Valbruzzi, 2005). It was argued that the Italian political system is in fact undergoing a process of Americanisation by selective imitation, adaptation and reversals, rather than as a result of longer-term endemic change (Pasquino, 2005). In this process, of course, the structures and praxis of political communication matter greatly. The mediatisation of politics, along with the declining significance of social cleavages, are partly responsible for the 'presidentialisation' of the Italian political system (Calise, 2005), which in turn feeds even more personalisation of political issues and polarisation of the opinion climate, within and across electoral cycles (Campus and Pasquino, 2006). It is true that personality politics has come to the fore in Italy to an unprecedented extent. This is a trend that originated in Italy in the early 1980s; before then, the media did not probe politicians' personal lives and opinions to any significant extent (Roncarolo, 2004). Since 2001, the increasingly 'informal' nature of Berlusconi's premiership has come to epitomise the incipient blurring of the lines between public and personal life. The prominence of personality is reflected in the increasing orientation of Italian voters towards party and coalition leaders, who have become a major object of political and electoral evaluation for an increasing proportion of the electorate, estimated at about 20 per cent (Barisione, 2005). According to Barisione, however, it is still very difficult to disentangle ideology from personality, and personal votes for the leader, from medium-term identification. More in-depth research suggests that personality and ideology, electoral organisation and communication surface and blur in novel – some claim, post-modern – ways (Grandi and Vaccari, 2004).

In this context, the distinction between majoritarian versus consensual campaigning rationales (Roncarolo, 2002) loses part of its power to explain variance in electoral communications. While it is true that Italy has moved from a largely consensual to a more combative political communication environment, also due to the parallel transition of the political system, the outcomes of the transition are far from clear (Roncarolo, 2004). There are many unresolved tensions between the two models. Beyond the themes highlighted, three more 'anomalies' are worth noting with regard to the 2006 election. First, although television has become the dominant electoral arena, politics has an even higher degree of control of private and public service broadcasting today than in the days of the First Republic. The Gasparri Law, approved in May 2004, aimed at increasing pluralism in the media system, does very little to fragment existing media concentration in the broadcast sector (Haraszti, 2005). Furthermore, the broadcast system, it is commonly suggested, unfairly favours the centre-right coalition. Second, the dramatic change in electoral law just months before the elections further exacerbated the tension between candidate-based and party-based styles of campaigning. In short, it encouraged *partitocrazia*, minor candidate apathy and major candidates' prominence (chapter 1), moving away from the mixed majority/proportional model first used in 1994. Finally, the law regulating electoral communication, approved in February 2000 and known as '*par condicio*', did not prevent the saturation of the media-electoral space by the centre-right coalition. The dispute between Berlusconi and President Ciampi prior to the election regarding the date when the chambers would be dissolved, and the *par condicio* kick in, rested on the desire of the centre right to shorten the formal campaign to avoid fair competition.

The Internet and elections

The contradictions in the system of political communication in Italy go well beyond the usual argument concerning the 'Italian anomaly', and touch upon the unfinished transition between a consensual and a majority model of political communications (Roncarolo, 2002). Others have argued that this is not simply a transition, but rather the inception of a new mode of political communication that blurs the lines between pre-modern and modern campaigns (Blumler and Kavanagh, 1999; Norris, 2001). In this scenario, it has been claimed that new information technologies, particularly the Internet, have an important role to play. Cyber politics is seen as a central aspect of the 'third age', as it reflects the intensified professionalisation, centrifugal diversification and fragmentation of the audience associated with a changing communications landscape (Blumler and Kavanagh, 1999). The claim is that the Internet has contributed to an increasingly direct, segmented and interactive electoral repertoire of parties as campaign organisations. As Farrell and Webb (2000: 105) argue, 'the third main stage of campaign professionalisation can be seen to have coincided with the arrival of new telecommunications technology'.

Most research on online elections has focused on two main aspects of 'the new media age' – pluralism and citizen engagement (Lusoli, 2005a; Ward, 2005). The former debate concerns familiar equalisation versus normalisation theses. The main point of contention is whether the Internet increases resource-poor, third-party and challenger candidates' chances of electoral success. While early research points towards 'equalisation' (Fielding and Duritz, 2001; Greer and LaPointe, 2001), later studies pointed to better chances for large-party, resource-rich incumbents (D'Alessio, 2000; Stromer-Galley *et al.*, 2001). In a range of countries, mainstream parties outperformed 'minority' parties in terms of site presence and sophistication (Davis, 1999; Margolis and Resnick, 2000; Bentivegna, 2002).

The capacity of the Internet to engage, rather than just inform, citizens is also under scrutiny. Unlike traditional media, interactive campaigns are consumer-driven rather than producer-driven (Harpham, 1999), possibly complementing traditional strategies. The Internet, it is claimed, tilts the political communications field from a vertical to a horizontal orientation: co-production may challenge producers' control of political messages; the release of creative energies favours dissident thought, while 'viral' mobilisation allows citizens to activate other citizens (Schneider and Foot, 2002). The concept of interactivity is thus strongly linked to the distinction between 'electronic democracy' where citizens can talk back to the campaign, and 'electronic marketing', which implies managed, unidirectional communication to the citizen-consumer (Miani, 2002). The number of campaign web sites offering interactivity and the full range of services – e-mail feedback, online discussion boards, blogs – have greatly expanded over time. However, most online campaigns are not yet truly interactive, and citizens often opt out of interactivity in favour of efficiency of delivery (Lusoli and Ward, 2005).

Online elections in Italy, 1996–2006

Most major Italian parties set foot in cyberspace between 1995 and 1996, with newer and smaller parties following shortly thereafter (Mosca, 2002). As De Rosa (2000: 11) noted, the 1996 Italian elections witnessed 'the debut of political communication on the Internet'. New media were quickly embraced by Italian parties in an attempt to surf, or survive, the 'renovation' wave pervading the system (Bentivegna, 1999). Or, more mundanely, they started to set up web sites in order to 'keep up with the Jones's' (Newell, 2001). There is general agreement that the first Italian election online, in 2001, was a disappointment: just one in ten Chamber candidates had a functioning web site, while 17 per cent of Senate hopefuls set one up (Bentivegna, 2001). Overall, the figure was a mere 13 per cent. Candidates from major parties in the centre-left and centre-right coalitions tended to dominate the online election, accounting for almost 90 per cent of all election websites. While candidates did relatively well in providing baseline information about themselves, and re-packaged to a large extent material created for the offline campaign, mobilisation was lacking; most relevant mobilisation features, for instance joining or downloading material, were present on about or below 10 per cent of websites (Bentivegna, 2001). A further, in-depth study of candidates in the Bologna province found that only 14 per cent of candidates had a website, divided equally between the two coalitions (Miani, 2002). Most sites were a conduit for one-off publishing of essential information on the candidate, rather than providing a steady source of communication. The sites attempted negligible mobilisation and fund-raising. Moreover, third-party candidates had no web sites, let alone interactive ones, although according to interview data, the national party website was an important medium for third-party campaigns. Overall, the data support a 'limited marketing' model of the use of the Internet for election purposes.

In terms of parties, there were some signs of levelling of the online playing field in 2001; although the largest two parties were more visible online, all small parties surveyed had web sites, which were listed in open directories and linked to relatively frequently from the wider net (Gibson *et al.*, 2002). On the margins, however, much smaller parties made very limited use of the Internet, creating static web sites that may have hindered, rather than assisted, their campaign efforts. Regardless of size, position or coalition, information provision and outward linkage to the web were the main aspects of all sites; conversely, voter and resource mobilisation, and participation scored much lower across party websites. Strikingly, these results reflect closely those of a previous survey of Italian parties, conducted in non-electoral times (Bartali, 2000). There were, however, signs of numerical improvement at the 2004 European parliament election. Miani (2004) shows that 251 of 995 candidates from relatively large parties ran an election web site, about 25 per cent of the total. Furthermore, there was a significant gap between major and minor parties and coalitions. About 72 per cent of candidates from the centre-left coalition (Lista Prodi – Uniti nell'Ulivo) were online; Forza Italia's candidates scored 54 per cent, while the Greens had 38 per cent and two centre parties, the UDC and UDEUR, had 30 per cent. Candidates from other parties were well below the one-in-four average. Therefore, Miani (2004: 5) argues, only candidates from major parties were really competing on a personal basis, many of them being 'prominent political leaders, or incumbents from various offices already endowed with some sort of on line presence'; smaller parties' candidates largely ran more compactly, under the party banner. Finally, while information prevails over participation features in most election websites, parties were head-and-shoulders above the competi-tion, including individual candidates, in providing interactive, engagement opportunities.

Nevertheless, most studies point to the lack of relevance of the Internet for election purposes, due to citizens' unwillingness to use it as a source of electoral information. In 2001, only 8 per cent of the population used the Internet to access electoral information. Three years later, data for the 2004 European Parliament elections found that Italians were less likely than other EU25 citizens (except for Greeks), to access campaign information online, both in absolute terms (5 per cent) and controlling for socio-demographics, political interest and activity and, crucially, Internet access (Lusoli, 2005b). As Italian citizens are no less interested in EU elections than their EU25 counterparts (possibly more so), it seems safe to conclude that Italians are near the bottom of the European Internet adoption league for electoral purposes.

Research questions and methodology

Based on our examination of the literature on online campaigning, we are mainly interested in four interrelated themes: First, what was the extent of online activity amongst candidates and political parties in 2006, and how does it compare with previous elections? Second, what are the patterns of competition online – that is, who and how many parties had live web sites for the election? Was cyberspace dominated by mainstream party candidates? Did candidates play a role, or was it parties that monopolised the online campaign? Third, how effective were campaign web sites as a campaign communication tool? Were any new, innovative, forms of campaigning developed? Finally, can online campaigning in the 2006 Italian election be related to wider systemic trends in Italian political communications?

To examine these issues, we conducted an in-depth feature analysis of 24 party websites. Although there were 37 parties fielded in 27 constituencies (one uninominal), our list included all members of the centre-left and the centre-right coalitions in addition to other national parties presented in most constituencies (Appendix 1). A feature analysis coding scheme was constructed based on similar party surveys conducted in the past, in Italy and elsewhere (Appendix 2) (Gibson *et al.*, 2002). Along with baseline data on party, date of coding and visibility online (using Google in-links), the coding scheme included multiple measures for: static information provision; dynamic information provision (such as RSS feeds, blogs and podcasts); provision for electoral discussion and campaign talk-back (such as discussion boards, WIKI and party email); provision for vertical mobilisation (such as facilities for making donations) and horizontal campaigning. The scheme also included measures for modes and sophistication of message delivery online (such as the presence of audio and video). Only one wave of coding was conducted, two weeks before the election; multiple waves were ruled out because previous studies suggested that features hardly changed at all during the campaign (Gibson *et al.*, 2002; Miani, 2002).

Additionally, we conducted a numerical survey of candidates' election web sites, to understand how many went online from which parties. Official sources' web sites (those of the Ministry of the Interior and the regions) and party web sites were used to compile an inventory of all candidates at the election. Overall, there were 10,492 candidacies in 27 districts, and 8,571 individual candidates.[1] Three main strategies were adopted to find website addresses. First, party websites and specialised directories (for instance www.ilcandidato.it) were browsed to identify candidate websites. Second, URLs were generated using candidate name and surname, for a range of Internet domains (.it, .com, .info), for candidates without a web site after phase one. This additional crop, including a large proportion of 'lay', non-electoral sites was then parsed to check existence; entries were added if electoral content was found. Third, when neither of these strategies yielded valid results, we conducted automated Google searches for every candidate using the search string ["name surname" + candidato + elezioni politiche + 2006]. The first ten results per search were examined to ensure they contained electoral information and appended to the data sheet. The resulting data sheet contained 572 candidate web sites; these were visited manually to ensure that they were genuine candidate web sites. This process left 551 valid candidate web sites.[2]

The online election in 2006: results

The first, remarkable result is the scarcity of candidate web sites, outside coalition and party leaders and prominent candidates. Only about 550, or 6.5 per cent of all candidates, had a functioning website at the election, while all parties had a web presence. We found a predominance of large parties' candidates over small parties' in terms of web presence: 11 versus 4 per cent. Also, candidates for northern and central Italy (8.5 per cent) were more likely to set up web sites than candidates in the south (5.2 per cent). Although, it will be argued, this may be explained away by the relative importance the Internet had for the two coalitions, it may also depend on the greater Internet penetration in the north. In terms of the two coalitions, the centre left leads the centre right, as the Unione had one-third more candidates with an online presence than the Cdl. Finally, a small contingent of candidates had functioning weblogs, or blogs; these are online campaign diaries that allow visitors to leave feedback on the site, and to link directly to the candidate from their own web sites. Antonio Di Pietro, Antonio

Bassolino and Dario Franceschini all had relatively well-maintained, interactive blogs where they posted messages throughout the campaign. Some blogs were written on behalf of the candidate, as in the case of Gianfranco Fini (http://fini2006.splinder.com), while other candidates appeared to provide most of the content, and the interaction with readers, as in the case of Di Pietro (www.antonio dipietro.com/index.html). Overall, the number of candidates with functioning web sites decreased from 2001 and 2004. Partly, this can be explained by the much larger number of candidates at this election, and the much smaller number of candidates with a realistic chance of being elected, given their positions on their parties' lists. On the other hand, there was very little incentive for candidates to seek to gain a personal profile, as their names were not shown on the ballot and a personal preference could not be indicated. Furthermore, B- and C-list candidates were chosen late on, with very little time, just weeks, to set up and advertise their web presence. The combination of these factors proved a killer-blow for the importance of the Internet as a campaign tool in 2006, at least at candidate level.

Slightly more positive results emerge from the analysis of online campaign strategies at party level. With regard to party web sites, once again the provision of campaign information superseded all other website features (Table 9.1). In aggregate, parties score 8.7 on the 0–14 scale of possible information features. While basic information on party structure, ideology and policies was available on most sites, information directly related to the campaign (candidate profiles, campaign diaries, speeches) was surprisingly scarce on smaller parties' web sites. On the other hand, the three top web sites in the overall index – Forza Italia, the DS and the Margherita – came close to offering the full range of static information services included in our coding scheme, including a campaign calendar, a diary, voting information,

Table 9.1 Features of Italian parties' websites at the 2006 election

	Score	Range
Static information	8.7	0–14
Dynamic information	2.3	0–6
Discussion tools	2.2	0–7
Vertical mobilisation	2.5	0–5
Horizontal mobilisation	1.4	0–4
Sophistication	1.7	0–7
Total index of campaign potential	19	43

Note: Figures are average values for the entire sample, n = 24.

Table 9.2 Content indicators by party

	Static information	Dynamic information	Discussion/ talk-back	Vertical mobilisation	Horizontal mobilisation	Sophistication
Forza Italia	13	4	4	4	3	4
Margherita	12	5	4	5	2	3
DS	12	5	3	4	3	4
Greens	11	3	4	4	3	3
Italia dei Valori	11	3	2	2	2	2
la Rosa nel Pugno	10	3	2	3	2	2
Radicals	10	3	2	3	1	3
PdCI	9	2	3	3	2	2
AN	10	2	2	3	3	2
Tricoloured Flame	9	1	3	2	1	1
RC	9	3	3	3	2	2
UDC	8	2	2	2	1	1
UDEUR	9	1	2	3	0	1
DC	9	2	2	2	1	1
Northern League	8	2	2	3	1	2
European Republican Movement	8	3	1	2	0	2
Fronte Sociale Nazionale	8	1	1	2	1	1
New PSI	6	2	3	1	0	1
SDI	7	1	1	2	1	2
Pensioners	7	1	2	2	2	1
Azione Sociale	7	2	1	2	0	1
MPA	5	1	1	1	1	0
PRI	6	2	0	1	1	1
Rauti	5	2	2	2	1	0
Average	8.7	2.3	2.2	2.5	1.4	1.7

Note: Figures are index values per individual party.

speeches and a whole range of services that transcend those available to citizens through the traditional media. In these cases, there is a deliberate attempt at harnessing the full potential of the Internet for propaganda purposes. Smaller, 'lifestyle' parties, such as la Rosa nel Pugno, and the Greens, follow closely, demonstrating that the web can be a cost-effective way of raising issues with large audiences.

However, even on the sites of major parties, more advanced ways of disseminating information – ones that are continuous and integrated with other media (news feeds) or the wider web (RSS) – are much less widespread, the sites scoring on average 2.3 on a maximum of 6. With some exceptions (such as, for instance, the site of the DS), there was no attempt to engage with younger audiences by producing podcasts for users to download to their MP3 players or by sending SMS messages with the 'soundbite' of the day. Most web sites, however, contained contact information in the form of e-mail; a large proportion (more than four in five) had some form of subscription e-newsletter, to which users could subscribe to follow the campaign more closely. Surprisingly, a responsiveness test revealed that hardly any campaigns (again, with exceptions: Prodi, the Greens and the DC) responded to specific or general enquiries using e-mail (Smargiassi, 2006). Overall, even if web sites are updated pretty frequently, on average once or twice a week for the sample, we are far from the 24/7 campaign witnessed during the 2004 US presidential campaign.

When we consider engagement, rather than information, some more marked differences emerge between web sites in the top tier and basic web sites. A range of free, easy tools are now available to parties, in the shape of blogs, WIKIs, discussion boards, chat rooms and the traditional letter-to-editor format, allowing users and voters to talk back to the campaign. The overall average for the discussion indicator, 2.2 over 7, conceals significant differences. While the sites of FI, the Margherita and the Greens featured a variety of channels that allow users to contribute, the websites of a large contingent of parties, such as the PRI, the Movimento per l'Autonomia (Movement for Autonomy; MPA), Azione Sociale, the SDI and the Fronte Sociale Nazionale, did not contain even the basic element of interactivity. It is striking that a number of parties who had a serious chance of being in government – such as the Northern League, the PdCI, the UDC and AN – did not strive to appear more engaged with their voters in the course of the campaign. Similarly, one of the most important claims about the new media is that they can help parties and organisations to mobilise supporters and, what is more, allow supporters to mobilise themselves, thus lightening the organisational burden. Results are much lower for mobilisation of either type (about 4 over a maximum 9), than for information (see Table 9.2). However, most parties were much better at using the Net to mobilise their supporters directly, by offering the chance to volunteer, donate and join (good examples include the Margherita, the DS and the Greens) than they were at allowing supporters to get organised (again, the exception here is AN).

In broader, comparative perspective, there are some interesting findings regarding party size, coalition and online content and visibility. Three main trends are worth noting here. First, the six scales of online election performance are strongly correlated with each other (see Table 9.3); exploratory factor analysis suggested that they could be reduced to a single factor, accounting for 74 per cent of the variance in online campaign features.[3] In other words, web sites that are good in

Table 9.3 Correlations between party website indicators

Sophistication	Static	Dynamic information	Discussion information/talk-back	Vertical mobilisation	Horizontal mobilisation	mobilisation
Static information	1	.73 (**)	.67 (**)	.84 (**)	.67 (**)	.86 (**)
Dynamic information		1	.56 (**)	.72 (**)	.52 (**)	.80 (**)
Discussion/ talk-back			1	.72 (**)	.57 (**)	.58 (**)
Vertical mobilisation				1	.64 (**)	.80 (**)
Horizontal mobilisation					1	.64 (**)
Sophistication						1

Note: ** marks significant Pearson correlations at $p < 0.01$ (2-tailed).

Table 9.4 Website content by party size, mean index scores

	Size of party			
	Very small	Small	Medium	Large
Static information	6.9	**9.7**	8.3	**11.8**
Dynamic information	1.4	**2.7**	2.3	**4.0**
Discussion/talk-back	1.6	2.3	2.3	**3.3**
Vertical mobilisation	1.8	2.7	2.7	**4.0**
Horizontal mobilisation	.8	1.6	1.3	**2.8**
Sophistication	.9	**2.1**	1.7	**3.3**
Total index	13.4	**21.1**	18.6	**29.2**
Number of links in	90	655	629	825

Notes: Figures are index values by party size. Results in bold are significantly different from the overall average [$p < 0.05$]. Party size is defined in endnote 4.

one respect are also very likely to score highly in other respects. This also implies that 'what you see is what you get', and that relatively little valuable content is hidden. Second, it is not necessarily large parties that are able to fund and staff sophisticated online campaigns (see Table 9.4). On the one hand, it is true that large parties[4] – FI, the DS, the Margherita, AN – are significantly more likely to top the chart in terms of information, engagement and sophistication. Web sites belonging to large parties such as Forza Italia, the DS and the Margherita are significantly more likely to outperform other web sites on all indicators: information, discussion, mobilisation and total campaign value. However, small, 'radical' parties are more likely than medium-sized parties to provide informative and sophisticated web sites, and overall a better online campaign experience. This can be explained by reference to the exceptional performance (relative to their size) of la Rosa nel Pugno, the Greens and Italia dei Valori. Furthermore, the most notable result is that 'very small' parties fail to deliver altogether in terms of the new media. Whether they fail to reach the critical dimension that allows an organisation to produce and maintain an effective campaign website is a hypothesis that needs further testing; certainly, they appeared 'too thin to win' on the web in 2006. Third, there are a number of significant differences between centre-left and centre-right parties in terms of online performance. Specifically, centre-left parties were better on the counts of static information, vertical mobilisation and sophistication. No significant differences were found concerning more innovative uses of the web. Having said that, it is not traditional left parties, but rather mainstream parties and 'lifestyle' parties that out-powered the opposition; the relative lack of such centrist parties and the long ideological tail of the centre-right (numerically) also helps explain this result.

Discussion and conclusions

Overall, it may safely be claimed that the Internet played a marginal but significant role in the 2006 election. What is striking is the integration of the Internet into the political communications structure of contemporary Italy. Parties and candidates alike used the new media rationally – that is, very much in line with the opportunity structures and constraints of the Internet as an election medium. Unfortunately, for those who hope that the new media can advance the role citizens play at election time, beyond casting their ballots, this had depressing consequences. Candidates made hardly any use of the Internet, and only parties and party leaders with a clear incentive to diversify into the digital domain clearly did so. The change in the electoral law prompted by the Berlusconi government in the months leading to the election, which restored proportional representation, suggests that candidates may not be prominent online. Increasing evidence suggests that electoral law matters in the extent to which candidates go online in Anglo-Saxon countries, the UK, the US and Australia (Gibson *et al.*, 2003), as well as in the context of EU Parliament elections (Jankowski *et al.*, 2005). In 'open' systems, candidates have a clear incentive to set up digital election platforms; conversely, in closed-list systems, where candidates are 'parachuted' into large electoral districts, there are no evident advantages for candidates to focus on marginal or personal votes. Yet, if the reasons candidates create web sites relate to their technological inclinations, the availability of IT resources and support at the local level (Miani, 2002), then a change in the electoral law itself is not likely to yield any positive effects. Indeed, the absence of candidates can also be explained by the lack of 'new' candidates at the election. The 2006 election saw the highest number of incumbent MPs standing for election and the highest incumbency (post-hoc) since 1994 (chapter 11, this volume). Old hands have much less of an incentive to set up web sites than candidates new to the arena. Although in some countries incumbents are better placed than challengers to set up an online campaign, this is clearly not the case in Italy. To make matters worse, the lack of electronic responsiveness of Italian politicians is truly remarkable, as Italian MPs are less likely than any other EU MPs to respond to e-mail enquiries, except their Polish counterparts, at 7 per cent (Trechsel *et al.*, 2003). The apparent lack of engagement by election candidates and parties with new media is put in starker perspective by the activities of social movements and extremist networks online.

Ten years after the introduction of the Internet for campaigns in Italy, superficially the picture seems to have changed only marginally; however, there are a number of qualifying notes indicating possible avenues for change in the future. First, the Internet is not, as yet, ingrained in the oligopolistic logic of the Italian media system and the way in which parties adapt to it. In the context of the wider media campaign, there were two distinct strategies adopted by the centre-left and the centre-right coalitions. The communications strategy of the first was rooted in the territory, and based on the government's track record; the second was a largely media campaign, based on emotional appeals (Campus, 2006). Although we would have expected the web to reflect these differences, it most definitely did not. Neither were more mobilisation features available on centre-right sites, nor was more detailed programme information available on the sites of the centre left. The web largely followed endogenous dynamics, linked to parties' cultural and financial resources, and incentives. In terms of the integration of online and offline campaigns, the online campaign obtained very little coverage in the mainstream national press, and close to no coverage on television. Having to compete with a very integrated media system, which currently does not encompass the Internet despite the provisions of the Gasparri Law, the election online struggled to achieve any significant prominence.

Second, the Internet clearly has a large potential to equalise the electoral playing field. Our results suggest an interesting comparison between the Internet and other media with respect to electoral rules. Whereas the broadcast media allocated a 'majority premium' to large coalitions and to the top candidates, especially Berlusconi, and the space devoted in the printed press to candidates was largely proportional to the strengths of individual parties in electoral terms, the Internet largely complied with the spirit, if not the letter (as it is to date unregulated), of the *par condicio* rules. Ironically, however, whereas media access of the traditional sort requires little more than a spokesperson, readily available in the ranks of any party, an (effective) Internet web site seems to require resources that are out of the reach of very small parties, and not committed by medium-sized, traditional parties. These resources were, however, available to small 'radical' parties, who found a favourable battleground on the Internet.

Third, with regard to citizen engagement, perhaps we are looking in the wrong place (Lusoli, 2005a). A number of alternative spaces, beyond party web sites, were available on the Internet for those who wanted to follow the election. For instance, a large number of web sites, blogs and discussions sprang up following Berlusconi's infamous remark about centre-left voters. Speaking at the conference of Confcommercio, the association representing the interests of trade and commerce, Berlusconi claimed he did not believe that Italian voters were such '*coglioni*' (variously translated in the English-language press as jerks, idiots and assholes) as to vote against their interests. The website 'Sono un coglione' (http://sonouncoglione.splinder.com) is only one of the dozen or more websites that allowed tens of thousands of people to 'come out' as '*coglioni*', to organise rallies, to download material, to buy '*coglione*' merchandise, and to spread the gospel. The website, according to its founders, attracted the pledges of about 100,000 people. This was very much in the spirit of the 'Girotondi' and of the independent, 'subversive' use made of the Internet by the 'No Global' movement. Perhaps, these are the loci where people are willing to engage in politics – that is, politics of a 'lighter' kind. Furthermore, a number of websites (such as www.chivotare.it, www.voisietequi.it, www.elezioni.it/demandi) allowed more than one million people to test their party positions by answering a range of questions about current affairs. Such preference locators, which harness the dynamic information potential of the Internet, have been common in other countries over the last year, and seemed to make a breakthrough in the 2006 Italian campaign.

Fourth, there is a reasonable expectation that the regulatory framework in Italy may be conducive to innovation in the digital domain. Today, e-democracy constitutes one of the five main pillars of the Italian e-government project, launched in 2004 by the Department for Innovation and Technology.[5] Between June 2005 and the election, 57 e-democracy projects were approved for government funding.[6] In particular, the historical importance in Italy of the 'civic' model of e-democracy, whereby local authorities and not-for-profit organisations play a central role in promoting citizen online engagement (Tsagarousianou *et al.*, 1998), suggests different outcomes for digital-isation of the social contract (Tedeschi, 2005) than are predicted in most other advanced industrial democracies. Rather than facilitating the construction of direct, deliberative or communitarian democracy, or the new citizen-consumer via technological means, citizens are at the centre of complex fluxes of political and public communication under the rubric of managerial/continuous democracy (Calise and De Rosa, 2003). In this scenario, 'virtual' or cyber-parties have an important linkage function to play, through the articulation and aggregation of citizens' electoral and non-electoral preferences (Lusoli and Ward, 2004; Margetts, 2005). And, the lack of party and candidate engage-ment in closed-list systems may be misplaced. Citizens of countries that are more advanced on the digital ladder are more likely to go online to search campaign information, regardless of the electoral law (Lusoli, 2005b).

Finally, the previous combined majority/proportional system ensured that both candidate and party campaign logics coexisted, acti-vating at the same time specific locally based constituencies with the tools of 'post-modern' campaigning and the larger electorate via tradi-tional persuasion/mobilisation techniques (Plasser and Plasser, 2002). This makes it is hard to compare the 2006 online campaigns in Italy both to recent ones in countries with a majority system, and to the previous 2001 Italian election. To date, our evidence suggests that the Internet reflected the greater prominence that leading candidates from a range of parties enjoyed in the campaign, perhaps tilting the political communication field more in favour of candidates other than Berlusconi, who monopolised both television and the press.

Notes

1 The difference between the number of 'candidacies' and the number of 'candidates' is, of course, explained by the tendency of at least the larger parties to field some of their flagship candidates in more than one constituency – in some cases many more than one: see chapter 11.
2 While we envisaged carrying out a basic feature analysis of candidates' websites, the small number found advised against committing resources to the task.
3 PCA with Varimax rotation, 6 items, .40 threshold for commonality.
4 Party size is defined, according to ex-post electoral result, as the percentage of the total vote received in the Senate contest. Parties receiving 10 per cent or more (four parties) were labelled 'large'; those receiving between 4 and 10 per cent (three parties) were labelled 'medium'; those receiving between 2 and 4 per cent (seven parties), 'small'; those receiving below 2 per cent (ten parties), 'very small'. Although this measure is less than ideal, it gives a relatively robust indication of party size.
5 Ministero per l'Innovazione e le Tecnologie, see www.innovazionepa .gov.it.
6 See www.crcitalia.it/e_government_fase_2/e_democracy. A number of papers at the 2006 annual conference of the Italian Political Science Society (SISP) examine preliminary results from a number of these projects (www.sisp.it/sisp_convegnoannuale_overview .asp).

References

Barisione, M. (2005), 'Il leader politico: star mediatica, euristica apolitica?', paper presented to the 19th annual conference of the Italian Political Science Society, Cagliari, 21–23 September.

Bartali, R. (2000), 'La nuova comunicazione politica: il partito telematico, una ricerca empirica sui partiti italiani', Working Paper No. 40 of the Dipartimento di Scienze Storiche, Giuridiche, Politiche e Sociali of the Università degli Studi di Siena.

Bentivegna, S. (1999), *La politica in rete*, Rome, Meltemi.

Bentivegna, S. (2001), 'La prova generale del 2001: candidati e elettori nel mare di Internet', *Comunicazione Politica*, 2, 183–204.

Bentivegna, S. (2002), 'E-campaigning in the 2001 Italy's election', paper presented to the Annual meeting of the American Political Science Association, 29 August – 1 September, Boston, MA.

Blumler, J. G. and Kavanagh, D. (1999), 'The third age of political communication: influences and features', *Political Communication*, 16:3, 209–230.

Calise, M. (2005), 'Presidentialization, Italian style', in T. Poguntke and P.

Webb (eds), *The Presidentialization of Politics: A Comparative Study of Modern Democracies*, Oxford, Oxford University Press.

Calise, M. and De Rosa, R. (2003), 'Il governo elettronico: visioni, primi risultati e un'agenda di ricerca', *Rivista Italiana di Scienza Politica*, 23:2, 257–284.

Campus, D. (2006), 'La campagna elettorale', paper presented to the workshop, 'Il voto del 9 e 10 aprile 2006: Analisi dei risultati e delle loro conseguenze sistemiche', University of Pisa, 15–16 June.

Campus, D. and Pasquino, G. (2006), 'Leadership in Italy: the changing role of leaders in elections and in government', *Journal of Contemporary European Studies*, 14:1, 25–40.

D'Alessio, D. (2000), 'Adoption of the World Wide Web by American political candidates, 1996–1998', *Journal of Broadcasting and Electronic Media*, 44:4, 556–568.

Davis, R. (1999), *The Web of Politics: The Internet's Impact on the American Political System*, New York, Oxford University Press.

De Rosa, R. (2000), *Fare politica in Internet. Come le nuove tecnologie influenzano la politica*, Milan, Apogeo.

Della Porta, D. (2001), *I partiti politici*, Bologna, Il Mulino.

Farrell, D. and Webb, P. (2000), 'Political parties as campaign organizations', in R. J. Dalton and M. P. Wattenberg (eds), *Parties without partisans*, Oxford, Oxford University Press.

Fielding, P. and Duritz, N. (2001), 'Net savvy challengers win online and at the ballot box', in S. Coleman (ed.), *Elections in the Age of the Internet: Lessons from the United States*, London, Hansard Society.

Gibson, R. K., Margolis, M., Resnick, D. and Ward, S. (2003), 'Election campaigning on the WWW in the USA and UK: a Comparative Analysis', *Party Politics*, 9:1, 47–75.

Gibson, R. K., Newell, J. L. and Ward, S. (2002), 'The new technologies: the first Internet election?', in J. L. Newell (ed.), *The Italian General Election of 2001*, Manchester, Manchester University Press.

Grandi, R. and Vaccari, C. (2004), *Cofferati anch'io. Un anno di campagna elettorale a Bologna*, Milan, Baldini Castoldi Dalai.

Greer, J., and LaPointe, M. (2001), 'Cyber-campaigning grows up', paper presented to the Annual meeting of the American Political Science Association, 30 August – 2 September, San Francisco.

Haraszti, M. (2005), *Visit to Italy: The Gasparri Law (Observations and Recommendations)*, Vienna, OSCE.

Harpham, E. J. (1999), 'Going on-line: the 1998 Congressional campaign', paper presented to the Annual meeting of the American Political Science Association, 2 – 5 September, Atlanta.

Hopkin, J. (2005), 'Towards a chequebook democracy? Business, parties and the funding of politics in Italy and the United States', *Journal of Modern Italian Studies*, 10:1, 43–58.

Jankowski, N. W., Foot, K. A., Kluver, R. and Schneider, S. M. (2005), 'The Web and the 2004 EP election: comparing political actor Web sites in 11 EU

Member States', *Information Polity*, 10:3–4, 165–176.

Lusoli, W. (2005a), 'The Internet and the European parliament elections: theoretical perspectives, empirical investigations and proposals for research', *Information Polity*, 10:3–4, 153–163.

Lusoli, W. (2005b), 'A second-order medium? The Internet as a source of electoral information in 25 European countries', *Information Polity*, 10:3–4, 247–265.

Lusoli, W. and Ward, S. (2004), 'Digital rank-and-file: party activists' perceptions and use of the Internet', *British Journal of Politics and International Relations*, 6:4, 453–470.

Lusoli, W. and Ward, S. (2005), 'Logging on or switching off?', in S. Coleman and S. Ward (eds), *Spinning the Web: Online Campaigning in the 2005 General Election*, London, Hansard Society and ESRC.

Margetts, H. (2005), 'The cyber party', in R. Katz and W. Crotty (eds), *Handbook of Party Politics*, London, Sage.

Margolis, M. and Resnick, D. (2000), *Politics as Usual: The Cyberspace 'revolution'*, Thousand Oaks, CA, Sage.

Mazzoleni, G. (1996), 'Patterns and effects of recent change in electoral campaigning in Italy', in D. L. Swanson and P. Mancini (eds), *Politics, Media and Modern Democracy*, Westport, CT, Praeger.

Miani, M. (2002), 'I siti elettorali dei candidati tra marketing politico e democrazia elettronica. Italia, Stati Uniti, Gran Bretagna e Francia a confronto', *Rivista Italiana di Comunicazione Pubblica*, 11.

Miani, M. (2004), 'EP election: Italy country report (Final report)', Bologna, Internet and Elections Project. Available online at www.mattiamiani .it /pubblicazioni/index.htm (accessed on 26 October 2005).

Mosca, L. (2002), *Internet – A New Potential for European Political Communication? Case Report: Italy* (WP 4: Internet No. 4D.1), Berlin, Europub.com.

Newell, J. L. (2001), 'Italian political parties on the web', *Harvard International Journal of Press / Politics*, 6:4, 60–87.

Norris, P. (2001), 'Political communications and democratic politics', in J. Bartle and D. Griffiths (eds), *Political Communications Transformed: From Morrison to Mandelson*, Basingstoke, Palgrave.

Pasquino, G. (2005), 'Italy and America: politics and culture – Americanization of Italian politics?', *Journal of Modern Italian Studies*, 10:1, 3–9.

Plasser, F. and Plasser, G. (2002), *Global Political Campaigning: A Worldwide Analysis of Campaign Professionals and their Practices*, Westport, CT, Praeger.

Roncarolo, F. (2002), 'Virtual clashes and political games: the campaign in the print and broadcast media', in J. L. Newell (ed.), *The Italian General Election of 2001*, Manchester, Manchester University Press.

Roncarolo, F. (2004), 'Mediation of Italian politics and the marketing of leaders' private lives', *Parliamentary Affairs*, 57:1, 108–117.

Schneider, S. M. and Foot, K. A. (2002), 'Online structure for political action:

exploring presidential campaign web sites from the 2000 American Election'. *Javnost – The Public*, 9:2, 43–60.

Smargiassi, M. (2006), 'Margherita OK, AN bocciata: ecco il parlamento elettronico', *La Repubblica*, 3 April, p. 10.

Stromer-Galley, J., Foot, K. A., Schneider, S. M. and Larsen, E. (2001), 'What citizens want, where they went, and what they got online in the U.S. election 2000', in S. Coleman (ed.), *Elections in the Age of the Internet: Lessons from the United States*, London, Hansard Society.

Tedeschi, M. (2005), *Gli strumenti e le tecnologie per la partecipazione democratica*, Milano, Formez-Progetto CRC.

Trechsel, A. H., Kies, R., Mendez, F. and Schmitter, P. C. (2003), *Evaluation of the Use of New Technologies in Order to Facilitate Democracy in Europe: E-democratizing the Parliaments and Parties of Europe* (STOA research report), Strasburg, European Parliament, STOA.

Tsagarousianou, R., Tambini, D. and Bryan, C. (eds) (1998), *Cyberdemocracy: Technology, Cities and Civic Networks*, London, Routledge.

Valbruzzi, M. (2005), *Primarie. Partecipazione e leadership*, Bologna, Bononia University Press.

Ward, S. (2005), 'The Internet, e-democracy and the election: virtually irrelevant?', in A. Geddes and J. Tonge (eds), *Britain Decides: The UK General Election 2005*. Basingstoke, Palgrave.

Appendix 1: Party website addresses

	URL
AN	www.alleanzanazionale.it
Azione Sociale	www.libertadiazione.net
DC	www.lademocraziacristiana.it
DS	www.dsonline.it
Tricoloured Flame	www.fiammatricolore.net
Forza Italia	www.forza-italia.it
Fronte Sociale Nazionale	www.frontenazionale.it
Italia dei Valori	www.italiadeivalori.it
Northern League	www.leganord.org
Margherita	www.margheritaonline.it
Movimento Idea Sociale	www.misconrauti.org
Movimento per l'Autonomia	www.movimentoperlautonomia.it
New PSI	www.nuovopsi.com
PdCI	www.comunisti-italiani.it
Pensioners	www.partitopensionati.it
RC	www.rifondazione.it
PRI	www.pri.it
Radicals	www.radicali.it
European Republican Movement	www.movimentorepubblicanieuropei.org
la Rosa nel Pugno	www.rosanelpugno.info
SDI	www.sdionline.it
UDC	www.udc-italia.it
UDEUR	www.popolariudeur.it
Greens	www.verdi.it

Appendix 2: Coding scheme for party websites at the 2006 election

Static information [0–14 index]

- Organisational history
- Party structure
- Values/ideology
- Policies
- Manifesto
- Media releases
- Speeches
- People / Who's Who

- Leader focus
- Candidate profiles
- Campaign calendar
- Campaign diary or blog
- [no feedback]
- Voting information
- Frequently Asked Questions

Dynamic information [0–6 index]

- E-mail details/form
- E-mail newsletter
- Mobile phone / PDA delivery

- RSS, other feeds [out-sourcing]
- Syndicated content [in-sourcing]
- Podcast

Discussion, talk-back channels [0–7 index]

- Survey/polls
- Letters to editor/post-it/ guestbook [no response]
- Letters to editor/post-it/ guestbook [response]

- Online Q&A
- Discussion board / Chat rooms
- Blog [with feedback]
- WIKI

Vertical mobilisation [0–5 index]

- Donate
- Join
- Buy

- Volunteer [offline]
- Volunteer [online]

Horizontal mobilisation [0–4 index]

- Social software tools
- E-mail/forward site material

- Download campaign material
- Write to the media

Sophistication [0–7 index]

- Separate election site
- Audio/video downloads
- Music background
- Streaming video
- Games / other gimmicks
- SMS/PDA support
- Any Web 2 features

Freshness [0–6 measure]

- Updated: Many times a day (6)
- daily (5)
- 1–2 days (4)
- 3–7 days (3)
- every two weeks (2)
- monthly (1)
- never since set up (0)

Visibility   Number of links in (Google in-links)

IV

The outcome

10

How Prodi's Unione won by a handful of votes

Alessandro Chiaramonte

A narrow victory

The success of the Unione in the elections of 2006 is not the story of a victory foretold. All the indications – from the results of the 2004 European elections to the even clearer results of the 2005 regional elections, and the surveys of the principal polling organisations, which gave the centre left a 4- to 5-point advantage throughout the campaign, even on the days of the vote itself – suggested that the coalition led by Prodi would beat the line-up headed by Berlusconi. And in fact the centre left was victorious. However, in contrast to what was predicted, the victory was the product of a handful of votes that was so small that it was necessary to wait until the last ballot had been counted before the result could be announced. Indeed, in the case of the Chamber of Deputies election, it was necessary to wait a further week in order for the national returning officer to be able to examine and assign the contested ballots and thus to declare the results official. Even after this declaration, however, Berlusconi refused to recognise the victory of his adversaries, announcing that he would make further appeals for a recount of the ballots declared invalid. Despite this the Prodi government was formed and obtained the confidence of a majority of deputies and senators.

The unexpected recovery of Berlusconi and his coalition made the victory of the Unione seem, to many, to be a partial defeat or, at the most, a tie. Among the ranks of the centre left, the victory that had for so long been savoured was celebrated quite quietly given the way in which it had come about. However, from a perspective less contaminated by political propaganda and by the unreal predictions that preceded the vote, the election result can be seen for what it was: a narrow victory on the part of a centre-left formation which, following the elections of 2001, had been able to eliminate a gap, in terms of votes expressed in the proportional arena, of almost 10 per cent, indeed of almost 15 per cent if one takes account of the fact that RC had then run independently of the Ulivo (the centre-left formation of that time). And this happened despite the stability that had been assured to the country by Berlusconi and his majority, which, on the whole, turned out to be more compact than many had predicted. In short: it is not true that the vote revealed the existence of a *clear* majority disappointed with Berlusconi; but it is true that at the end of the five years he had led the country, the majority of Italians preferred the centre-left alternative.

In order to understand how the result just described came about, it is necessary first of all to examine the workings of the new electoral systems that were used for the vote. These, as we shall see, were decisive in bringing about the final result. We shall then provide a description of the results of the Chamber and Senate elections, referring to the votes and seats obtained both by the coalitions and by the party lists. After that we shall try to identify the main reasons why the centre left was able to overturn the heavy defeat of five years before and to regain its hold on the government of the country. To that end we shall focus on two aspects in particular: the reconstruction of the coalition that was presented to voters, and changes in electoral geography. Finally, we shall conclude by analysing the prospects for the new governing majority and for the party system as a whole.

The new electoral systems

In December 2005, just four months before the legislature came to the end of its life, a parliamentary majority consisting only of the parties of the Cdl approved a new electoral law for the Chamber and the Senate.[1] The timing of the reform and the hostility shown by the forces of the opposition are in themselves evidence that the centre right's aim was to change the rules to its own advantage in order to prevent a defeat predicted by many, or at least to minimise its dimensions. But if we look at what the new electoral law stipulates and, above all, at what it *doesn't* stipulate, then the evidence becomes proof. It does not, in fact, provide for the single-member colleges that were part of the previous law. At the last two general elections (in 1996 and 2001) these had heavily penalised the centre right – whose common candidates had obtained far fewer votes than those obtained, separately, by their lists in the proportional arena – and favoured the centre left – which obtained more votes here than in the proportional arena.[2] In other words, at the previous elections the centre right showed that it was less a *coalition* than an *aggregate of parties*, its electorate less willing compactly to support its own common candidates, and thus that it was less cohesive than the centre left; by contrast, the centre left showed that it was more a *coalition* than an *aggregate of parties*, such that it did better where it presented a common symbol, that is, in the single-member colleges. From the point of view of electoral advantage, it is not therefore surprising that the Cdl's reform abolished the 'coalition vote', that is the one for common candidates in single-member colleges, replacing it with a vote given solely to a party list (which then automatically goes also to the coalition of which the chosen list forms part). At this point, however, it is necessary to analyse in more detail the principal characteristics of the two new electoral systems for the Chamber and Senate.

The electoral system for the Chamber of Deputies is, for the most part but not entirely, a proportional system with a majority premium. Indeed, with regard to the distribution of the 630 Chamber seats, it is necessary to distinguish between three arenas, in each of which different electoral regulations operate. A first arena consists of the 26 multi-member, regional or sub-regional, constituencies, which cover the whole of the national territory, to the exclusion of the small Valle d'Aosta region. Each of the 26 constituencies is assigned a number of seats in proportion to its resident population, for a total of 617 seats. The second arena consists of the single-member college of Valle d'Aosta, to which, obviously, one seat only is assigned. The third arena, finally, consists of the twelve seats reserved for Italians resident abroad and nominally assigned to a single 'foreign' constituency, but in fact assigned to four geographically separate divisions. Now, the mixed 'proportional-plus-majority-premium' formula is applied in the first arena, which is by far and away the most important, but not in the other two where the relevant formulae are – respectively – the plurality system and the proportional system (where seats are distributed using the Hare quotient and there is preference voting among the parties' lists of candidates).

The 617 seats assigned to the first arena are distributed as follows. In the first instance, seats are distributed proportionally, at national level. To that end the total number of votes obtained by the coalitions and independent lists that have succeeded in surmounting the thresholds are considered. Coalitions are formed by party lists which, though fielded independently of each other, have declared in advance a mutual association, identified a coalition leader and registered a common election platform. For coalitions, the threshold is set at 10 per cent of the votes provided that at least one of their constituent lists has obtained at least 2 per cent; for independent lists, on the other hand, the threshold is 4 per cent.

Once the seats have been proportionally assigned, it is established whether the coalition or independent list with the largest number of votes nationally has obtained at least 340 seats. If this is not the case, then it triggers assignment of the majority premium, which 'annuls' the purely proportional distribution of seats, attributes 340 to the winning coalition or list and distributes proportionally the remaining 277 between the other coalitions and lists.

The majority premium thus has three distinctive characteristics: 1) its attribution is something that is *possible*, in the sense that this does not happen always, come what may, but only under certain conditions; 2) its size is *not predetermined*, since it consists of the number of seats that is sufficient to allow the winning coalition or list to reach the figure of 340; 3) it is 'majority-assuring', insofar as the winning coalition or list obtains in any case – and therefore independently of the proportion of votes it has obtained – at least 340 seats, a number equivalent to about 54 per cent of the total of Chamber of Deputies seats and thus more than the absolute majority of its members.

After the number of seats due to each of the coalitions and independent lists has been established, seats are then distributed, for each coalition, among the various lists of which it is composed. The lists that participate in this distribution, which again takes place proportionally, at the national level, are those that have obtained at least 2 per cent of the vote, as well as, for each coalition, the list with the largest number of votes below the 2 per cent threshold.

Finally, within each of the 26 constituencies seats are distributed, first to the coalitions and independent lists, then to the lists belonging to coalitions. This is done in accordance with a complex procedure which aims to ensure that every constituency in the end receives the number of seats due to it on the basis of its population. For each constituency list there is thus elected a number of candidates equivalent to the number of seats assigned to it. Candidates are elected according to the order in which they appear on the list since there is no provision for preference voting meaning that the lists are thus 'closed'.

The electoral system for the Senate has certain similarities with that for the Chamber, but also important differences. These concern, above all, the level at which the distribution of seats takes place, the mechanisms for assignment of the majority premium and the size of the vote thresholds. The first of these features is decisive; for the distribution of seats takes place separately and independently, in each region. That is, unlike in the Chamber, there is no (quasi) national-level benchmark. Rather, the majority premium and the vote thresholds are applied region-by-region – but not in all of them, however.

In seventeen regions – that is, in all of them except Molise, Valle d'Aosta and Trentino-Alto Adige – the system is the same. Seats are in the first place distributed proportionally[3] among the coalitions and/or independent lists that have surmounted the relevant vote thresholds – respectively, 20 per cent (provided that the coalition in question includes at least one list with at least 3 per cent) and 8 per cent of the votes. It is then established whether the coalition or independent list with the largest number of votes in the region has obtained at least 55 per cent of the seats (rounding upwards) due to the region itself. If this is not the case, then it triggers assignment of the majority premium (always region by region) and the winning coalition or list is assigned as many additional seats as are necessary to reach the proportion of 55 per cent, while an equivalent number of seats is taken from the other coalitions or independent lists.

In this case too assignment of the majority premium is something that is *possible, not inevitable*; but in contrast to what happens in the case of the Chamber, there is no guarantee that the coalition or independent list with the largest number of votes nationally will obtain an absolute majority of the seats in the Senate. This is a not insignificant difference whose effects we will understand better after we have analysed the outcome of the 2006 elections in the two chambers of Parliament.

Once the number of seats due to each coalition has been determined, these are then distributed, internally, among those of the coalition's lists that have received at least 3 per cent of the votes in the region. Here too the lists are 'closed', and thus for each list candidates are elected in accordance with the order in which they are presented.

As far as the other three regions and the 'foreign' constituency are concerned, the electoral systems are different. In Molise, the two seats in contention are distributed proportionally and there is no majority premium. The Valle d'Aosta consists of one, single-member college, where the winning candidate is the one that obtains the most votes, exactly as happens in the case of the Chamber. Trentino-Alto Adige consists of six, single-member colleges, where the plurality formula is applied, while the remaining seats due to the region (currently one) are distributed using the method of proportional recoupment: that is, they are distributed among those candidates who have not already been elected in one or the other of the single-member colleges. Finally, in the 'foreign' constituency – or, rather, in each of its four geographical 'subdivisions' – a list system of proportional representation is used and the six senators are elected by means of preference voting.

The results

A comprehensive analysis of the election outcome needs to distinguish not only between what happened in the Chamber and in the Senate, but also, for each chamber of Parliament, between what happened in the different arenas in which seats are distributed.

The Chamber results given in Table 10.1 are thus shown separately for the three arenas: the one in which the counting of votes serves the purpose of deciding the possible attribution of the majority premium, the Valle d'Aosta single-member college and the 'foreign' constituency. As we have already said, the first of these arenas is the decisive one, since it is here that the line-up that wins, even by a margin of just one vote, obtains an absolute majority of seats. Here there was a difference of just 24,755 votes between the Unione (which obtained a little over 19 million) and the Cdl (which obtained just under 19 million), less than 0.1 per cent of the total of over 38 million valid votes cast. This was indeed a minimal vote difference – to which however, thanks to the majority premium, there corresponded a much larger difference in terms of seats: the Unione was assigned 340, the Cdl 277, a difference of 63 seats (equal to 10 per cent of the total number of deputies). The results in the other two arenas were also favourable to the Unione, though they added only four seats to its margin of victory. Overall in the Chamber, the final outcome of the distribution of seats was such as to give 348 to the Unione, 281 to the Cdl and 1 to the Association of Italians in South America.

As far as the Senate election is concerned, Table 10.2 shows the results of the 'domestic' segment and of the 'foreign' segment separately. Within the national territory alone, the election was won by the Cdl, even though by a narrow margin both in terms of votes and in terms of seats. In fact here the Cdl obtained 269,998 votes more than the Unione – equivalent to 0.7 per cent of the valid votes cast – and obtained just one seat more – that is, 155 seats as against the 154 obtained by the Unione. The upshot of this is that the victory of the Unione in the Senate was obtained thanks to the votes cast by the Italians resident abroad. The latter, in fact, tended to favour the coalition of the centre left, which won four of the six seats up for grabs, while the two remaining seats went, respectively, to Forza Italia (and thus to the Cdl) and, as in the Chamber, to the Association of Italians in South America. The overall result was such that the Unione emerged in front with 158 seats, as against the 156 seats of the Cdl and 1 seat for an independent list. This is a result that placed the winning coalition just beyond the threshold of an absolute majority of the Senate's

Table 10.1 Election results, Chamber of Deputies 2006

| | Italy (Majority-Premium) | | | | Valle D'Aosta | | Foreign Constituency | | Total | |
| | Votes | | Seats | | Votes | Seats | Votes | Seats | Votes | Seats |
Lists/coalitions	No.	%	No.	%	No.	No.	No.	No.	No.	No.
L'Ulivo	11,930,983	31.3	220	35.7					11,930,983	220
Communist Refoundation	2,229,464	5.8	41	6.6					2,229,464	41
la Rosa nel Pugno	990,694	2.6	18	2.9					990,694	18
PdCI	884,127	2.3	16	2.6					884,127	16
Italia dei Valori	877,052	2.3	16	2.6			27,432	1	904,484	17
Greens	784,803	2.1	15	2.4					784,803	15
UDEUR	534,088	1.4	10	1.6			9,692	0	543,780	10
Pensioners' Party	333,278	0.9	0	0.0	1,135	0			334,413	0
SVP	182,704	0.5	4	0.6					182,704	4
Other Unione parties	255,405	0.7	0	0.0					255,405	0
Autonomie Liberté Democratie	–	–	–	–	34,167	1			34,167	1
L'Unione-Prodi	–	–	–	–			422,330	6	422,330	6
UNIONE (tot.)	19,002,598	49.8	340	55.1	35,302	1	459,454	7	19,497,354	348
Forza Italia	9,048,976	23.7	137	22.2			202,407	3	9,251,383	140
National Alliance	4,707,126	12.3	71	11.5					4,707,126	71
UDC	2,580,190	6.8	39	6.3	2,282	0	65,794	0	2,648,266	39
Northern League-MPA	1,747,730	4.6	26	4.2	1,566	0	20,227	0	1,769,523	26
DC–New PSI	285,474	0.7	4	0.6					285,474	4
Alternativa Sociale	255,354	0.7	0	0.0	1,587	0	7,102	0	264,043	0
Fiamma Tricolore	230,506	0.6	0	0.0	430	0	1,133	0	232,069	0
Other Cdl parties	122,487	0.3	0	0.0					122,487	0
Forza Italia-AN	–	–	–	–	13,372	0			13,372	0
Per l'Italia nel mondo	–	–	–	–			73,289	1	73,289	1
CASA DELLE LIBERTA' (tot.)	18,977,843	49.7	277	44.9	19,237	0	369,952	4	19,367,032	281
OTHERS (tot.)	172,902	0.5	0	0.0	24,118	0	146,008	1	343,028	1
Total	38,153,343	100.0	617	100.0	78,657	1	975,414	12	39,207,414	630

Table 10.2 Election results, Senate 2006

Lists/coalitions	ITALY				FOREIGN CONSTITUENCY		TOTAL	
	Votes		Seats		Votes	Seats	Votes	Seats
	No.	%	No.	%	No.	No.	No.	No.
DS	5,977,313	17.2	62	20.1			5,977,313	62
Margherita	3,664,622	10.5	39	12.6			3,664,622	39
Communist Refoundation	2,518,624	7.2	27	8.7			2,518,624	27
'Together with the Unione'	1,423,226	4.1	11	3.6			1,423,226	11
Italia dei Valori	986,046	2.8	4	1.3	26,134	0	1,012,180	4
la Rosa nel Pugno	851,875	2.4	0	0.0			851,875	0
UDEUR	476,938	1.4	3	1.0	13,265	0	490,203	3
Pensioners' Party	357,731	1.0	0	0.0			357,731	0
L'Unione-SVP	198,153	0.6	3	1.0			198,153	3
Partito dei Socialisti (Craxi)	126,625	0.4	0	0.0			126,625	0
SVP	117,500	0.3	2	0.6			117,500	2
Alleanza Lombarda	90,943	0.3	0	0.0			90,943	0
Consumers' List	72,139	0.2	1	0.3			72,139	1
L'Ulivo	59,499	0.2	1	0.3			59,499	1
Autonomie Liberté Democratie	32,553	0.1	1	0.3			32,553	1
L'Unione-Prodi	27,629	0.1	0	0.0	387,145	4	414,774	4
Other Unione parties	136,948	0.4	0	0.0			136,948	0
UNIONE (tot.)	17,089,756	49.1	154	49.8	426,544	4	17,516,300	158
Forza Italia	8,201,688	23.6	78	25.2	185,438	1	8,387,126	79
National Alliance	4,234,693	12.2	41	13.3			4,234,693	41
UDC	2,311,448	6.6	21	6.8	57,200	0	2,368,648	21
Northern League-MPA	1,531,939	4.4	13	4.2	18,455	0	1,550,394	13
Fiamma Tricolore	219,707	0.6	0	0.0	8,433	0	228,140	0
Alternativa Sociale	215,392	0.6	0	0.0			215,392	0
DC–New PSI	190,724	0.5	0	0.0			190,724	0
Casa delle Libertà	175,137	0.5	2	0.6			175,137	2
Other Cdl parties	279,026	0.8	0	0.0			279,026	0
Per l'Italia nel mondo	–	–	–	–	63,474	0	63,474	0
CASA DELLE LIBERTA' (tot.)	17,359,754	49.9	155	50.2	333,000	1	17,692,754	156
OTHERS (tot.)	330,917	1.0	0	0.0	120,389	1	451,306	1
Total	34,780,427	100.0	309	100.0	879,933	6	35,660,360	315

members and just two seats in front of the opposing coalition. It must in addition be stressed that though it was defeated in the Senate contest, the Cdl nevertheless obtained more votes than the Unione, even taking account of those cast by Italians resident abroad.

Table 10.2 highlights the decisive role played by the 'foreign' constituency in ensuring that the final result would be one that favoured the Unione. In the 'domestic' segment, aggregation of the data masks how the Senate's electoral system (or, rather, electoral *systems*, in the plural) actually worked, given that what counts is not the national, but the regional, distribution of the vote. Indeed the majority premium, where provided for, and the seats, are assigned in each of the regions separately. This alternative perspective is shown in Table 10.3, which shows precisely the regional breakdown of the Senate election results. It may be observed that of the seventeen regions where the majority premium was at stake, the Cdl won seven and the Unione ten. The Unione also won the Valle d'Aosta seat; it won by five seats to two in Trentino-Alto Adige, and it drew in Molise. In total, twelve regions went to the centre left, seven to the centre right and one was drawn. How was it, then, that in the 'domestic' part of

Table 10.3 Electoral support for coalitions by region, Senate 2006

Regions	% of votes			No. of seats		
	Unione	Cdl	Others	Unione	Cdl	Others
Piemonte	49.5	50.5	0.0	9	13	0
Valle d'Aosta	45.6	22.4	32.0	1	0	0
Lombardia	42.6	56.9	0.4	20	27	0
Trentino-Alto Adige	62.7	33.1	4.2	5	2	0
Veneto	39.5	57.1	3.4	10	14	0
Friuli-Venezia Giulia	44.4	54.8	0.7	3	4	0
Liguria	53.3	46.7	0.0	5	3	0
Emilia Romagna	59.4	40.6	0.0	12	9	0
Toscana	61.3	38.7	0.0	11	7	0
Umbria	57.2	42.8	0.0	4	3	0
Marche	54.4	45.6	0.0	5	3	0
Lazio	49.1	50.2	0.6	12	15	0
Abruzzo	53.2	46.8	0.0	4	3	0
Molise	50.5	49.5	0.0	1	1	0
Campania	49.6	49.1	1.3	17	13	0
Puglia	47.9	51.9	0.2	9	12	0
Basilicata	60.4	39.2	0.5	4	3	0
Calabria	56.8	42.6	0.7	6	4	0
Sicilia	40.5	57.8	1.7	11	15	0
Sardegna	50.9	45.3	3.8	5	4	0
Foreign constituency	48.5	37.8	13.7	4	1	1
Total	49.2	49.6	1.3	158	156	1

the Senate the Cdl obtained more seats than the Unione? It is explained by the fact that the Cdl won many 'weighty' regions, those where even a single-vote victory brought about a large margin of victory in terms of seats. These regions include Lombardy, Sicily and Veneto, where victory for the Cdl was a foregone conclusion. But they also include regions that were thought to be marginal and were confirmed as such, like Piedmont, Lazio and Puglia, as well as Friuli-Venezia Giulia. Only Campania, among the larger regions, saw a (narrow) victory on the part of the Unione.

The 'neck-and-neck' race between the two strongest coalitions, the Unione and the Cdl, brought about an extraordinary concentration of votes on them, to an extent never before reached in the history of the 'Second Republic'. Together, the two largest line-ups received 99.1 per cent of the total of the valid votes cast in the Chamber elections, and 98.7 per cent of those cast for the Senate race. In terms of parliamentary representation, or the assignment of seats, bi-polar concentration was even higher: 99.8 per cent in the Chamber and 99.7 per cent in the Senate. Figure 10.1 compares the figure for the Chamber with the equivalent figures for the three preceding elections. Following a rather linear path beginning in 1994, the bi-polar structure of the Italian party system has not only become increasingly pronounced, but it has gone as far as almost completely to 'eliminate' 'third' forces. In the

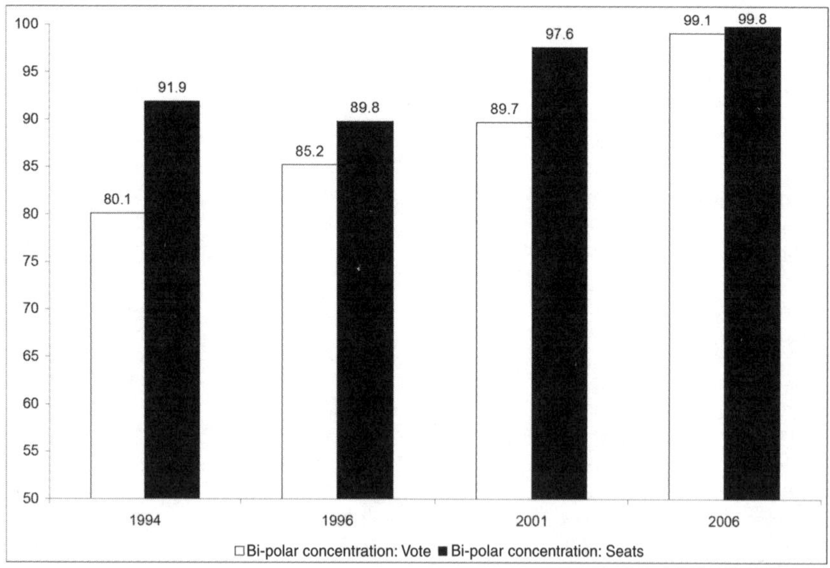

Figure 10.1 Bi-polar concentration of votes and seats, Chamber 1994–2006

elections of 2006, in fact, the latter were reduced to about 1 per cent of the votes and a single seat in both chambers of Parliament. This was made possible by two principal factors.

The first has to do with the way in which the political supply was structured, where the coalitions were inclusive as never before. Once the divisions previously running through both the Unione and the Cdl had been overcome, the two coalitions in presenting themselves for election closed ranks. Not only that: both incorporated within themselves a series of minor political formations with the aim of enlarging, to the greatest extent possible, the sizes of their 'catchment areas'.[4] It must be remembered that, with the new electoral system, a vote expressed for any list is automatically attributed to the coalition of which it is a part; and that for the coalition the vote counts for the purposes of the distribution of seats, even if the list in question fails to surmount the vote threshold. If, as in fact happened, the election outcome is subsequently decided by a handful of votes, the packet of ballots, though small, contributed by a minor party can turn out to be decisive for the victory of a coalition, which thus has an incentive to incorporate it.

The second factor that accounts for the extraordinary level of bipolar concentration of the vote at the 2006 elections resides in the type of election campaign that was conducted and in the consequent behaviour of voters. Given that he had to climb back from an initial disadvantage, Berlusconi sought to dramatise the campaign in order to mobilise voters who, though inclined towards the centre right, were – whether through disappointment or apathy – undecided about whether to vote or not. On the other hand, the political formations, and the electorate, of the centre left had for long been cohesively lined up against Berlusconi and his government. It is not surprising, then, that the 'third' forces, whose numbers and political relevance had already been reduced, were relegated to the margins of media attention. Nor is it surprising that voters responded to these stimuli by choosing to vote for one or the other of the two major coalitions, helped as they were in this by the wide range of party options that in both cases were presented to them. Electors wanted to make their votes count and to do so they had no option but to turn their backs on lists outside the two coalitions. A further demonstration of the point is given by the significant decline in the number of non-valid ballots as compared to previous elections.

A final aspect of the election results that is worth emphasising concerns the performance of the party lists, in relation to which the data given in Tables 10.1 and 10.2 is once again relevant. In the

Chamber, the list that obtained the largest number of votes was the Ulivo, consisting of the DS, the Margherita and the European Republican Movement (MRE) – parties which, in the case of the Senate election, ran separately. It can be seen that, with a vote total of 31.3 per cent, the Ulivo in the Chamber contest did better than its party components in the Senate race, where the combined total of their votes amounted to 27.8 per cent. This confirms that recently, unlike the past, the aggregation of parties within single entities has 'worked', bringing with it 'added value'. However, the Ulivo is not yet a new single entity, a new party in a de facto sense. The upshot is that the party with the largest following is still Forza Italia, with slightly fewer than 24 per cent of the valid votes – equivalent to about 5 per cent less than its vote tally at the previous general election. In contrast, the percentage of votes obtained by the UDC went up, as did, to a lesser extent, those obtained by RC and AN. The remainder of the profile of lists represented in Parliament is made up of the numerous minor parties that just managed to cross the vote threshold. Not counting those returned by the foreign constituency, the lists winning seats amount to fourteen in the Chamber and sixteen in the Senate. These elections too, then, confirmed the very high level of party fragmentation which, together with the consolidation of bi-polarity, has characterised development of the Italian party system over the past twelve years.[5]

The reasons for the victory and the defeat

When election outcomes are decided by small margins of votes, explanations for the victory of one side and the defeat of the other have to reckon with a fortuitous component. In our case there are actually two elections whose outcomes were decided by a handful of votes. Not only did the Unione beat the Cdl by just 24,755 votes (equivalent to 0.07 per cent) in the arena that was decisive for the Chamber outcome, the one involving attribution of the majority premium, it also won in Campania, in the Senate contest, by a margin of just 15,771 votes: if this difference had gone in favour of the Cdl, the overall result of the Senate election would have been victory for the centre right. But the result could have been quite different even without imagining shifts of the vote from one side to the other. In the Chamber, for example, the 92,002 votes obtained by Progetto Nordest – a minor list that was fielded independently of the two coalitions but which certainly drew its support from the centre right's potential reservoir – would have been sufficient to allow the Cdl to overtake the Unione; as would the votes of the Pensioners' Party – which allied with the Unione in these elections but which, sub-nationally, has often been a partner of the Cdl – or the votes of Alleanza Lombarda, another small party hosted by the Unione but clearly supported by voters not of the left.

Certainly, all this is not only the fruit of chance. It must be acknowledged that the Unione was able to build a coalition that was highly inclusive, to the point of incorporating within it political formations that would perhaps have felt more comfortable in the Cdl if only they had been accepted – political formations which in the end turned out to be decisive. The Cdl, which also gathered together many minor political forces and brought them within its own line-up, was evidently unable to do as much. But there is more. The Cdl made a strategic mistake – one which, in retrospect, was decisive – concerning the way it competed in the foreign constituency for the Senate. As already mentioned, this constituency has a total of six proportionally distributed seats. The point is that it consists of four 'geographical subdivisions', each *distinct* from all of the others, in half of which there are two seats and in the other half one. This means that though formally proportional, election of the representatives of Italians resident abroad is in practice majoritarian. The Unione understood this and tailored the nature of its offering to this logic: that is, it presented a single, joint list (apart from the minority defection of UDEUR and Italia dei Valori (IdV) in the latter case in one 'subdivision' only) in order to avoid its votes being wasted. The Cdl by contrast fielded separate lists for each of its principal parties and by doing that ended up 'wasting' many of the votes that it received here. In fact, had the votes obtained by its lists separately been cast for a joint list, the Cdl would have obtained two extra seats, which would have come precisely from the centre left's tally. In other words, the winning coalition in the Senate contest would have been the Cdl.

Aside from the contribution of certain micro-lists to the centre left's victory, or the strategic mistakes made by the Cdl in the Senate foreign constituency, the construction of the coalitions is one of the principal factors explaining the outcome of the 2006 election. The change in the party composition of the two line-ups compared to what happened in 2001 in fact helped by itself to bring about a considerable readjustment in the distribution of support between them.[6]

In 2001 in the Chamber contest the lists forming part of the Ulivo and competing in the proportional arena had a combined vote total of 35.0 per cent, those of the Cdl 49.6 per cent. Vast though this difference is, it is one that was considerably reduced in the majoritarian segment (that is, in the single-member colleges), where the Ulivo reached 43.8 per cent and the Cdl was limited to 45.4 per cent. This was due to the greater attractiveness of the Ulivo's candidates in the single-member colleges as compared to the attractiveness of its proportional lists; and, on the other hand, to the inability of the centre right's candidates to attract the votes of all of those who supported its lists in the proportional arena. But it was also due to the fact that RC – which was not a member of the Ulivo – refrained from presenting its own candidates in the single-member colleges in order not to damage those of the Ulivo.[7] In 2006, however, the elections were to take on a colouring more similar to that of the proportional arena in 2001, as a result of which the centre left lost the advantage of a 'return on coalescing' greater than that accruing to the Cdl and which had been revealed precisely in the single-member colleges now abolished.[8] In other words, without the inclusion of all of the forces active in its part of the political spectrum, the centre left would never have closed that 15 per cent vote gap that had been registered in the proportional arena in 2001.

The years spent in opposition to the Berlusconi government were, indeed, profitably utilised by the parties of the centre left to build a new political entity – the Unione – one able, through enlargement of the coalition beyond the boundaries of the 2001 Ulivo, to offer a competitive alternative to the centre right. Thus it was that the Unione ended up absorbing RC, IdV and the Radicals,[9] that is, three parties which in 2001 had taken part in the elections outside both of the two principal coalitions, managing in the process to obtain 5.0, 3.9 and 2.2 per cent of the vote respectively in the proportional arena. Besides which, as we emphasised above, the Unione negotiated entry to the coalition of various small parties which, in 2001, had stood alone (the Pensioners' Party, Alleanza Lombarda, the Liga Fronte Veneto) or even been part of the Cdl (Bobo Craxi's Socialists) and had nevertheless scraped together a few votes.

In the period between 2001 and 2006, the Cdl too took steps to strengthen itself – first, by incorporating Democrazia Europea, which as an independent entity had obtained 2.4 per cent of the votes in 2001 and now merged with the CCD and the CDU to give life to the UDC; second, by establishing, in the run-up to the 2006 elections, ties with a series of minor parties, in particular, parties of the extreme right such as Alternativa Sociale and the Fiamma Tricolore.

In order to assess the impact of the reconstruction of the coalitions on the outcome of the 2006 elections, we shall compare the results of the Unione and the Cdl in 2006 with two types of data relating to the previous election: 1) the results for the Ulivo and the Cdl as they were then made up; and 2) those for a *virtual* centre left and centre right, as similar as possible, in terms of their party composition, to the Unione and the Cdl of 2006. In other words, we will estimate the level of support for the two coalitions compared to the past on the basis of both constant and variable political supply. To that end, we shall use the votes cast in the proportional arena in 2001 and ignore for both elections those cast in the Valle d'Aosta single-member college. The data in question are shown in Table 10.4, subdivided by the country's three main geo-political areas.

The importance as an explanatory factor of the restructuring of political supply emerges clearly. If, at the elections of 2001, the coalitions had been composed as they were in 2006, then in the proportional arena the centre right would indeed have retained a certain advantage in votes over the centre left, but such advantage would have been much smaller than the one that was in fact registered. In the nineteen regions all together, in fact, the centre right would have reached 52.4 per cent (2.8 per cent more than its actual result) and the centre left 46.8 per cent (a good 11.9 per cent more than its actual share). Thus, the distance between them would have been drastically reduced, going from 14.7 to 5.6 per cent – this on the assumption that the voting choices of the supporters of 'third' forces would have remained unchanged notwithstanding the change of positioning of their chosen parties. This is a plausible assumption, even while it is not necessary, in order to establish the importance of reconfiguration of the coalitions to the 2006 outcome, that there be no empirical exceptions to it.

Table 10.4 Election results for actual and 'virtual' coalitions by geopolitical area, Chamber 2001–2006

Geopolitical area[a]	Centre left 2001–2006			Centre right 2001–2006		
	Ulivo 2001	Virtual centre left 2001[b]	Unione 2006	Cdl 2001	Virtual centre right 2001[c]	Cdl 2006
North	31.5	45.1	45.5	52.3	54.1	53.8
Centre	46.9	58.5	59.7	40.1	41.3	40.3
South	32.8	43.2	49.5	51.2	55.9	50.1
Italy (19 regions)	34.9	46.8	49.8	49.6	52.4	49.7

Notes: [a] North: Piemonte, Lombardia, Veneto, Trentino Alto Adige, Friuli-Venezia Giulia, Liguria; Centre: Emilia Romagna, Toscana, Marche, Umbria; South: all the other regions; [b] The virtual centre-left coalition in 2001 includes: DS, Margherita, Girasole, PdCI, RC, IdV, Lista Pannella-Bonino, SVP, MRE, Pensioners' Party; [c] The virtual centre-right coalition in 2001 includes: FI, AN, CCD-CDU, Northern League, New PSI, Democrazia Europea, Fiamma Tricolore, Fronte Nazionale, Forza Nuova.

Taking account of the 'virtual' coalitions of 2001, and thus para-meterising the change in composition of the coalitions, highlights both *how much* and *where* the centre left caught up with the centre right between 2001 and 2006. In the north, the restructuring of the political supply appears to explain the recovery *by itself*. Indeed the percentages of votes obtained by the two 'virtual' coalitions in 2001 (45.1 and 54.1 per cent) coincide almost exactly with the results obtained by the Unione and the Cdl in 2006 (45.5 and 53.8 per cent). Essentially the same is true in the central regions, where the relevant percentages are: 58.5 and 59.7 for the centre left, 41.3 and 40.3 for the centre right. It cannot be ruled out that in both areas there were self-cancelling vote flows between the two coalitions – flows of limited dimensions to judge from recent analyses of Italian voting behaviour – but there is no doubt that the nature of the supply was a much more important factor.

The area where recomposition of the coalitions explains *quite a bit but not all* of the change in the distribution of support between the centre right and the centre left is the south. Here, the proportion of votes obtained by the Unione in 2006 is in fact significantly higher not only than that obtained by the Ulivo in 2001, but also than that obtained by the 'virtual' coalition of the centre left. For the Cdl on the other hand, such share of votes is significantly lower. Given that turnout in 2006 was about the same as in 2001, it must be assumed that in the south there was also a change of voting opinions, with voters switching directly from the Cdl to the Unione or else refusing to follow the party supported in 2001 as it repositioned itself within the coalition of the centre right.

On the other hand, a decline in the centre right's southern support was to some degree expected in light of the results of the regional elections of 2005. Many observers had already drawn attention for some time to the existence, within the governing majority, of a 'special relationship' between Forza Italia and the Northern League – dubbed the 'northern axis' – which not by chance aroused the impatience of those parties, such as the UDC and AN, whose bases of support lay predominantly in the south. The issue of constitutional reform might also have had an influence, especially the so-called devolution measures which had been approved by the Cdl under pressure from the Northern League. The fact remains that the centre right, though not undergoing a collapse did suffer a set-back, against which the centre left enjoyed an advance of even larger proportions, one large enough to determine the overall outcome of the elections.

To those who are already familiar with the history of Italian voting outcomes since the start of the 'Second Republic', the factors that explain the outcome of the 2006 elections and which we have analysed in this chapter will, if one leaves aside the impact of the recently introduced electoral system, be anything but new. In fact, both the structure of political supply and southern voting behaviour were crucial factors at the three preceding general elections. As far as the first of these is concerned, it is enough to remember that in 1996 the centre right lost as a result of the Northern League's defection from the coalition, while in 2001 the absence of an alliance with RC was probably the principal cause of the centre left's defeat. Secondly, that elections are often decided in the south is testified to by the fact that this is the only area of the country where the relative strengths of the two line-ups are evenly matched and, above all, where there exists a significant proportion of volatile voters, willing, that is, to change the direction of their vote from one election to another. From this point of view, notwithstanding the alternation in government it produced, the result of the 2006 elections appears marked more by elements of continuity than of discontinuity with the past.

Prospects

Had the distribution of votes differed slightly from the actual distribution, the result of the 2006 elections would have been a completely different story. Instead of the victory of the Unione, we would have been here analysing the reconfirmation in office of Berlusconi, or else imagining complex present and future scenarios consequent upon a tied result arising from a victory of the centre left in one chamber of Parliament and a victory of the centre right in the other. The victory of the Unione, however small, was nevertheless unequivocal and it brought about another alternation in the government of the 'second republic'.

The journey that awaits the Prodi government will, however, be anything but easy. The majority on which it can count is large enough in the Chamber but very small in the Senate. In a system of symmetric bicameralism where the government is responsible to both chambers of Parliament, this means that the majority is very small *tout court*.

It will obviously be in the Senate that we will best be able to evaluate the real degree of cohesion of the Unione and the possibilities of the executive remaining in office: here, in fact, every party component of the centre-left coalition – including the one representing the German linguistic minority (the Südtirolervolkspartei [South Tyrolese People's Party; SVP] with two seats) and the component representing

Italians resident abroad (with four seats) – is indispensable for maintenance of the majority; and therefore the defection of just one of these could compromise the government's fortunes.[10] In these conditions it is easy to predict that any issue that is in the slightest bit divisive for the partners of the Unione – and there are not a few of them especially in the areas of economic and foreign policy – will be kept off the government's agenda on pain of paralysis or worse. But the government will not always be able to control the agenda and therefore its prospects will depend crucially on unexpected events that require drastic decisions, potentially disruptive of the coalition's unity, related to international and/or economic developments. Or else, as some have predicted, the so-called northern question might flare up – that is, the protest of the most economically advanced area of the country, which is currently underrepresented in the Government.[11]

The prospects for the Cdl, currently in opposition, are not on the other hand that dissimilar to those of the Unione. While Berlusconi's leadership has not been especially weakened by the elections of 2006 given that the overall result for the centre right exceeded expectations, it is also true that the cohesion shown by the Cdl in the immediate aftermath could vanish along with the idea that the Prodi government is not capable of lasting for any length of time. In the absence of any short-term possibility of replacing the Unione at the head of the country it cannot be ruled out that the internal tensions that had already surfaced in the Cdl in the last legislature will emerge again and perhaps with greater intensity – with consequences that are currently impossible to predict.

In short, despite having moved in the last decade in the hoped-for direction of fully fledged bi-polarity, the Italian party system continues to reveal its weak side: the fragility of the coalitions, too internally fragmented to become genuinely autonomous political entities capable of translating into government policy outputs the programmes they have given themselves. From this point of view the new electoral law has actually worsened the situation by abolishing the provision for single-member colleges and with them an important incentive for the coalitions to remain united. Though it is now clear that electoral law reform cannot – on its own – resolve the problem, it will nevertheless be necessary once more to start from here, hoping that at least this time the reform will find sufficient support in both coalitions to enable it to last.

Translated by James L. Newell

Notes

1 For a more detailed analysis of the new electoral systems and their potential effects see D'Alimonte and Chiaramonte (2006).
2 See Bartolini and D'Alimonte (2002) and Chiaramonte (2002).
3 In this case too the distribution takes place by using the Hare quotient together with the largest remainders.
4 In some cases the incorporation of a minor list within a coalition was agreed to on the basis of remuneration, such as – for example – the candidacy of one or more representatives of the minor list, in itself unable to obtain seats, within a larger list and in positions such as to assure their election.
5 On this latter aspect see also Bartolini, Chiaramonte and D'Alimonte (2004) and Di Virgilio (2006).
6 The importance of the political supply to the outcome is also stressed by Feltrin, Natale and Fabrizio (2006). For further details on the party composition of the Ulivo and the Cdl, and more generally on the structure of political supply at the elections of 2001, see Di Virgilio (2002), Donovan (2002), Rose (2002).
7 In contrast to the Chamber, in the Senate contest, RC presented its own candidates in the single-member colleges. The reason for this was that in the Senate there was only one arena of competition, and the votes not used to secure victory in the single-member colleges were counted for the purposes of assigning the proportionally distributed seats.
8 In more precise terms, by 'return on coalescing' we mean the average difference between the votes obtained, in single-member colleges, by a coalition's common candidate, and the combined vote total obtained by the lists presented by the same coalition in the proportional arena.
9 As far as the Radicals are concerned, it should be remembered that, having fielded the Pannella–Bonnino List in 2001, a majority of them joined la Rosa nel Pugno, which became part of the Unione, but that a minority, however, formed a party (called i Riformatori liberali) which became part of the Cdl.
10 Some help for the new majority may also come from the life senators – whose numbers currently amount to seven – or from some of them.
11 On this issue see the comments of Ricolfi, Ferragutti and Dallago (2006) who caution, however, against the assumption that the favourable outcome for the centre right in the north was due to disproportionate levels of support for the coalition among the most economically advanced strata.

References

Bartolini, S. and D'Alimonte, R. (2002), 'La maggioranza ritrovata. La competizione nei collegi uninominali', in R. D'Alimonte and S. Bartolini (eds), *Maggioritario finalmente? La transizione elettorale 1994–2001*, Bologna, Il Mulino.

Bartolini, S., Chiaramonte, A. and D'Alimonte, R. (2004), 'The Italian party system between parties and coalitions', in *West European Politics*, 27:1, 1–19.

Chiaramonte, A. (2002), 'How the centre right won', in J. L. Newell (ed.), *The Italian General Election of 2001: Berlusconi's Victory*, Manchester and New York, Manchester University Press.

D'Alimonte, R. and Chiaramonte, A. (2006), 'Proporzionale ma non solo. La riforma elettorale della Casa delle libertà', in *Il Mulino*, 56:1, 34–45.

Di Virgilio, A. (2002), 'L'offerta elettorale: la politica delle alleanze si istituzionalizza', in R. D'Alimonte and S. Bartolini (eds), *Maggioritario finalmente? La transizione elettorale 1994–2001*, Bologna, Il Mulino.

Di Virgilio, A. (2006), 'Dal cambiamento dei partiti all'evoluzione del sistema partitico, in L. Morlino and M. Tarchi (eds), *Partiti e caso italiano*, Bologna, Il Mulino.

Donovan, M. (2002), 'The process of alliance formation', in J. L. Newell (ed.), *The Italian General Election of 2001: Berlusconi's Victory*, Manchester and New York, Manchester University Press.

Feltrin, P., Natale, P. and Fabrizio, D. (2006), 'La sorpresa di aprile. Una prima analisi delle elezioni politiche 2006', in *Polena*, 3:1, 145–169.

Ricolfi, L., Ferragutti, P. and Dallago, F. (2006), 'Le elezioni di aprile e la "questione settentrionale"', in *Polena*, 3:1, 170–176.

Rose, S. (2002), 'The parties of the centre left', in J. L. Newell (ed.), *The Italian General Election of 2001: Berlusconi's Victory*, Manchester and New York, Manchester University Press.

11

The election and the XV legislature[1]

Licia Papavero and Luca Verzichelli

The 2006 elections and the puzzles of the Italian parliament

The effects of legislative election outcomes can be classified as *immediate* and/or *systemic*. If some of the immediate effects of the 2006 elections have been considered elsewhere in this volume, then the core question underlying this chapter is: to what degree has the 2006 outcome had significant systemic effects – in terms of the structure of Parliament and its influence on political processes – if any? Of course, an adequate answer to this question will be possible only with the passage of time. However, some partial (but critical) effects can already be discerned from an analysis of the characteristics of the new parliament and its members.

The centre right's electoral-law reform created the conditions for a number of significant changes in the processes of parliamentary recruitment. First, the nature of the reform was such that profound modifications in the modes of selection of parliamentary candidates were almost inevitable, as were changes in the relationship between candidates and territorial units, and in the role of the various actors (from the national party leaders to the least-known party activists in the peripheries) involved in the candidate-selection process. However, it is unlikely that the effects of the new law have simply been direct and mechanical. Rather, it is reasonable to suppose that the closed-list system and the incentives created by the majority premium (incentives whose effects are even more complicated in the Senate because of the way in which the premium is segmented on a regional basis) will also have had an effect by virtue of their impact on politicians' expectations and thus on their strategic reactions. Hypotheses that institutional environments are significant for political behaviour (Norris, 1997) here find striking confirmation, for the new form of party competition – one offering no space for the visibility of individual candidates – that was ushered in by the new law seemed likely to bring with it a transformation in the social and political profile of parliamentarians. We will use some classic indicators in order to verify such a hypothesis.

At a more general level of analysis, the birth of the new legislature was expected to bring with it definitive moves towards simplification of the party-political scene. In particular, it seemed that the institutional back-drop might encourage the emergence of a 'more perfect two-party system',[2] given that both Prodi and Berlusconi had in their different ways promised to revive the construction of unitary party actors in their respective camps, once the election had taken place.[3] The results of the elections clearly showed that such a scenario still faces many obstacles, but a look at the changes in the 'parliamentary context' at the start of the new legislature can help us to shed light on the likely future relationship between parliamentary dynamics and party-system change.

The hypotheses that can be derived from our initial conjectures are too numerous to be discussed in detail. We have therefore decided to concentrate on the hypotheses about possible change or persistence in the political composition, and in the profile of the members, of Parliament. In the following section we deal with the process of candidate selection. Our main argument is that party centralisation has re-emerged as the most important feature of this process. Territorialisation, which had made a timid appearance with the three consecutive applications of the mixed majoritarian system between 1994 and 2001, has been easily overcome, while 'local involvement', once assured by the preference vote and by a locally active party-faction structure, is no longer a visible phenomenon.

The third section is devoted to the social, political and occupational features – and changes therein – of the members of Parliament and explores, among other things, the role of the new electoral system in bringing about the enhanced level of female representation that was registered by the 2006 outcome.

The fourth section is devoted to the formation of Parliament's internal bodies – the parliamentary groups, standing committees and chairpersons' offices – at the beginning of the XV legislature. Do they really look different to their counterparts in the previous parliament? Are they committed, formally or by means of informal practices, to enforcing bi-polar competition? And how did they perform in the early days of the legislature, when a number of fundamental decisions about programmes and appointments had to be taken? We will answer these questions by looking in particular at the cohesion of the parliamentary groups and the internal organisation of the chambers in the first two months of the legislature.

Candidate selection, parliamentary recruitment and parliamentary turnover in 2006

As a closed-list system of proportional representation (PR), the new electoral law has reduced the potential gap between the expectations of those who design the candidate lists, and actual outcomes in terms of parliamentary recruitment. Indeed, each party was easily able to identify, in advance, a large number of places on the constituency lists that could be considered 'safe'. An immediate and obvious effect of the new system has thus been a strong centralisation of the process of candidate selection. Centralisation was further encouraged by those provisions of the law that made it possible to field as a candidate the same individual in an unlimited number of constituencies. By thus allowing the national party leaders to occupy the top positions on the lists presented in large numbers of constituencies and – in some cases – all of them, the law more or less guaranteed the loyalty and obedience of ambitious outsiders placed further down the lists, since these outsiders were well aware that their chances of election might depend heavily on the constituency that party leaders elected in several different places in the end chose to represent.

Of course, the parties could argue that by maximising the exposure of the most charismatic figures, multiple candidacies on the part of their leaders were likely to maximise their electoral support. However, more specific and more egoistic factors may have been at work – such as awareness that the practice allowed leaders to mark the distance with their 'lieutenants' and/or to reduce the institutional presence of troublesome internal factions. It was not to be wondered at, therefore, that in all of the parties the process of candidate selection was far from painless.

The use that was made of multiple candidacies varied between the two coalitions. On the centre right, the fact that Berlusconi, Fini and Casini were fielded as the heads of their respective lists in all 26 of the constituencies for the Chamber of Deputies indicated that their parties wanted to use the provisions of the electoral law as a mechanism for testing the relative popularity of their leaders. A similar strategy was also followed by the Northern League, which placed its leader, Umberto Bossi, in the top position in all of the Chamber constituencies of the northern and central regions down to Rome. The heads of the lists presented for the Senate elections, and the candidates occupying the second to the fifth places on the lists for the Chamber, were in many cases the other national leaders, whose precise placements were rotated in such a way as to avoid surprising exclusions from the new legislature.

The core parties of the centre left pursued a contrasting strategy: having supported Romano Prodi in the October 2005 primary elections, they decided to present joint lists for the Chamber – the Ulivo – where the top positions were shared between Prodi (who headed the list in fifteen constituencies) and the leading spokespersons of the Ulivo's constituent parties.[4] On the other hand, the minor parties were much more likely to 'use' their national leaders to head their Chamber lists more or less everywhere, and to rotate other leading figures among the safest positions.[5]

However, the number of top positions taken by candidates fielded in more than one constituency was high in all the parties, with the result that a very large number of members of Parliament found that they had been elected in several constituencies: in the Chamber, the proportion of members in this position was over 17 per cent, with about 110 deputies achieving at least two 'passes' to Montecitorio. As mentioned, such a strategy is an impressive tool of centralisation of the recruitment process. However, its costs were probably underestimated: many parties found themselves in deep trouble, in the weeks following the elections, because of internal disputes involving outgoing parliamentarians who had failed to achieve re-election, 'lucky losers' who got in because of leaders' choices of constituency, and 'unlucky losers' penalised by these same choices.

The game of options and renunciations on the part of members with several 'passes' was time consuming: only at the end of April did the profile of the new parliament emerge with any clarity. This was due, among other things, to the various legal prohibitions on multiple office-holding – meaning, for example, that a successful candidate who also happened to be a regional councillor was obliged to make a choice between the two offices – which thus necessitated, for those involved, complex decisions whose results looked, in some cases, as though they might not be known for some months.[6]

It is therefore difficult to predict how stable the parliamentary elite will be during the XV legislature; and in fact reliable measurement of the rates of persistence and turnover of parliamentarians will be possible only at a later stage, when all the choices arising from the various office-holding incompatibilities have been made and when the outcomes of future local, European and regional elections have told us how many parliamentarians prefer to leave Rome to occupy more visible or politically remunerative positions. However, the evidence collected during the first couple of months of the XV legislature confirms what we had already observed in previous years: namely, that offices at the sub-national and European levels seem to

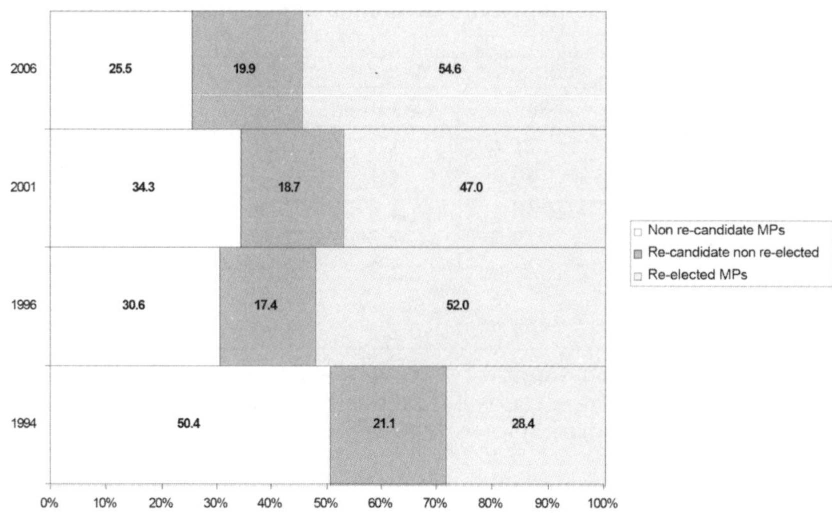

Figure 11.1 Continuity and retirement among parliamentarians, 1994–2001

Notes: The data refer to the deputies and senators in office during the previous legislature, excluding those who died during the legislature but including those who resigned before it came to an end. The raw numbers are 960 parliamentarians in 1994 (that is, at end of the XI (1992–94) legislature), 961 in 1996, 974 in 2001 and 958 in 2006.

Source: Data archive on Italian Parliamentary personnel, CIRCaP – Siena.

be of growing attractiveness as compared to a seat in Parliament.

The extent of continuity in patterns of recruitment within the parliamentary elite can be measured by considering, among outgoing members of Parliament, the percentages of those who are successfully re-elected, those who fail to secure re-election and those who retire. Figure 11.1 suggests that the new electoral system had little impact on the figures – which remain broadly in line with those for previous years – concerning the general process of parliamentary recruitment. This in turn suggests that the new – bi-polar although extremely fragmented – party system had become fairly well consolidated by the time of the 2006 elections; for the level of persistence of the political elite remains essentially the same despite the change in the 'rules of the electoral game'.

The overall proportion of newcomers at the start of the XV legislature (Table 11.1) was very close to the average for the last two elections (41 per cent in the Chamber and 40.4 per cent in the Senate). On the centre-left, of course, the percentage of newcomers (49.2 per

Table 11.1 Turnover, seniority and circulation of parliamentarians after the 2006 elections

	% newcomers		Average seniority		Interval re-elected	
	Chamber	Senate	Chamber	Senate	Chamber	Senate
RC	65.9	71.4	1.5	0.68	2.3	7.1
Ulivo	43.0	39.8	2.1	1.31	3.2	6.9
UDC	35.9	38.1	2.4	1.38	–	4.8
FI	26.9	19.0	2.3	1.73	3.0	5.1
AN	23.0	22.0	2.7	2.05	–	4.9
Total MPs	41.5	35.2	2.2	1.65	3.6	5.2

Notes: Average seniority is calculated as the mean number of successful elections for each group of representatives. 'Interval re-elected' refers to the percentage of representatives who served in parliament before 2006, although not during the 14th legislature (2001–06).

Source: Data archive on Italian Parliamentary personnel, CIRCaP – Siena.

cent in the Chamber and 53.9 per cent in the Senate) is maximised by the increase in the number of available seats. But the figures for the centre-right (31.3 per cent in the Chamber and 28.9 per cent in the Senate) are also remarkable, confirming the tendency towards a relatively high rate of 'early retirement' by the new politicians which we had already remarked upon during the 'majoritarian decade' (Verzichelli, 1998; Verzichelli and Zucchini, 2002).

Other indicators of persistence and turnover of the parliamentary elite confirm the trends of the recent past: the 'new parties' are normally less likely to be characterised by high levels of 'parliamentary seniority'. Especially relevant is the difference between Forza Italia and the two centre-right parties that are connected with the traditional party politics of the 'First Republic'. On the centre left, the core parties of the Ulivo, despite the obviously high rate of turnover of their parliamentarians, have a consistently large number of senior members, unlike the 'movement-based' parties, such as Rifondazione Comunista, which is inclined to change the composition of its parliamentary elite more frequently.

However, persistence and turnover among the parliamentary elite seem to be growing increasingly complex. The increasing mean age of members of Parliament (now about 52 years) suggests that the path that must be trod before developing a parliamentary career is getting longer and longer, with some remarkable differences among the parties. Very striking is the figure for the mean age of the 'beginners'

(49.4 years), which is particularly high in the DS and the Margherita (50.9 years) and somewhat lower in parties like RC, AN and FI (where it is 47.4, 48.5 and 47.6 respectively). It is interesting to note that the most remarkable difference between the two parties of the centre right on the one hand, and the DS and the Margherita on the other, refers to female recruitment: women who enter Parliament for the first time as representatives of FI or AN are much younger (at 43.9 and 46 respectively) than those in the two parties of the centre left (where the average ages are 49.3 and 50.6 for the Margherita and the DS respectively). Finally, the Northern League proves to be the youngest group in the Chamber of Deputies, where the average age of its representatives is 42 and the average age of its newcomers, 40. These latter figures suggest a shortening of the length of the political training undertaken by the Northern League's representatives before they enter Parliament.

The new parliamentary elite: social and political characteristics

The 2006 elections saw a significant, though still less-than-satisfactory, increase in the proportions of female members of Parliament. These, at 17.5 per cent for the Chamber and 13.9 per cent for the Senate, are the highest figures ever reached in Italy. Indeed, the under-representation of women has been one of the most persistent of the characteristics of Italy's parliamentary elite and the decline to around 11 per cent in the proportion of female parliamentarians in 1996 persuaded several scholars (Nevola, 1997; Cotta, Mastropaolo and Verzichelli, 2000) that the proportion was unlikely to be increased without special legal supports. This was also the opinion of the majority of the female (and several male) legislators at the end of the XIV legislature, when the centre-right coalition passed the current, proportional, electoral law. The activism of the Minister for Equal Opportunities, Stefania Prestigiacomo, led the Cabinet, in February 2006, to propose the introduction of a female quota of at least 30 per cent of the places on all electoral lists. The fact that the system of PR introduced by the electoral law reform was of the closed-list variety seemed to suggest that, in terms of its results, the quota mechanism would prove particularly effective. After several impassioned debates during which several other aspects of the electoral law were also discussed,[7] Parliament rejected the proposal by a small majority, the votes of male representatives of minor parties – who saw their chances of re-election as seriously jeopardised by the proposal – being decisive.

Why, despite the absence of a mechanism supporting greater balance in the gender distribution of candidates and members of Parliament, did the proportion of female representatives increase in 2006? We suppose it to be the outcome of the interaction of a set of variables of which the re-introduction of a proportional electoral system and the shift in the distribution of seats from centre right to centre left are the most important. Comparative studies on female legislative recruitment (Beckwith, 1990; Lovenduski and Norris, 1993; Matland, 2002) have provided a wealth of evidence supporting the hypothesis that female representation is favoured by PR rather than majority electoral systems as the latter but not the former give parties a rational incentive to present a 'balanced ticket' (Matland, 1993; Norris, 1996). The comparative literature has also stressed the role played by party ideology: women are more likely to be fielded by, and elected for, left-wing parties; and in the legislatures where those parties have a majority, the presence of female legislators is higher (Caul, 1999).

Our data provide some corroboration for these two hypotheses. When we compare the percentages of women candidates and members of Parliament elected in the 1994, 1996 and 2001 with the corresponding percentages for the 2006 election and the current legislature, the effects of the change of electoral system are quite clear. The share of women candidates and members of Parliament (Figure 11.2 and Table 11.2) has increased in both the two main coalitions. In the Chamber, parties like the Margherita on the centre left and FI and AN on the centre right have significantly increased the proportions of women among their delegations. Among the parties of the centre left, the DS and RC confirm their role as the leading parties in terms of the proportions of their representatives who are female, without any significant change for the first, but a significant decline for the second. The decision to run joint lists with the Margherita probably hampered the possibility of a more significant increase for women among the DS members of Parliament – the coalition between the DS and the Margherita having limited the growth of female representation simply by virtue of the fact that the overall limitations on the candidatures available to each party necessarily also reduced the slots available for women. On the other hand, the decline in the proportion of female parliamentarians in the two Communist parties, RC and the PdCI, may reflect little more than the fact that in 2001 their representatives were too small in number to be able to reflect true tendencies.

Two further factors – both of which made female (under)representation a relevant issue at the time of the electoral campaign – may be relevant to the increased female representation brought by the 2006 outcome. The first is the failure of the referendum to repeal law no.

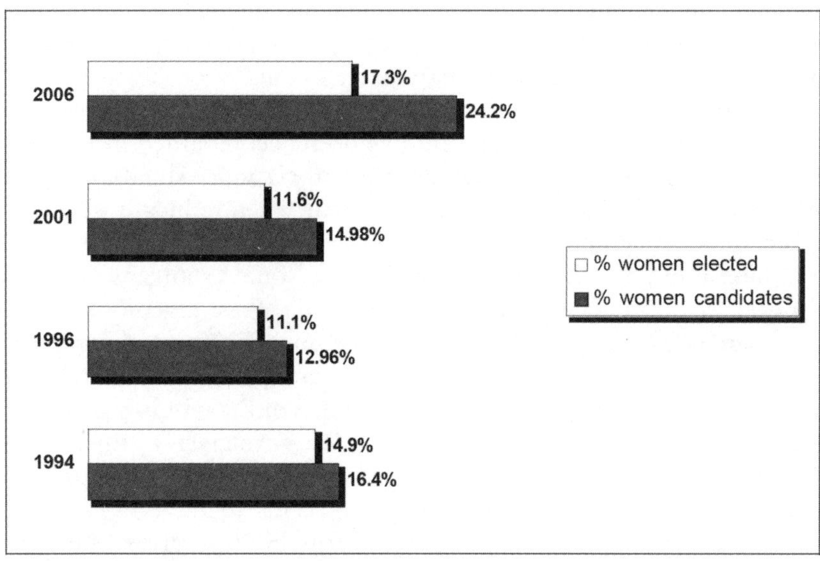

Figure 11.2 Percentage of female candidates and members of the Chamber of Deputies, 1994–2006

Source: Data provided by the Ministero degli Interni. A detailed elaboration can be found in Papavero (2006).

Table 11.2 Percentage of women elected to the Chamber, by coalition and by party, 1994–2006

	1994	*1996*	*2001*	*2006*
Centre left	19.4	14.6	16.7	19.5
Centre right	10.5	6.3	6.7	14.6
DS			25.4	26.8
Margherita			6.3	14.5
Ulivo (DS + Margherita)			–	20.9
RC			50.0	31.7
PdCI			30.0	12.5
la Rosa nel Pugno (SDI + Radicals)			–	11.0
Greens			28.6	18.8
UDEUR			0.0	7.1
AN			3.2	16.7
FI			7.7	17.0
LN			11.5	8.7
UDC			5.7	7.7
Others			8.0	7.4

Source: Data archive on Italian Parliamentary personnel, CIRCaP – Siena. A detailed elaboration can be found in Papavero (2006).

40/2004, on artificial insemination, held in June 2005. This event generated a mobilisation of women in parties, labour unions and pressure groups, which at least the main parties could not easily ignore. As a consequence of that failure, the re-emergence of the debate concerning law no. 192/1981 on abortion has been accompanied in both the coalitions by strongly expressed demands for a more significant presence of women in Parliament, at a moment when 'ethically sensitive' issues, often affecting women's lives in a specific and direct way, are becoming more and more relevant. The personal involvement of the Minister for Equal Opportunities, Stefania Prestigiacomo, in the campaign in favour of modification of law no. 40/2004, and her subsequent activism in promoting a more balanced gender distribution among parliamentarians by taking advantage of the window of opportunity opened by the new PR electoral rules, have given to the issue of female representation very high levels of visibility. At the same time the very failure of Prestigiacomo's initiative seems to have induced the main parties to attempt to compensate for the 'bad press' they may have received among the female electorate as a result of the issue – possibly also giving potential female candidates within the parties strong arguments to be included on lists in viable positions.

The process of re-professionalisation of the parliamentary elite that had already emerged in the 2001 legislature (Verzichelli and Zucchini, 2002) emerges even more strongly in 2006. It is probably related both to the contingent circumstances of the outcome itself and to the changes brought about by the new electoral law. On the one hand, the positive performance of the parties of the left, in which the weight of the representatives with a professional political background has always been higher than in other parties, has increased the proportion of parliamentarians with such a background. Indeed, the DS, RC and the PdCI are the parties with the highest percentage of party professionals among their representatives (almost 35 per cent). They are also the parties in which the weight of this professional category has most evidently increased vis-à-vis 2001. To a lesser extent, this also happened to AN, which on the centre right is the party with the highest proportion of political professionals, and which shares with the leftist parties the characteristic of having the oldest established party organisation. However, the phenomenon of professionalisation has also involved parties – such as FI and the Margherita, around 10 per cent of whose parliamentarians have professional political backgrounds[8] – the organisations of which have been established more recently. In addition, some smaller formations – such as the alliance between the New PSI and Gianfranco Rotondi's Christian Democratic

Party, Italia dei Valori, UDEUR and to some extent also the alliance between the Radicals and Socialists – have recruited political personalities from 'old' parties, like the Socialists, the Christian Democrats and the Radical Party, looking for new placements within the party system.

These data suggest that behind the increases we are talking about there is probably a systemic dynamic at work. In particular, two different and divergent mechanisms seem to have been activated by the new rules of the game. On the one hand, the closed-list system introduced by the electoral-law reform, in limiting the visibility of individual candidates and favouring a major centralisation of the recruitment process, may have created, especially in the larger parties, an incentive to recruit candidates among politicians, in order to enforce party discipline once in parliament. Today, with these rules of the game, the parties are probably less interested in recruiting visible, but also potentially more 'independent' personalities. In other words, the closed list system seems to promise a higher level of party cohesion. On the other hand, the growing weight of 'pure politicians' among members of Parliament may also reflect the fragmentation of the Italian party system. Indeed, since fragmentation encounters no limit in the new PR system, it is likely that intra-party struggles will have promoted 'political entrepreneurs' from within parties' machineries as against 'policy entrepreneurs' or 'constituency servants' with predominantly non-political backgrounds.

If we exclude the increase in the proportion of political professionals, the variations in the occupational profile of parliamentarians (Table 11.3) are more clearly related to the electoral fate of the different parties. There was a slight decrease in the proportions of representatives coming from the liberal professions (down from 7 per cent in 2001 to 6 per cent in 2006) – with especially large declines for architects, engineers (down from 2.5 to 1.9 per cent) and lawyers (down from 15 to 11.1 per cent) – reflecting the electoral defeat of the centre-right parties, which however continue to be the main representatives of these professional categories. Other professional groups, like primary and secondary school teachers, and university professors, are slightly less represented in the new parliament than in the past, despite the positive electoral performance of the parties which in these professional categories are more deeply rooted. In 'old' parties, such as the DS, it is mainly at the expense of these professions that the weight of 'pure politicians' has grown; while within the Margherita the presence of university professors has increased, balancing the emerging political professionalism. This picture confirms the differentiation between the professional profiles of the representatives of the two coalitions, but a closer look reveals additional, intra-coalition, differences reflecting a complex process of 're-positioning' in the structure of interest representation. Private-sector occupations, and mainly liberal professionals and industrialists, are more heavily represented in the parties of the centre right. However, among these professional categories, senior private-sector managers have strongly increased their presence among parliamentarians of the centre left: the Margherita, in particular, shows rates close to those of the centre-right parties (with an increase from 2.9 per cent in 2001 to 8.6 per cent in 2006). The centre-left parties continue to draw relatively large proportions of their representatives from the public sector, in particular from among teachers and academics, but the proportion of junior public officials, which has

Table 11.3 Professional background of MPs, Chamber of Deputies, 2006 (%)

	DS	Margherita	AN	FI	All MPs
Professional politicians	36.8	2.9	23.9	10.4	20.2
Trade unionists	8.0	3.7	0.0	0.0	2.9
Workers	2.4	1.2	0.0	0.0	0.6
Liberal professionals	1.6	2.5	5.6	12.6	6.0
Landowners	0.0	0.0	0.0	1.5	0.3
Industrialists	0.0	1.2	0.0	5.2	1.9
Lawyers	1.6	7.4	15.5	16.4	11.1
Architects and engineers	0.8	8.6	4.2	3.0	1.9
Medical professionals	4.8	8.6	4.2	6.0	5.7
Commercial consultants	0.8	4.9	4.2	4.5	3.4
Other professionals	2.4	0.0	4.2	3.7	2.9
Teachers	9.6	8.6	4.2	3.0	6.3
University professors	4.8	14.8	1.4	3.0	6.4
University-based liberal professionals	0.8	1.2	0.0	0.7	0.7
Judges	0.8	1.2	0.0	0.0	0.5
Army officers	0.0	0.0	2.8	0.0	0.3
Senior public officials	2.4	3.7	4.2	4.4	3.4
Junior public officials	9.6	6.1	5.6	2.2	6.3
Senior private-sector managers	3.2	8.6	8.5	11.9	6.8
Private-sector clerical workers	5.6	1.2	0.0	1.5	3.1
Journalists	4.0	7.3	11.3	6.7	7.8
Others	0.0	0.0	0.0	3.0	1.3
Total	100.0	100.0	100.0	100.0	100.0

Source: Data archive on Italian Parliamentary personnel, CIRCaP – Siena.

Table 11.4 Professional background of parliamentarians belonging to the main political parties, Duncan index 1994–2006

Parties	Legislatures			
	1994	1996	2001	2006
FI–PDS/DS	61.39	55.31	48.01	58.94
AN–FI	57.16	41.63	30.76	27.81
LN–FI	40.17	67.20	53.71	51.08
LN–AN	37.18	64.93	64.66	56.46
AN–PDS/DS	41.28	40.92	46.31	45.97
PDS/DS-LN	53.84	67.40	66.06	66.11
DS–Margherita	–	–	34.31	45.57
Margherita–FI	–	–	34.39	41.78
Margherita–AN	–	–	33.12	40.98
Margherita–LN	–	–	50.41	65.37

Note: The Duncan Index is a measure of the differences between two distributions. It is calculated as the sum of absolute percentage point differences between the proportions of each of the two distributions across each category, divided by two. A value of zero signifies complete identity; a value of 100 signifies complete difference. For examples of its use, see Wessels (1997: 89), Martinelli and Zucchini (2001: 846), and Verzichelli and Zucchini (2001: 232).

Source: Data archive on Italian Parliamentary personnel, CIRCaP – Siena.

doubled as compared to 2001, has increased especially in the DS. At the same time, AN, the party in which, among those of the centre right, the latter professional category was most deeply rooted, shows a decline in the proportion of its representatives with such a professional background.

These variations can be better evaluated when we use the Duncan Index, a synthetic index that has allowed us to measure the degree of dissimilarity between the distribution of professional categories in different pairs of parties of the centre left and centre right (Table 11.4). The available data for the period 1994–2006 show two tendencies. On the one hand, between the main parties of the two coalitions there is a clear tendency towards a more accentuated differentiation in the professional profile of their parliamentarians. Particularly interesting is the case of the DS and FI which, after a partial reduction in the distance between them in 2001, have returned almost to the levels of differentiation of 1994. On the other hand, within the coalitions, FI and AN show a clear and steady tendency increasingly to recruit their representatives from the same professional fields, while the DS and the Margherita have further and significantly differentiated the categories from which they recruit. The Northern League confirms its peculiarities, being the party most distant, both from the parties of its own coalition and from the parties of the centre left (Martinelli and Zucchini, 2001).

A look at the backgrounds of the parliamentarians elected in the 'foreign' constituency reveals interesting elements to complete the picture of the legislative recruitment process in Italy. The representatives elected abroad are trade unionists (mainly from the international branches of the CGIL, and to a lesser extent the Catholic CISL), small businessmen, journalists and high civil servants from the European Parliament. Almost all of these newcomers have had long experience as representatives of Italian communities abroad, or as members of extensive networks of Italian regional and national associations (cultural associations, youth associations, industrial associations and so forth), or of the extensive network of bilateral (Italo-American, Italo-Argentine and so forth) chambers of commerce scattered all over the world. However, one of the most important channels of recruitment for these parliamentarians has been the General Council for Italians Resident Abroad (CGIE), a body set up within the Ministry of Foreign Affairs in 1989, which gives advice to the Cabinet and to Parliament on all matters concerning Italian living overseas.[9] In fact, most of the parliamentarians elected by the centre-left coalition have such a political background. As representatives of the complex (and, for the Italian public, still unknown) interests of the Italian communities abroad, these eighteen representatives have focused their parliamentary activity on specific legislative commissions in both the chambers: those for Foreign Affairs, EU Policies, Social Affairs (in the Chamber of Deputies) and Public Health (in the Senate). Moreover, in the Senate, two of the representatives elected abroad are members of the legislative commissions for agriculture, and for industry, commerce and tourism.

A look at the mean age of these parliamentarians suggests that the parties of the centre left have been able to develop deeper roots in the communities of the Italians abroad than have FI or AN. The mean age of the deputies elected by the centre left is 56.2, while the representatives elected by FI are very young (average age 38), suggesting the absence of a more structural and long-lasting tie of this party with the Italian communities abroad. On the other hand, the 75 years of the deputy elected by AN seem to be more a tribute to the homesickness of some proportion of first-generation emigrants than the reflection of an ability of the party to link the emergent needs and interests of a multi-faceted community with those of its country of origin. In other words, the parties that have supported the reform are also the parties that have been less able, at this election, to find channels of recruitment for representatives of this particular group of Italian citizens, probably suffering from their lesser organisational strength.

Parliamentary elites at work: the political environment of the XV legislature

Having analysed the patterns of turnover, and the social and political profiles of the parliamentarians elected in 2006, we think that a third dimension relevant to our attempt to assess the new parliamentary context concerns the degree of homogeneity and fragmentation within the legislature. Expectations, during the weeks before the vote, were quite contradictory: on the one hand, a high level of fragmentation was expected, this having been, in a sense, a conscious aim of the sponsors of the 2005 electoral reform. On the other hand, the supporters of the core parties both in the centre-right and in the centre-left coalition were hoping that their respective leaders, who were by far and away the most important protagonists of the election campaign, might reduce the spread of support among the several lists and therefore reinforce the positions of a few, relatively united, actors within the new parliament. Such expectations were directly related to what was the most significant question hanging on the outcome of the April election, namely the capacity of Parliament to sustain a government which, in the absence of some sensational outcome such as a perfect tie, had to be the expression of *one* of the two camps.

In order to explore these issues, we can begin by comparing the party composition of the new parliament with that of the previous legislature. Tables 11.5 and 11.6 suggest few very surprising changes, apart from those due to the small 'electoral swing' and the proportional effect of the new electoral system, already discussed. In the end, the party profile of the new parliament confirms the decisive role of the political supply side (Chiaramonte, chapter 10) and the substantial stabilisation of a fragmented (but slightly simplified) party system (Di Virgilio, 2006). A closer look at what happened in the days following the election shows that the slight reduction in fragmentation is due only to the formation of 'combined' parliamentary groups such as that of the Ulivo in both the chambers: if we use a standard measure, such as the effective number of parliamentary parties,[10] we discover that the decision to allow the formation of very small parliamentary groups in both chambers[11] brings about an increase in the actual numbers of groups, alongside effective numbers that are quite close to those for the end of the XIV legislature.

Table 11.5 Parliamentary groups at the end of the XIV and at the beginning of the XV legislature, Chamber of Deputies

End of XIV legislature			XV legislature		
Group	N	%	Group	N	%
RC	12	2.0	RC	41	6.5
			PdCI	16	2.5
			Greens	16	2.5
DS	129	21.1			
			Ulivo	220	34.9
Margherita	80	13.1			
			IdV	18	2.9
			la Rosa nel Pugno	18	2.9
			UDEUR	14	2.2
'Mixed' group	68	11.1	'Mixed' group	13	2.1
UDC	38	6.2	UDC	39	6.2
			DC–New PSI	6	1.0
FI	167	27.3	FI	134	21.3
LN	26	4.2	LN	23	3.7
AN	92	15.0	AN	72	11.4
Total seats	612		*Total seats*	630	
Actual of groups	8		Actual number number of groups	13	
Effective number of groups	5.64		Effective number of groups	5.17	

Note: The mixed group (Gruppo Misto) is a residual parliamentary group to which are automatically assigned all those deputies who, during the initial parliamentary session, do not request affiliation with any other group.

Source: Our elaboration on official data from www.parlamento.it.

Further worrying signs came a few weeks after the vote, with the effective start of the legislature, confirming that the Italian parliament remains a 'transformative' arena, especially when political appointments and specific, visible, issues are at stake. In such circumstances, parliamentary actors expect to be able to discuss and to modify without restriction proposals made by the government and/or the leadership of the majority. This is not to deny the highly adversarial nature of the party system: indeed, the election of RC leader, Fausto Bertinotti, as President of the Chamber of Deputies and the – obvious-

Table 11.6 Parliamentary groups at the end of the XIV and at the beginning of the XV legislature, Senate

Group	N	%	Group	N	%
			RC	27	8.4
			PdCI–Greens	11	3.4
Greens	10	3.1			
DS	64	20.0			
			Ulivo	101	31.4
Margherita	35	10.9			
			UDEUR		
Autonomie	10	3.1	Autonomie	10	3.1
'Mixed' group	34	10.6	'Mixed' group	17	5.3
UDC	30	9.4	UDC	21	6.5
			DC–other CdL	10	3.1
FI	74	23.1	FI	71	22.1
LN	17	5.3	LN	13	4.0
AN	46	14.4	AN	41	12.7
Total	320		*Total*	322	
Actual number of groups	9		Actual number of groups	10	
Effective number of groups	6.62		Effective number of groups	5.49	

Note: The Mixed group (Gruppo Misto) is a residual parliamentary group to which are automatically assigned all those senators who, during the initial parliamentary session, do not request affiliation with any other group.

Source: Our elaboration on official data from www.parlamento.it.

ly more difficult – election of a leader of the Margherita, Franco Marini, as Senate speaker, represented 'victories' for the majority – as did the election of the President of the Republic, a few days later, when the official candidate of the majority, Giorgio Napolitano, was elected at the fourth ballot (that is, as soon as the achievement of a simple majority became sufficient to secure election: at the first three ballots, majorities of two-thirds of those entitled to vote are required). However, signs of uncertainty among parliamentarians were already evident during these episodes, confirming the 'critical role' of a number of parliamentary actors including certain senior members, the leaders of certain small parliamentary groups, the leaders of factions within parliamentary groups, members of the mixed group, life senators and the handful of members elected in the constituencies representing Italians resident abroad.

The lengthy negotiations that preceded formation of the government – and which led to the formation of what was (at 102 members, among ministers, junior ministers and under-secretaries) the largest government in the Republic's history – confirmed these difficulties, highlighting once more the 'post-electoral' nature of the process of government formation in Italy, notwithstanding the consolidation of a 'presidential' style of leadership selection in 2006. Finally, the processes underlying selection of the chairs of the permanent committees in both the chambers were complex and in some cases surprising. Again, the 'majority rule' was at work, being suspended in the single instance of the chair of one of the Senate committees, but the candidatures were always widely debated, and in one case the chairperson in question was elected with the decisive votes of the opposition, against the 'official' candidate of the majority.

Conclusion: the paradox of the parliamentary role in Italy

Our analysis suggests that the current Italian parliament reflects the workings of a curious mix of old and new factors. Three features of the new parliament stand out. First, despite marked differences in the recruitment strategies and in the characteristics of parliamentarians *between* the two coalitions, there remains a considerable degree of fragmentation and heterogeneity *within* each of them. Second, there is a persisting democratic deficit in processes of recruitment: the closed-list system of PR has favoured the centralisation of candidate selection within each party, limiting the chances of 'alternative' candidates such as the ones that were fielded in many of the single-member districts between 1994 and 2001. At the same time, the new PR system has provided a crucial means of helping to bring about a positive effect – an increase in female representation – something that faces considerable obstacles in Italy, despite the repeated declarations of intents of countless political actors. A third feature is the persistence of an aged and in many respects multifaceted parliamentary elite. Patterns of parliamentary recruitment are still oriented to the selection of skilled and experienced politicians (and, as we have noted, there has been an increase in the proportion of parliamentarians with purely political backgrounds). But, once again, features such as this are unevenly distributed among the parliamentary parties. Nor do 'party specific' features, such as the young age of representatives of the Northern

League, or the difference between Forza Italia and the other large parties in terms of rates of seniority, appear to be getting any less marked with the passage of time.

Together, these features point to a series of contrasts with important implications for the functioning of Parliament as an institution. On the one hand, the new electoral system, by centralising candidate selection, has contributed to a return to levels of political professionalisation more typical of those extant before the party system upheavals of the early 1990s and this is likely to facilitate the enforcement of discipline within the parliamentary groups. On the other hand, the overall proportional redistribution and the results achieved by the minor parties in each coalition have created (especially on the centre left) 'dangerous' levels of fragmentation.

Second, the political and professional backgrounds of the current members of Parliament speak to the persisting polarisation of two distinct groups of elements characterising political recruitment in the two coalitions, and confirm that bi-polarity has become a consolidated feature of the party system as much in the parliamentary as in the electoral arena. At the same time, by enabling the over-representation of a number of specific and sensitive social groups and interests, the closed-list system has helped each single party to preserve its own 'identity'. In the long run, this could obstruct the emergence of the minimum levels of bi-partisanship necessary for effective functioning of the legislature and, above all within the centre left, it could create problems for the deliberative action of the Cabinet and for the unity of the parliamentary majority.

This highlights the paradox that while Parliament appears to have been weakened by the 2006 outcome, it remains the arena in which the most sensitive decisions (including those concerning appointments, the standing orders, the electoral system and the Constitution) have to be made. It is no accident that, in seeking to re-revive bi-partisan discussion on the issue of constitutional reform in the aftermath of the referendum of 26 June 2006, Prodi said that a reduction in the number of parliamentarians was a necessary first step towards the achievement of inter-coalition agreement. The argument is quite obvious, but it is also very clear that in the 2006 legislature, with its large number of veto players and uncertainties, the difficulties in the way of reaching decisions such as this one seem to be greater than ever.

We can therefore conclude that, in terms of its 'systemic effects', the 2006 election does not appear, in comparison with previous elections, to have changed very much: despite the new electoral system and despite the unusual quality of the outcome in terms of the margin of victory of the winning coalition, the crucial element remains the capacity of Parliament to reform itself (especially through reform of its standing orders) and thus to make a positive contribution to the prospects for institutional reform more generally.

Notes

1 The chapter has been designed and developed jointly by the two authors. However, Licia Papavero has been responsible for drafting the first three sections, Luca Verzichelli for drafting the other two.

2 Of course, the use we make of this term differs from the classic definition of the 'imperfect two-party system' developed by Giorgio Galli (1966) to interpret Italian party politics in the period between 1948 and 1963. We simply mean here that a decisive step towards transformation of the two relatively stable (but fragmented) coalitions into the embryos of 'real' unitary parties, were it to happen, could be represented as a move in the direction of a 'more perfect two-party system'.

3 More precisely, Prodi and supporters of the Partito Democratico were pushing for the establishment of a unitary party already in October 2005, following the success of the primary election to decide the centre left's candidate for the premiership. Passage of the electoral law reform in December 2005 suggested a more cautious approach, but supporters of the Partito Democratico achieved two immediate results in the form of the joint, Ulivo, list for the Chamber and the promise of single groups bringing together Ulivo members in both branches of Parliament. Berlusconi, on the other hand, announced more than once during the election campaign that, whatever the result of the elections, he would work for unification of the centre-right coalition in the new legislative term.

4 They were Piero Fassino, Dario Franceschini, Rosy Bindi, Fabio Mussi, Vannino Chiti, Francesco Rutelli, Ciriaco De Mita, Massimo D'Alema, Luciano Violante and Arturo Parisi.

5 Particularly centralised were the strategies adopted by RC and the PdCI, whose respective leaders, Fausto Bertinotti and Oliviero Diliberto, headed their parties' lists in all 26 constituencies. More open, but still very personalised, was the strategy of Italia dei Valori (rotating the leader Antonio Di Pietro with former Mayor of Palermo, Leoluca Orlando), the Greens and la Rosa nel Pugno.

6 The most famous case is that of the President of the Lombardy region, Roberto Formigoni, who organised an internet poll to decide between his seat in the Senate and the regional office he already held. His final decision to remain in the regional government was formalised only at the end of June.

7 The position of centre-left parliamentarians was made difficult by a deliberative process that linked discussion of the quota system with discussion of the new electoral system to which they were opposed. Therefore,

notwithstanding declarations of support for the proposals of Prestigiacomo, voting behaviour in the chambers was coherently oriented to rejection of the entire package of proposals concerning the electoral system.

8 If we look at the data for the occupations that are most similar to the category of professional politicians, such as trade unionists and journalists, the trend towards re-professionalisation of the Italian political class becomes even more marked. Interestingly enough, both the categories have grown in significance on the centre left generally, but the largest increases have occurred in the Margherita.

9 Of the CGIE's 94 members, 65 are directly elected by Italian citizens living abroad, the rest being appointed, by the Government, national organisations of emigrants, parties with parliamentary representation, trade unions and other organisations.

10 We use here an adapted version of the well known Laasko and Taagepera (1979) index of effective number of parties, one that is calculated using the shares of seats of the parliamentary groups instead of the vote shares of the party lists.

11 The decision is consistent with the established practice of allowing the formation of groups with numbers lower than the thresholds (twenty in the Chamber, ten in the Senate) set out in the parliamentary standing orders when the groups in question represent organised nation-wide parties fielding a list in every constituency.

References

Beckwith, K. (1990), 'Candidature femminili e sistemi elettorali', *Rivista Italiana di scienza politica*, 20:1, 73–103.

Caul, M. (1999), 'Women's representation in Parliament: the role of political parties', *Party Politics*, 5:1, 79–98.

Cotta, M., Mastropaolo, A. and Verzichelli, L. (2000), 'Parliamentary elite transformations along the discontinuous road of democratization: Italy 1861–1999', in H. Best and M. Cotta (eds), *Parliamentary Representatives in Europe 1848–2000: Legislative Recruitment and Careers in Eleven European Countries*, Oxford, Oxford University Press.

Di Virgilio, A. (2006), 'Forza e debolezza delle coalizioni dopo le politiche di aprile', *Il Mulino*, 3, pp. 443–452.

Galli, G. (1966), *Il bipartitismo imperfetto*, Bologna, Il Mulino.

Laasko, M. and Taagepera, R. (1979), '"Effective" number of parties: a measure with application to West Europe', *Comparative Political Studies*, 12:1, 3–27.

Lovenduski, J. and Norris, P. (eds) (1993), *Gender and Party Politics*, London, Sage Publications.

Martinelli, A. and Zucchini, F. (2001), 'Profilo sociale e professionale, livello e tipo di istruzione ed esperienza politica dei deputati italiani. Evoluzioni e prospettive', in L. Violante (ed.), *Annali della storia di Italia. Vol. 17, Il Parlamento*, Turin: Einaudi.

Matland, R. E. (1993), 'Institutional variables affecting female representation in national legislatures: the case of Norway', *The Journal of Politics*, 55:3, 737–755.

Matland, R. E. (2002), 'Enhancing women's political participation: legislative recruitment and electoral systems', in *Women in Parliament: Beyond Numbers*, Stockholm, International IDEA, www.idea.int.

Nevola, G. (1997), 'Alla ricerca di un ceto politico: I candidati del ciclo 1994–1996 tra innovazione e consolidamento', in P. Corbetta and A. L. Parisi (eds), *Cavalieri e fanti: Proposte e proponenti nelle elezioni del 1994 e del 1996*, Bologna, Il Mulino.

Norris, P. (1996), 'Legislative Recruitment', in L. LeDuc, R. G. Niemi and P. Norris (eds), *Comparing Democracies: Elections and Voting in Global Perspective*, Thousand Oaks, CA, Sage.

Norris, P. (1997), *Passages to Power: Legislative Recruitment in Advanced Democracies*, Cambridge, Cambridge University Press.

Papavero, L. (2006), 'Revisiting the "Contagion Theory": Female Parliamentary Recruitment in Italy and Spain (1975–2005)', PhD thesis, University of Siena.

Verzichelli, L. (1998), 'Parliamentary elites and the Italian transition', *European Journal of Political Research*, 34, 121–150.

Verzichelli, L. and Zucchini, F. (2002), 'The new parliament and the start of a decisive legislature', in J. L. Newell (ed.), *The Italian General Election of 2001: Berlusconi's Victory*, Manchester and New York, Manchester University Press.

Wessels, B. (1997), 'Germany', in P. Norris (ed.), *Passages to Power: Legislative Recruitment in Advanced Democracies*, Cambridge, Cambridge University Press.

Conclusion: not an ambiguous outcome (even though of uncertain consequences)

James L. Newell

What is the significance of the outcome of the general election of 2006? This question can be answered from the point of view of what the election tells us about the nature of Italian voting behaviour and the party system, and from the point of view of its wider political consequences.

Voting behaviour

As a number of the contributors to this volume have implied or stated, the campaign run by Silvio Berlusconi was a reflection of his populism. Because they claim to be the authentic voice of 'the people', populist leaders are naturally intolerant of rules and institutions that limit their freedom to act on behalf of the ordinary citizens with whom they believe, genuinely or otherwise, they have a privileged relationship. It was not surprising then (and, indeed, as much had been predicted beforehand) that as soon as the results were known the centre right cried 'foul'. Initially, its claim was that victory had been stolen from it by irregularities in the way the votes had been counted and that their correction would be sufficient to overturn the result in its favour. As a propaganda weapon, the power of this claim lay, like so much in the armoury of Berlusconi especially, in its circularity: if the Cdl and Forza Italia in particular are the authentic representatives of the people, then if they lose an election it can only be due to irregularities (voters would not be such *coglioni* as to vote against their own interests). What is the evidence that there have been irregularities? – the fact that the Cdl has lost the election. But as Ignazi (2006: 435) points out, the claim was one that was bound to lose force with the passage of time and the failure of genuine evidence to materialise, and so it was not long before the claim that victory had been stolen metamorphosed into the claim that the victory was 'mutilated' – or in other words, that as well as being morally doubtful, the centre left's victory was numerically ambiguous.

In fact there was no ambiguity. The 24,755 votes that separated the two coalitions in the Chamber election were drawn from the arena that counted for the purposes of assigning the majority premium (and it is probably for this reason that claims that the victory was 'narrow' have had so much purchase). But as Chiaramonte points out in chapter 10, there were two additional arenas in which the Chamber election took place. Across the three arenas the victory of the centre left was clear cut: it outdistanced the centre right by 130,322 votes (Table 10.1). The fact that the centre left won fewer votes than the centre right in the Senate contest can hardly be adduced as a counter to the argument being made here: all that tells us – on the assumption that all, or the vast majority, of those voting for both branches do so in the same way (Agosta, 2006: 461) – is that the centre right had a moderate advantage among that part of the electorate consisting of voters over the age of 25 (Corbetta and Vassallo, 2006: 423). The fact remains that, among the voting population as a whole, the centre left had the support of a clear majority.

A second (and related) myth about voting behaviour in 2006 is that it bequeathed a country 'split down the middle'. Depending on the commentator, the split in question was numerical, ideological or geographical. Numerically, the country *was* closely divided, but this was true well *before* 2006[1] – in which year the salience of the division was heightened as the result of an electoral law that significantly reduced the vote for 'third' forces by pushing these to line up on one side or the other. In other words, the closeness of the division became more *visible* in 2006. Given the electoral law and its disincentives in the way of third-force candidacies – namely, the higher threshold they faced and the fact that the votes of all coalesced parties counted for the purposes of deciding the majority premium, not just the votes of those crossing the threshold – a decline in the share of the vote going to 'others' was almost inevitable simply because there were far fewer 'others' available to vote for in the first place. If the 99.1 per cent of the valid votes that then went to one or the other of the two main contenders in turn divided in the proportions 50.2 to 49.8, on what grounds was one to say that such a division was the sign of an electorate *significantly more* split than one divided in the proportions 52 to 48 per cent (say)?

Nor was it reasonable to infer, from the sharply bi-polar numerical division, the sign of an electorate sharply divided ideologically. While the bitterness of the campaign might have given plausibility to such an inference, by far the largest body of evidence about the outlooks of Italian voters points in the opposite direction. Indeed, if the evidence suggests that most voters are characterised by what Paolo Natale (2002) calls *fedeltà leggera*, or 'weak partisanship', then the effects of the latter are such as to sustain rather than weaken a division of voters sharply bi-polar in numerical terms; for weak partisanship is the kind of political tie that is insufficiently strong to ensure that voters will support their chosen party 'through thick and thin', but strong enough to ensure that, when they defect, their defection will rarely if ever take the form of voting for a party belonging to the opposing coalition.

Finally, much was made, especially by journalists, of the geographical distribution of the vote to argue that the country was split politically between an advanced north and a less productive south – the centre right apparently having improved upon its existing advantage in the more industrialised part of the country by successfully echoing demands for modernisation; the centre left having made its strongest gains in more depressed regions by successfully echoing demands for state protection. In short, if the centre right had lost the election, it remained the privileged representative of the country's most productive classes, the centre left having shown itself unable to speak to these strata. The interpretation is one that invites three comments. First, it is weakened by the fact that the persistence and growth of the centre right's northern support owed nothing to the party, FI, one thinks of as the most likely spearhead of modernisation (and which lost everywhere) and everything to the compensating growth of parties, AN and the UDC, most strongly associated with the south and with state intervention (Corbetta and Vassallo, 2006). Second, the interpretation falls victim to the ecological fallacy: as Corbetta and Vassallo (2006: 432–433) show, within the North, at a disaggregated level, there is no positive correlation between indicators of socio-economic modernity and support for the centre right; indeed, if anything, the opposite is the case. Third, to assume that the north represents the most economically advanced part of the country is to overlook the fact that it is at least matched if not exceeded by the central regions, the support of whose inhabitants goes, as it has always done, overwhelmingly to the centre left. In short, in its broadest outlines there was in 2006 nothing very new about the geographical distribution of support, to whose explanation the persistence of long-standing sub-cultural traditions continues to make a significant contribution, as Piero Ignazi (2006) has convincingly argued.

If, then, the electoral majority achieved by the centre left was neither mutilated nor ambiguous, how do we account for it? In chapter 2,

Michele Capriati shows that almost all the principal macroeconomic indicators moved in an unfavourable direction during the life of the Berlusconi government – whose calculations were all based on assumptions about growth that never materialised, and which was almost bound, therefore, to disappoint the expectations it had built up in 2001. Indeed, so great was the gap between expectations and reality (and the level of public disillusionment that came thus to be created) that it fed perceptions of the state of the economy and standards of living that were actually sometimes much worse than could reasonably be justified by official data (Guarnieri and Newell, 2005). Important in this was probably also what had been the emergence of leadership-centred campaigning combined with leaders' direct responsibility for platforms – which, as Donatella Campus notes, encourages citizens to seek to punish leaders for poor performances. The first, rather straightforward, explanation that suggests itself, then, is that on balance voters looked at the policy performance of the government and on the basis of what they (thought they) saw, voted it out of office. As Table I.1 on page 9 shows, the centre right was less successful than it had been in 2001 both in retaining its own support and in compensating for its losses by winning votes from those who had previously voted against it or abstained. Several things need to be said about this interpretation.

First, as Donatella Campus notes in chapter 7, if in First Republic Italy the nature of the party system made voting based on punishments and rewards unfamiliar to voters, then since 2001, 'both alternation and retrospective voting [have] become possible and available options'. In 2006, the centre left explicitly sought to elicit a vote based on retrospective judgements of the government's economic performance, something that was 'extremely well suited to the characteristics and the peculiarities of the Unione'. In the weeks leading up to polling day, opinion poll evidence showed that economic issues ranked highest in the list of priorities for most electors in deciding how to vote.

Second, the interpretation is one that is supported by the data on geographical variations in voting. If FI's losses in the north were counterbalanced by gains for AN and the UDC, then in the south – where as Biorcio shows they declined (AN) or grew less strongly (UDC) – the two parties were unable to compensate for FI's losses. Here, as Chiaramonte shows, the parties of the centre left made above-average gains. On the one hand, then, it was as if (and it may actually have been that) northern centre-right voters reacted to the government's performance as 'weak partisans' defecting from the party most closely identified with the cause of their disappointment without defecting to the other side. On the other hand, if there were nevertheless some net centre-left gains to be had from disappointment with the government's performance then the expectation had to be – as was in fact the case – that such gains would be greatest in the south where, by comparison with those in the north, voters are less partisan and less consistent in their electoral behaviour.

Third, the idea that the centre left's majority was essentially based on voters' retrospective judgements would appear to be of most help in seeking to make sense of the centre right's campaign. As has been repeatedly emphasised in the preceding chapters, this was monopolised by Berlusconi who sought to defend himself from the implications of voters' retrospective assessments first by denying the evidence of his economic performance and then, if pocket-book issues *were* to be the basis on which the election would be decided, shifting the spotlight onto the centre left's tax proposals. From this point of view, if the thesis of a Berlusconi 'comeback' has credence then, as the entrepreneur lost, it would have to be – and by most observers is – conceded that the fears he managed to arouse were, as Biorcio notes, insufficient 'to outweigh the effects of the attitudes of mistrust (or hostility) against the centre-right government that had become widespread during the preceding years and that had given rise to a kind of general mobilisation against Berlusconi'.

The party system

Despite the fact that the election was fought on the basis of a new electoral law, its outcome was such as to leave the most fundamental characteristics of the party system unchanged. At the same time, the new law has brought about significant shifts in the distribution of power within each of the two main coalitions.

The most essential characteristic of Italy's party system, its 'fragmented bi-polarity', has gradually consolidated itself over the course of the four general elections that have taken place since 1994. The polarised pluralism of the First Republic began to give way to bi-polarity as an intimate consequence of the PCI's transformation after 1989 and the disintegration of the DC and its 'satellites' from 1992. On the one hand, the former process (and the consequent end of the (now ex-) communists' 'ineligibility' for government) removed the last of the three pillars (Catholicism, clientelism and anti-communism) on which support for the DC and its allied parties had traditionally rested, thus hastening their demise under the pressure of the then corruption scandals. On the other hand, their demise and thus the end of their role as a dam against the opposing extremes removed the most fundamental, and previously insurmountable, obstacle in the way of the overriding ambition of the Movimento Sociale Italiano to find a partner or partners in the construction of a conservative anti-left pole (Newell, 2000: 124). The 1993 electoral law subsequently ensured that the emerging bi-polarity would remain fragmented, for if the law strongly encouraged the formation of coalitions, then it was introduced at a time when the traditional parties of government were disintegrating while new parties' positions had not yet been consolidated, thus allowing the continuation of reciprocal blackmail in the formation of coalitions; while the coalitions themselves were required in the electoral arena: in the parliamentary arena the parties faced no such imperatives. Consequently, if the new party system, unlike the old, has had coalitions, as well as parties, as its constitutive units; and if bi-polar competition between these coalitions has enabled them to produce alternation in government (Di Virgilio, 2006: 444), then their fragmented character has prevented the emergence of strong governments able to impose discipline on their parliamentary followers. Even in the electoral arena, pressures towards unity have not always been strong enough to overcome the coalitions' centrifugal tendencies.[2] As a result, of the eight governments that held office between May 1994 and the general election of 2006, the composition of only one – the one that was sworn in on 12 June 2001 – could claim to have been the unmediated reflection of the choices of a majority of voters (Massari, 2005: 448). All of the others were governments that owed their positions to post-election negotiations among parties in the parliamentary arena. From the perspective of party-system characteristics, then, the most significant consequences of the 2006 election have been: the installation of a government whose composition directly reflects the choices of a majority of voters for only the second time in the Republic's history; perpetuation of the party-system's fragmentation.

There are a number of ways to measure the latter. As Papavero and Verzichelli point out in their chapter, the decision, at the start of the new legislature, to allow the formation of very small parliamentary groups – a consequence of the practice of allowing groups with fewer than the minimum numbers set by the standing orders when the groups represent organised, nationwide forces – has led to an increase in the actual number of groups: from the eight to the current thirteen in the Chamber, for example. However, as the authors recognise, focusing on actual numbers is a potentially misleading way of assessing fragmentation as it takes no account of the relative weights of the groups. Using Laasko and Taagepera's (1979) index which does take account of these, they find that the effective number of parliamentary groups is 5.17 in the Chamber and 5.49 in the Senate. The effective number of groups in the Chamber of Deputies rose from 3.2 in 1976 to 6.2 in 1994 and 6.1 in 1996 and remained at 5.3 in 2001 (Newell, 2006). So despite the return to proportional electoral arrangements, the level of fragmentation has remained substantially unaltered.

Aldo Di Virgilio (2006: 445) explains the continuity of party-system characteristics in terms of two factors: first, the fact that the electoral system is not only proportional, but is, in fact, a mixed system. Indeed, the system is both proportional and majoritarian in the sense that with *one and the same* vote, the voter makes a choice *both* of party (to which seats are allotted in proportion to its vote) *and* of coalition (where the coalition with most votes wins an automatic majority of seats). Consequently, if the previous electoral law encouraged 'strategic coordination' as a consequence of the imperatives created by the single-member colleges, the new law encourages the same kind of strategic coordination as a consequence of the majority premium. Second, if the previous electoral law was introduced at a moment when the emerging bi-polar party system had yet to be consolidated, the new law was introduced at a moment when it already was consolidated.

The law has had significant effects within each coalition, however. On the centre right, FI, which, as coalition maker and largest Cdl party had once had to pay a forfeit to its allies, in 2006 no longer had to do so. In other words, once it had had to concede candidatures in the single-member constituencies to its allies as the price of their cooperation and this meant that proportionally its parliamentary following tended to be less than its electoral following. With the new electoral law there was no such imperative so that, paradoxically, though its electoral weight within the coalition declined substantially, its parliamentary weight as compared to that of its allies remained substantially unchanged. The UDC meanwhile saw its vote rise from 3.2 to 6.8 percent while its share of seats actually went down to 39 from the 40 it had won in 2001. Within the Unione, there was a significant shift in the distribution of power from the parties of the centre and reformist left to the parties of the radical left (Di Virgilio, 2006: 447–451). Whereas the latter parties' strength in terms of seats had always been less than their strength in terms of votes, in 2006 for the first time, the reverse relationship applied, with the relative weight of these parties within the centre left's Chamber of Deputies contingent as a whole going up by some two thirds as compared to the two previous elections (Table C.1). There was a similar shift in the case of the Senate (Di

Table C.1 Comparison of Chamber-of-Deputies vote and seat shares won by Forza Italia and the radical left, 1994–2006

	% votes	% seats	Votes as % of coalition total	Seats as % of coalition total
Forza Italia				
1994	21.0	15.7	45.3	27.0
1996	20.6	18.7	48.9	48.0
2001	29.5	30.0	59.4	51.4
2006	23.6	22.2	47.8	49.8
Radical left				
1994	10.6	8.9	30.9	26.3
1996	11.1	7.9	25.5	15.6
2001	12.8	6.0	29.1	14.6
2006	12.2	14.1	24.6	25.6

Note: 'Radical left' = RC, Greens, Rete in 1994; Progressisti 1996, Greens in 1996; RC, PdCI, Girasole, IdV in 2001; RC, PdCI, Greens, IdV in 2006. In 2001, the bases on which the percentages in the two right-most columns are calculated are the totals for the Ulivo plus those for RC and IdV.

Virgilio, 2006: 448–449). Such shifts throw a spotlight on the broader political consequences of the outcome.

Political consequences

In the immediate aftermath of the campaign the belief that Berlusconi had staged a dramatic comeback to bring his coalition within a handful of votes of victory meant that his position as leader of the centre right was strengthened. If it is true that the Cdl as a whole did better than many were expecting, then Berlusconi's was an odd sort of comeback given that his own party had suffered losses of electoral support almost without parallel in the history of the Italian republic. However, as W. I. Thomas (1923), famously remarked, 'a situation defined as real is real in its consequences', and the strengthening of Berlusconi's leadership gave his coalition the compactness required to enable it to attempt to weaken the incoming government – both through the insinuations of electoral irregularities mentioned above and through the argument that the government's position was necessarily of doubtful legitimacy given that the country was 'split down the middle' (and therefore the government could claim to be backed at the very most by only half the country).

Again, it was a case of interpretations with potentially real consequences diverging from the reality of the situation; and, in relation to this point, three observations seem called for. First, there was a sense in which the centre right's argument might have turned out to be incontestable. That is, to the extent that (sufficient numbers of sufficiently influential) people could be made to believe that the vote distribution rendered the government's position doubtfully legitimate, then of course it *would* be doubtfully legitimate, at least from a broad political point of view. Second, however, it was also true that, from a constitutional point of view, the distribution of the vote was irrelevant to the legitimacy of the incoming government's position and that in this Italy is no different to parliamentary regimes elsewhere. As Piero Ignazi (2006: 436) points out, in such regimes governments are legitimised by votes of confidence of the legislature where majorities in terms of seats may or may not correspond to majorities in terms of votes. In Britain, for example, Tony Blair and the Labour Party govern with full authority despite being backed by considerably less than half the voters.

However, while Blair is backed by a single party with a secure parliamentary majority, Romano Prodi is backed by a multi-party coalition with a small parliamentary majority – and this leads naturally to the third observation. That is, empirical political scientists might well be tempted to argue that as far as they, at least, are concerned, the distribution of the vote adds to rather than detracts from the government's legitimacy broadly understood; for, together with the narrowness of the parliamentary majority, it empowers citizens by being particularly effective in ensuring the Government's sensitivity to public opinion, and democratic accountability, and is therefore to be welcomed, not derided. And – they might continue – in a dangerous world in which government decision-making is concerned with issues of ever greater moment, especially in the international arena, the individual citizen is perhaps more likely to feel secure in the face of an executive whose position is somewhat precarious than s/he is in the face of one – such as that of the UK, for example – whose power of independent initiative is directly enhanced by the backing of a large and cohesive parliamentary majority (and is therefore a source of worry to both MPs and ordinary citizens alike).

However plausible this argument may or may not be, what does seem to be beyond doubt, comparatively speaking, is that the Italian election outcome was absolutely normal in terms of all the usual criteria. If the victory was of modest proportions, then it stood at the head of a long line of modest victories in western democracies.[3] If it was a product of voters' judgements concerning the economy and taxes, then this too was perfectly normal (Corbetta and Vassallo, 2006: 422).

It remains the true, however, that the Italian case is unusual in two important respects. One is the fragmented character of the Italian government's small parliamentary majority, rendering it un-typically fragile. The second is that the two main coalitions continue to fail to accord each other – whether through charges of conflicts of interest or of allegations of 'communist conspiracies' – full legitimacy as potential governing actors. These two factors make it possible to envisage two possible scenarios for the new government: either that it succumbs to opposition attempts to exploit the divisions in its ranks and therefore fails to last for any length of time, or that it finds that the very precariousness of its position is, paradoxically, its strength, giving it a degree of cohesion it might otherwise not have had. Current indications point in both directions.

In favour of the first scenario are two considerations. In the first place, it may be argued that the prospects for the talked-about merger of the DS and the Margherita in a Partito Democratico – which Prodi considers essential to cohesive government – have been improved by the election outcome. The reason is that the 'added value' of the two parties' joint, Ulivo, list argues in favour of the view that it was essential to the coalition's victory in the Chamber, and that it is essential to balance the coalition's 'extremes': in the Chamber contest, so the reasoning goes, some of RC's voters were prepared to reinforce Prodi and the entire coalition by voting for the Ulivo; in the Senate contest, where the Ulivo symbol was not present, they voted for their own party (which did exceptionally well). In the second place, a very significant number of the leaders of the centre left's parties have joined the new government or assumed positions close to government. Thus, DS President Massimo D'Alema has become Foreign Secretary and Deputy Prime Minister; Margherita leader Francesco Rutelli has become Minister for Culture and the Arts and Deputy Prime Minister; IdV leader Antonio di Pietro has become Minister for Infrastructure; UDEUR leader, Clemente Mastella has become Justice Minister; Emma Bonino of la Rosa nel Pugno has become Minister for European Policy; and Fausto Bertinotti of RC has become President of the Chamber of Deputies. In this respect, the new government reflects the one that was formed in 2001 by Berlusconi in a move that was unusual for post-war Italy but that could be expected to increase the stability of the administration. Traditionally, there had been a tendency for the most senior party leaders to remain outside government, delegating ministerial tasks instead to less powerful party figures.

> The advantage of this from the parties' point of view had been that it had allowed them to keep Cabinet and Prime Minister in a state of relative

weakness, with Cabinet Ministers owing their positions essentially to agreements between party secretaries who would often agree policy away from the arena of Cabinet altogether within the framework of periodic 'majority summits'. If, as Cotta (1996) argues, this distance between parties and government made it difficult for the former to benefit from the fund of authority and legitimacy that goes with the assumption of public office, the reverse side of this coin was that it made it easier for parties to decline responsibility for, and avoid the electoral consequences of, unpopular policies. (Newell and Partridge, 2002: 242)

So, by including the party leaders in his cabinet, Prodi appeared to be imitating Berlusconi five years earlier in attempting to bind the prospects of any one of the parties individually closely to the success or otherwise of the government as a whole, in the process strengthening his own hand vis-à-vis the parties and that of the executive vis-à-vis Parliament.

In favour of the scenario according to which the government fails to last there are also two considerations. First, there are signs that the Partito Democratico might have considerable difficulties in taking off with some, especially in the DS, arguing that the project should be delayed on the grounds that far from balancing the 'extreme left' the project could increase its vote (De Marchis, 2006: 10). And its chances of success have to be considered much less than even in any event simply because of the fundamental ideological incompatibilities of the two parties involved (the one having roots in the communist tradition, the other in Catholicism) and because of the potential losers from the project in both parties (Dilmore, 2005; Newell, 2006). Second, the new government has taken office at a time of considerable economic difficulties, the pressures to reduce the budget deficit and the level of public debt bequeathed by its predecessors leaving it very little room for popular public spending measures. Some have therefore been prepared to argue that the most likely scenario is that of a government diligently delivering austerity measures and thereby paving the way for defeat at the next election by a right-wing coalition once again enjoying all the conditions necessary to allow it to raise levels of public spending and reduce taxes (D'Eramo, 2006). Under pressure to accept labour-market and welfare reforms, supposedly essential to the recovery of international competitiveness, the position of RC is likely to be particularly uncomfortable, entrapped as it is between a government whose survival depends on it, and the aspirations of its working-class supporters.

Finally, the election outcome seems to have had a significant bearing on two of the most important institutional developments in Italian

politics in recent years. The first of these is the election of a new
President of the Republic that took place at the outset of the new legislature in order to replace Carlo Azeglio Ciampi whose seven-year
mandate was about to expire. By common consent, the supreme function of the President is to mediate and regulate with the aim of
ensuring that political processes are carried on without threatening
national integration and it is for this reason that election – which is by
an assembly that includes not only the members of the two branches of
the legislature, but also three delegates from nineteen of the twenty
regions and one from the Valle d'Aosta region – requires the support
of two-thirds of the members of the assembly at the first three rounds
of voting, a simple majority thereafter – the rationale being to ensure,
as far as possible, that the winning candidate enjoys the support of
forces extending beyond those of the government of the day. A government with a bear majority *can* elect a president on its own – but only
if it is cohesive. In fact, high levels of fragmentation and majorities
lacking in cohesion have nearly always rendered dialogue with non-
governing forces essential in presidential elections. And, since a vote is
cast simply by writing, in secret, the name of a person on a blank piece
of paper (meaning that the choice of person for whom to vote is not in
any way limited by any prior process of nomination of candidates) the
number of rounds of voting required has often been large.[4] The 2006
election of ex-communist Giorgio Napolitano – whose support was
confined to the governing majority and came at the fourth round –
therefore represented something of an unusual case, reflecting as it did
the difficulties, referred to above, of the two coalitions in according
each other legitimacy. The delicacy of the president's position is, then,
rendered the greater by a constitutional curiosity of once minor political significance. This is the power of the President, conferred by
article 59 of the Constitution, to nominate five life senators from
among individuals who have distinguished themselves in the 'social,
scientific, artistic and literary fields'. It remains to be seen how the
nominations of Giorgio Napolitano will be received (assuming he
decides to make nominations within the life of the current parliament)
in the light of the wafer-thin Senate majority achieved by the centre-
left just one month prior to his own election.

Second, the outcome of the referendum that took place in June on
the proposed constitutional changes passed by the centre right in the
previous legislature was, as Pasquino notes in his chapter, a foregone
conclusion given the superior mobilising capacity of the centre left.
Nevertheless, it is interesting to speculate about the impact of the election outcome on the size of what was a very large majority against the

proposals.[5] And although, as Pasquino argues, the referendum result may ensure that constitutional issues continue to occupy a prominent place on the political agenda with a continuation of the so-called 'Italian regime transition', it might be argued that it has brought the transition to an end. If, by definition, the term 'regime transition' refers to the interval of time separating one regime from another, then the fulfilment of two conditions would seem necessary for the onset and successful conclusion of a transition of this kind. One is a disintegration of consensus on the desirability of maintaining the existing 'rules of the game'; the other is support for an alternative set of rules on the part of a group of actors at least potentially capable of bringing it into existence and making it stick. If the first of these conditions may continue to apply, the second appears to have gone unfulfilled for quite some time. Already with the instigation of the 1997 parliamentary commission for constitutional reform – which began its work almost five years after the 1992 election had revealed the first major cracks in the old 'regime' – much of the enthusiasm for large-scale reform had passed its peak and it then fell victim to the parties' interlocking vetoes. In producing such an unambiguous outcome, the June 2006 referendum could be interpreted as implying that the electorate has decisively turned its back on, and thus rendered highly unlikely, the possibility of establishing any radically new institutional framework for the Republic for the foreseeable future.

Conclusion

The general election of April 2006 thus marked a further milestone, and possibly a turning point, in the recent trajectory of Italian politics. In bringing about the second alternation in government since the party-system upheavals of the early 1990s, the outcome appeared to represent the consolidation of a bi-polar party system based on fragmented coalitions. However, precisely because of the system's fragmentation and the seeming precariousness of the in-coming government's position, there appeared to be room for considerable doubt about the likely direction of future party-system developments, and political developments more generally. In short, if the election appeared to represent the confirmation of past trends, in other respects it looked as though it might also represent the start of a new period of uncertainty. It is precisely this uncertain quality which, for the academic observer, gives Italian politics their fascination.

Notes

1 In 2001, for example, the two coalitions were separated by just 1 per cent in the Chamber majoritarian arena (Ignazi, 2006: 436).
2 Thus it was that, in 1994, the centre right was unable to form a single coalition but was obliged to present two: the Polo delle libertà (between FI and the League) in the north, and the Polo del buon governo (between FI and AN) in the south. Therefore, it was nowhere possible to vote for a candidate backed by all of the parties that then went on to form the government. In 1996, the centre left's inability fully to integrate RC led to stand-down arrangements between the latter party and the Ulivo – so that candidates representing the coalition that went on to form the government were not present throughout the country.
3 The Israeli Knesset contest of 1981 saw Menachem Begin's Likud party beat Labour by just 10,405 votes or 0.5 per cent of the total. The United States presidential contest in 2000 was decided by just 537 votes in the state of Florida. The German federal election in 2005 saw the CDU/CSU emerge ahead of the SPD by just 1 per cent of the vote.
4 The record was set by the election of Giovanni Leone in 1971, which required 23 rounds of voting.
5 The referendum was held on 25 and 26 June 2006 and, on a turnout of 53.6 per cent, resulted in the proposals being rejected by 61.3 to 38.7 per cent.

References

Agosta, A. (2006), 'I risultati deformi del voto alla Camera e al Senato', *il Mulino*, 3, 461–468.

Corbetta, P. and Vassallo, S. (2006), 'L'Italia divisa ... dalla recessione e dalle tasse', *Il Mulino*, 3, 422–433.

Cotta, M. (1996), 'La crisi del governo di partito all'italiana', in M. Cotta and P. Isernia (eds), *Il gigante dai piedi di argilla*, Bologna, Il Mulino.

D'Eramo, Marco (2006), 'Maledetto popolo', *Il Manifesto*, 18 April, www.ilmanifesto.it /Quotidiano-archivio/18–Aprile-2006 (accessed on 18 August 2006).

De Marchis (2006), 'Ds, si apre la partita sul vertice', *La Repubblica*, 12 April, p. 10.

Dilmore, N. (2005), 'Fragili e stabili: Le alleanze nel sistema politico italiano', *Il Mulino*, 2, 239–249.

Di Virgilio, A. (2006), 'Forza e debolezza delle coalizioni dopo le politiche di aprile', *Il Mulino*, 3, 443–452.

Guarnieri, C. and Newell, J. L. (2005), 'Introduction: 2004 – A year "on hold"', in C. Guarnieri and J. L. Newell (eds), *Italian Politics Quo Vadis?*, New York and Oxford, Berghahn.

Ignazi, P. (2006), 'Leggende metropolitane e comportamento elettorale', *Il Mulino*, 3, 434–442.

Laasko, M. and Taagepera, R. (1979), '"Effective" number of parties: a measure with application to West Europe', *Comparative Political Studies*, 12:1, 3–27.

Massari, O. (2005), 'La crisi di governo e il bipolarismo difettoso', *Il Mulino*, 3, 442–450.

Natale, P. (2002), 'Una fedeltà leggera: i movimenti di voto nella "Seconda Repubblica"', in R. D'Alimonte and S. Bartolini (eds), *Maggioritario finalmente? La transizione eletorale 1994–2001*, Bologna, Il Mulino.

Newell, J. L. (2000), *Parties and Democracy in Italy*, Aldershot, Ashgate.

Newell, J. L. (2006), 'Two coalitions in search of a victory: the *Cdl*, the *Unione* and their electoral prospects', paper presented to the Association of the Study of Modern Italy and the American University of Rome conference on the 2006 Italian General Election, American University of Rome, 24–25 March.

Newell, J. L. and Partridge, H. (2002), 'Conclusion', in J. L. Newell (ed.), *The Italian General Election of 2006. Berlusconi's Victory*, Manchester and New York, Manchester University Press.

Thomas, W. I. (1923), *The Unadjusted Girl*, Boston, Little, Brown, and Co.

Index

Note: 'n' after a page number indicates the number of a note on that page